BLACK MARXISM and AMERICAN CONSTITUTIONALISM

An Interpretive History
from the Colonial Background
to the Great Depression

Malik Simba
—CALIFORNIA STATE
UNIVERSITY, FRESNO

Kendall Hunt
publishing company

Kendall Hunt
publishing company

www.kendallhunt.com
Send all inquiries to:
4050 Westmark Drive
Dubuque, IA 52004-1840

Printed in the United States of America
10 9 8 7 6 5 4 3 2 1

Dedicated to my father, Theoplis Taliferro Hogue, always the scholar and gentleman; to my mother, Maymie Bell Hogue, always the strength on which I leaned; and to my wife, Ceroasetta, always supporting, encouraging, inspirational, and challenging.

PREFACE

It is acceptable to now discuss the relationship among law, race, and society. However, students still tend to walk around in a fog when you ask them to convey a theoretical paradigm concerning the dynamics of such a relationship. What makes this strange is that since the 1960s there has been a proliferation of collegiate courses addressing this triumvirate. These courses cut across and appear in various disciplines, ranging from literature to history to criminology.

The closet effort at creating a concrete theory of the relationship among law, race, and society come from the critical legal theorists who now are referred to as the *critical legal studies movement*, which used the theoretical works of Max Weber, Karl Marx, and others to better understand the real workings of law, race, and society. However, the need to bring these theories and the works of the critics to real history has not been attempted to date. This book is an attempt to rectify that lacuna, and is based essentially on the very valuable body of primary and secondary scholarship produced by esteemed colleagues in the field of legal history. I have made reference to many, but not all, who helped make this book possible.

I believe students, teachers, professors, and laypersons will be intellectually enhanced and historically enlightened by the contents of this book. This book can be used in a wide variety of General Education courses that establish learning outcomes requiring students to be able to describe American slavery; American constitutionalism; the historical construction of race, class, and gender; and to develop a critical perspective on the praxis of a multicultural society. This book is the enabler for students to achieve those outcomes.

By an examination of the United States Supreme Court and its decisions on race through a theoretical lens, the students are able to use this history as a compass to explore and compare other social categories such as gender and class. Blacks, women, immigrants, and the poor have used constitutional law as an instrument to protect and shield their civil rights and civil liberties from class domination.

For those who take the opportunity to read, study, and understand the contents of this book, I hope that they realize that there is a dialectic to Gunnar Myrdal's *An American Dilemma: The Negro Problem and Modern Democracy* (New York: Harper & Bros.,1944), and that each generation must recognize the tension between the ideals of constitutionalism and the abject reality of America's minorities. I hope this book helps Americans understand that the Myrdalian gap can only be shrunk or eliminated by an informed, proactive, and educated citizenry. This book seeks to be that educative variable.

ACKNOWLEDGMENTS

During the research and writing of this book, I was supported by many colleagues to whom I owe a debt of gratitude. This book evolved out of a mentoring relationship that I had with the late Paul Murphy. He saw potential in a young graduate student at the University of Minnesota. Professor Murphy introduced me to the field of constitutional history. However, it was Joao Ries who started me down the road using a materialist approach to understanding the law, and John McClendon who mentored me in applying Marxist theory to my research. Funny, as I was mentored on this left-leaning intellectual road, I realized what Joao meant when he explained the Marxist theory of why a Volkswagen and a Mercedes Benz can never be the same car, even if both cars were built in the same way with the exact same components. In addition, recognition of other graduate faculty include Lansine Kaba, Allen Isaacman, Stuart Schwartz, Tony Martin, and the late Allan Spear. My graduate years at the University of Minnesota were long and difficult, and my survival was due, in part, to a few graduate colleagues who became lifelong friends and supporters of my research: Charles Cambridge, Ralph Crowder, the late Dolan Garrett, Sally Malone-Hawkins, Robert Fikes, Moussa Foster, Keith Parker, Robert Nathaniel Scott, Nate Smith, Ralph Peace, Tiffany Patterson, David Taylor, Quintard Taylor, Joe Trotter, and Herbert West. Other supportive individuals include James Caldwell, Savander Parker, Ronald Kent Richardson, Ronald Woods, Steve Ferguson, Terry Day, Chuck McKenzie, and Louis Ervin. In addition, Ricky Stewart and Alicia Rivera represent all my best and brightest students. A note of thanks to Cedric Robinson, who hired me at Binghamton University. Cedric, along with John McClendon, Martin Murray, and Tom Denyer, became fellow scholars and hoopsters. I thank all my fellow hoopsters who still have nightmares over my fade-a-way. That means you, Roberto Reyes and Gene Emory.

At California State University–Fresno I would like to especially thank the Dean of the College of Social Science, Luz Gonzalez, who supported my research efforts by granting me a much needed sabbatical. My chairs of the department of history Michelle DenBeste and Bill Skuban, and my colleagues Jill Fields and Jesus Luna provided the nutrient of friendship on a daily basis, as did all my colleagues in the department of history, especially the hoopsters. My colleagues in Africana and American Indian Studies provided strong collegial support. A special thanks to Servant Dr. Jerome E. Jackson for his inspirational sermons that always reenergized me and English Department chair, James E. Walton for the relaxing and intellectually stimulating lunch breaks. Ms. Diane Martinez, in the Africana and American Indian Studies program, is recognized for her assistance. Coordinating an academic program and researching simultaneously was and is a daunting task made easier by Ms. Martinez.

My National Endowment for the Humanities (NEH) Summer Seminars with Joel Grossman at The University of Wisconsin Law School aided my research on critical legal studies, and my other

NEH with Michael Johnson at The University of California–Irvine facilitated my research on the American laws of slavery. The manuscript benefited greatly from the comments, readings, and editing of several important colleagues. I recognize the efforts, which greatly improved the quality of the manuscript, of Steve Brown of Jefferson Community College (New York), Viscount "Berky" Nelson of The University of California–Los Angeles, and John H. McClendon, III, of Michigan State University. Thanks—Steve, for the hoops and John, for being there at each step. We all wait your return to the hardwoods. A very special thanks to Robert Fikes of San Diego State University for locating citations to various "lost" but important sources. I thank my Kendall Hunt Publisher Project Coordinator, Abby Davis, for her attention to detail and for making the process less stressful, and many thanks to my Kendall Hunt Publisher Acquisitions Editor, Joe Wells.

Finally, I acknowledge my late mother-in-law, Mrs. Martha Butts, who always kept me alert and focused in the wee hours of the morning by bringing a comic relief to the stress and strains of research and writing. Of course, I deeply thank my family, the Hogue clan of Denver, Colorado, who were always "acting out" as cheerleaders.

Even though I have recognized editorial support from those mentioned here, I take full responsibility for any errors of omission and downright absence of procedural attention to detail in this book.

CONTENTS

Introduction *1*

CHAPTER 1
The Colonial Background *17*

CHAPTER 2
Ideology, the American Revolution, and Constitutional Slavery *29*

CHAPTER 3
Law of Slavery, Law of Freedom: 1820–1860 ....*43*

CHAPTER 4
Reconstruction, Reform, and the Retreat from the Revolution in Race Relations *69*

CHAPTER 5
The Supreme Court's Legitimation of the Compromise of 1877 ....*89*

CHAPTER 6
Plessy v. Ferguson: Anatomy of Legal Hegemony *105*

CHAPTER 7
The Problem of the Twentieth Century Is the Problem of the Color Line *117*

Epilogue *143*

ABOUT THE AUTHOR

Malik Simba received his B.A. in History and Philosophy from University of Southern Colorado-Pueblo, and his M.A. and Ph.D. in Constitutional history from the University of Minnesota. His doctoral work also included course work in the History of African Peoples Program. He has held professorships in the departments of history at State University of New York at Binghamton and Clarion University in Pennsylvania. Presently, he is a senior professor and past chair of the History Department (2000-2003) and current Coordinator of the Africana Studies Program at California State University-Fresno. Dr. Simba was awarded fellowships from the National Endowment for the Humanities in 1979, 1987, and 1990. He serves on the Boards of the Ronald E. McNair Scholars Program at California State University-Fresno and Blackpast.org, the "google" of the African American experience.

Dr. Simba's publications include entries in the Encyclopedia of African History, Historical Encyclopedia of World Slavery, W. E. B. Du Bois Encyclopedia, Malcolm X Encyclopedia, African American Encyclopedia, Encyclopedia of Slave Resistance and Rebellion, and the Historical Dictionary of Civil Rights. Additionally, Dr. Simba has published the definitive analysis of race and law using critical legal theory in his "Gong Lum v. Rice: The Convergence of Law, Race, and Ethnicity" in American Mosaic. His essay, "J. A. Rogers: The Forgotten Contributions of a Pioneer Self-Trained Black Historian" appeared in Afro-American in New York Life and History. His essay, "The Obama Campaign 2008: A Historical Overview," appeared in the Western Journal of Black Studies. Dr. Simba's other published works include book reviews in the Chicago Tribune, Focus on Law Studies, Journal of Southwest Georgia History and Western Legal History.

Introduction

The revolution which the bourgeois class has brought into the conception of law, and hence into the function of the State, consists especially in the will to conform (hence ethnicity of the law and of the State). . . . The Bourgeois class poses itself as an organism . . . capable of absorbing the entire society, assimilating it to its own cultural and economic level.[1]

—ANTONIO GRAMSCI

A MATERIALIST CONCEPTION OF LAW

To use the term *Marxist theory of law* is problematic, because neither Karl Marx nor Frederick Engels ever fully wrote on the State and its relationship to the law; however, both men commented frequently on these topics. This book attempts to use those comments as tools of objective analysis in explicating the historical and cultural moment in which American slave law and American law of freedom, responding to the economic interests of a racial hierarchy within the social relationship of political economy, helped move African Americans from plantation to a certain kind of freedom.

Law, according to one leading Marxist writer, "is the repressive and negative aspect of the entire positive civilizing activity undertaken by the State."[2] Nowhere can this statement be more fully validated than by the historical relationship between American Constitutional law and America's citizens of African descent. Rarely have the problematics of law, race, and political economy been so demonstrably destructive of human rights as this history reveals. The historians who have examined the interrelationships of law, race, and political economy have, for the most part, restated

I

Frederick Douglass' queries of 1849: "The Constitution of the United States—What is it? Who made it? For whom and for what was it made?"[3] Those historians who have centered their research on attempting to answer Douglass' questions have been somewhat incensed, somewhat embarrassed, and, at the same time, disgusted that the first beacon of Western constitutionalism in the New World was fostered in part by slaveholders who protected their "peculiar institution" by the rule of law. The answers to Mr. Douglass' queries lie in this concrete fact and much more.

The realization that slavery was protected by democratic rule of law leads one to at least begin to understand that the history of the relationship between African Americans and American Constitutional law has been bound, since its inception, in the words a *travesty of justice*. Such concepts as fairness, equity, impartiality, equality before the law, and due process have been constitutionally interpreted to the detriment of this country's citizens of African descent as a class in or for itself.[4]

Very few, if any, historians, dissent from the previous statement. In fact, most use more severe words and description. However, fundamental differences arise among legal scholars in their theoretical understanding of why this travesty developed in the very way that it did and, thus, what it means for the juridical future. "Traditionalist" scholars assume that the rise of democracy, liberty, and the rights of man has been relentless, and that slavery, racial oppression, and class exploitation were paradoxical or merely exceptions.[5] More recently, "revisionists" have accepted the intimate relationship between the development of American liberty and American racial exploitation.[6] "Neo-revisionists" propose a knee-jerk relationship between the needs of economic growth and the emerging contours of American liberties.[7] Unlike traditionalists, who perceive racial oppression as a momentary anomaly, revisionists still seek to explain Americans as dedicated to liberty while trying to explain the unexplainable—the retentiveness of racial oppression. Neo-revisionists reject any such dedication and drive home the simplistic theory of the direct responsiveness of law, at all times, to the needs of the economic group dominant at any given moment. Because of this historiographical impasse, there is a serious theoretical lacuna on the exact and objective relationship among law, race, and political economy.

This book proposes that scholars of American Constitutional history will be better able to explicate its precise relationship to African Americans by conceptualizing *law* within a Marxist theory of law and the analytical works of the critical race and legal studies movement.[8] Scholars employing this approach, in using variants of the social theories of Karl Marx,[9] propose "Law and legal doctrine reflect, confirm, and reshape the social divisions and hierarchies inherent in a type or stage of social organization,"[10] and that law is "a constitutive element of race itself."[11]

Furthermore, this work suggests that law, even as it is embedded, and thus responsive to political economy, does have a "relative autonomy" from the needs of the economic base. Marx and critical legal scholars, in differing degrees, emphasize this essential point.[12] The rejection of economic and race reductionism leads to a creative and a clarified understanding of the praxis of law, race, and political economy.

The assumption in this work is that Marx and critical legal scholars put forth a legal theory that

> explains the way in which law ultimately reflects and sustains the social order, yet has
> its own internal logic, and unique modes of discourse and institutional patterns that

are to some extent independent of the will of powerful, non-legal, social and political actors and that represent an important constitutive element of the social totality in their own right.[13]

The law, in reflecting, confirming, and reshaping the social formation, reveals both its ideological aspects as well as its material predications. Although Marx analyzed the law's material foundations, both Max Weber and Antonio Gramsci addressed part of their scholarship to explaining the hows and whys of the ideological process of the law. Both men propose that law within capitalist production relationships, given its own unjustified social stratification, behave in such a way as to legitimize that particular economic system.

Weber, in a circuitous or inverted fashion, begins his analysis of the importance of legitimacy by noting that liberal-democratic-based, capitalist social formations need *formal legal rationality,* or a legal order that is logical and autonomous, so that economic growth can be developed and sustained. In his major work, *Economy and Society,*[14] Weber focuses on how the unique law of the West sets the juridical basis for the rise of capitalism. Although this theory is clearly anti-materialistic, it helps clarify certain ideological aspects of the alliance between law and capitalist relations of production.

According to Weber, formal legal rationality helps capitalism by relying on rules or principles that are clear and non-ambiguous and that are applied from case to case with specific jural cognition based on and proceeding from what was applied in previous legal decisions.[15] This guarantees that developed legal rules have an independence, an internal form and logic that existed before and beyond the actual litigants in any particular controversy.[16] This system of law governing capitalist speculative activity ensures, to a certain extent, a sense of predictability, neutrality, and thus security to one's investment against potential arbitrary sanctions from other capitalist factions that might hold state power at any given time or place.[17] The legal process did this by convincing all potential capitalists that they could calculate a return on their investments and speculate on entrepreneurial activity knowing the parameters of rule of law could protect their interests from all competitors, irrespective of their wealth, status, or power—e.g., planter or merchant capitalist. Cold, calculated speculation by these social groups within the law's dictate was the driving force of economic growth.

The assurance that power would be restrained and that force would be applied only through formal legal processes led to the legitimization of capitalism in the eyes of those within its sphere of influence. Planter and merchant capitalist sued and were sued to maximize their profits as American slavery and capital matured over several centuries. Legal formalism gave the actions of these classes a legitimacy as they exploited laboring classes composed of African slaves, Indians, and dispossessed indentured servants.

The legitimization of such exploitation under the aegis of law is explained theoretically by Isaac Balbus,[18] for whom Weber's contributions to our understanding of capitalism lay not in his inverted, anti-materialist assumption about the dialectics of law to capitalism, but in his explanation of how legitimacy is attained through formal legal rationality. Balbus and others argue that this concept has the greatest of ideological consequences. It convinces all aspiring capitalists (including those without property but with big dreams, e.g., indentured servants, free Blacks, and certain Indian groups) that the rule of law ensures they have the legal right to invest money into a commercial venture and they can take a grievance through the legal process if they believe they have been swindled. Thus, law, in holding out this type of opportunity coupled with its remedies or rectifying sanctions, ensures that the dreams of becoming a member of the bourgeoisie by the property-less shall not be torn asunder by the arbitrariness of more powerful and greedy individuals or groups.[19]

Balbus stressed that it is indeed difficult to convince the have-nots that the liberal-democratic, capitalist social structure is fundamentally unjust when the rights of economic activity are universal and are tied to the legal rights of expressing economic grievances through what appears to be non-politicized and neutral law.[20] For African Americans, this legitimization process occurred early in the late seventeenth and early eighteenth centuries when Black freeholders appeared throughout the colonies. These individuals were farmers and merchant capitalists who used law's formal rationality and rule of law to protect their contractual petit bourgeois interests.[21] The appearance of these freed Blacks within slavery's early development, in first instance, made law appear to have an internal logic separated from the growing race, class, and gender realities of colonial society. The hegemony of the law is illustrated by these freed Blacks and others.

It is this appearance that law, in its educative, symbolic, and disciplinary aspects, is standing above particularized interests that led Antonio Gramsci to formulate his concept of hegemony. Hegemony was the concept that Gramsci used to describe the ability or process that creates "the spontaneous consent given by the great mass of the population to the general direction imposed on social life by the dominant fundamental group" (i.e., the ruling or capitalist class).[22]

For Gramsci, law, even though appearing thrice removed from the influence of the State and social reality, was repressive and a negative process undertaken by the State and aimed at nationalizing the social consciousness of all the social strata—the interstitial classes, the workers, the *lumpen,* the petty bourgeoisie, and even the less-enlightened faction of the bourgeoisie—to the worldview and, thus, to the social and economic policies of the most enlightened faction of the ruling class.[23] For Gramsci, Weber's formal legality was the basis for Eugene Genovese's "hegemonic function of the law." However, by touting the rule of law as something desirable, Weber misunderstood its purpose, according to Gramsci. The *rule of law* (formal legal rationality) doctrine inverted the real world by giving individuals certain rights, powers, and interests that were in contradistinction from the class in which they belonged (e.g., individual Black freeholders existing simultaneously with mass racial slavery). The rule of law, in using this individuated construct, employed the adversarial system to deliver penalties and rewards on a case-by-case, win or lose, basis. The equalization of unequal social beings was best described by A.V. Dicey:

> When we speak of the rule of law as a characteristic of our country, we mean not only that with us no man is above the law, but (what is a different thing) that here every man, whatever be his rank or condition, is subject to the ordinary law of the realm . . . with us every official, from the Prime Minister down to a constable . . . is under the same responsibility for every act done without legal justification as any other citizen.[24]

The idea that both the oppressed and the oppressor are governed by an autonomous and reasoned legal order is maintained on a consensual level, in part because the celebrated procedural rules or guarantees that are offered up to everyone—the right to a lawyer, trial by jury, no double jeopardy, right to bear arms, right of free speech, and so forth. *Legitimacy,* or what people think is right or just, is achieved in part by the court holding closely to these procedures and by a certain degree of impartiality. In such *cause célèbre* cases as Quock Walker, Elizabeth Freeman, *Amistad,* Scottsboro, Angela Davis, Huey P. Newton, Jo Ann Little, O.J. Simpson, and even in cases when slaves violated slave codes. Even these individuals, according to one scholar, were given due procedure rule of law.[25] These rule-of-law procedures represent the height of the symbolic and educative aspects of the law's hegemony. It is difficult for the average citizen to see through this facade. Mass society does not see that the law is governed in the interests of those who have the gold (i.e. "the Golden Rule"). However, mass society sees that those like themselves without the gold have a competing chance to win under the rule of law. The law's formal legal rules give them this chance and, in doing so, create a consent, a legitimacy, therefore creating the hegemonic function of the law. The law can alleviate the harsh material conditions of the exploited individual, but never those of the exploited mass class to which that individual belongs. Any discussions concerning the ideological basis of mass social consciousness must relate it to an understanding of the material grounding of the real social structural forces of race and law. The material grounding of White over Black in concrete social relations of production is the springboard for hegemonic legal superstructure.

Understanding hegemony gives rise to another key question: How does law reflect a certain real equality when grounded in social structures of inequality? A Marxist analysis clarifies this dilemma by suggesting that our conception of commodities as things divorced from the person(s) who created them gives rise to a false equality between persons and things based on an assessment of value. Pashukanis, a leading Marxist legalist, went on to clarify this aspect of law and commodity form:

> [A]t the very same time that the product of labour is taking on the quality of the commodity form and becoming a bearer of value, man acquires the quality of a juridic subject and becomes the bearer of a right. If things are economically the rulers of men through the fetishism of commodities (Marx), then man is juridically dominant over the things because he, as an owner, is an abstract impersonal subject of rights in things.[26]

Procedural rules of law are supposed to ensure some degree of predictability and parameters on economic activities. If contract law rules are violated, these procedural rules provide a degree of fairness, due process, and impartiality in the resolutions of these disputes in the contracted exchange of commodities by their juridical owners, who are equal before the law despite class, race, gender, and religious differences. Violations of contract and litigation thereof could be legal cases between juridic owners of different class positions concerning the ownership and use of bridges, oxen, houses, slaves, and so forth. However, a Marxist analysis implies that this type of formalistic law extracts the juridic owners from their social class positions and, I argue, their racial and gender positions. In doing so, this formalistic law helps perpetuate a false sense of equality between social unequals.[27]

Thus, the material basis for equality before the law is grounded within these real economic relations. Only in this manner does legal formality express a certain degree of structural reality regarding what is occurring as economic activity. The mystifying aspect of law lies in this exact paradox, which is the law's ability to become the "universal political equivalent"[28] within capitalism by treating all individuals as equals—ignoring the distinct human needs, concrete interests, social position, and class relations of discrete individuals.[29] Law's legitimacy or hegemony comes about when it conveys the rightness of treating social unequals as political equals by obscuring or mystifying the fact that these juridic owners are, in reality, unequals within a set of hierarchal social relations of economic production.

An example of the law treating unequals as equals is demonstrated by the way the Supreme Court interpreted civil rights law or the Congressional "rights of man" axioms in the post–Civil War era. The axiomatic ideologies of the Thirteenth, Fourteenth, and Fifteenth Amendments, Enforcement and Civil Rights Acts of the early and mid-1870s, were the precise legal formulative responses to capitalism's victory over the economically backward, slave-based, quasi-capitalistic economy of the Old South. The legal basis that purported to give the ex-slaves "freedom" without material independence ("forty acres and a mule")[30] reflected the settling proposition of industrial capitalism that "the concentration of business, industrial and commercial (sectors) in the hands of a few . . . was not only beneficial, but essential to the future progress of the (White) race."[31] The ideological form of bourgeois freedoms as stated in the new laws (freedom from the vestiges/badges of slavery, right of petition and speech, right to own, lease and sell property, and the ultimate right—the power of the ballot) was, in a series of Supreme Court decisions between 1871 and 1901, contoured to the demands of late-nineteenth century industrial and monopoly capitalism. These decisions were predicated on the reality that the New South and the nation needed a politically prostrated and placated Black labor force. In their interpretive essence, these Constitutional decisions reduced the freedman

> to a second-class citizen, voteless, powerless, helpless in the face of White terror, denied access to places of public accommodations, forced to scrounge an cadge for education, segregated in every phase of life . . . with no place to turn for redress of his grievances except the Court that had approved the legal devices used to reduce him to helpless and almost hopeless degradation![32]

This is the exact paradox of law that is addressed in this work: law can only be law in its negation of its essence—justice. In making the freedpeople and their ex-masters equal before the law as both stood in the shadow of the plantation, the Court had to explain why federal protection should be withdrawn at the time when the reign of terror was swiftly developing. In the 1883 Civil Rights Cases, Justice Bradley noted,

> When a man has emerged from slavery, and by the aid of beneficent legislation has shaken off the inseparable concomitant of that state, there must be some stage in the progress of his elevation when he takes the rank of a mere citizen, and ceases to be the special favorite of the laws, and when his rights as a citizen, or a man, are to be protected in the ordinary modes by which other men's rights are protected.[33]

The Court's power to explain the freedpeople's stage in their progress from slavery to freedom is the power to interpret legal facts in the context of race. In rejecting the power of Congress via these new laws to remove the badges of slavery, the Court elevated ex-slave and ex-master to the same formal legal playing field and made these social classes equal in and before the law even though they were unequal in the reality: sharecropping, Klan violence, discrimination, and lynching as

White redeemers created a New South. In trying not to recognize the special protection because of Black folk's race and history, the Court recognized the superior race and dominant interests of Whites. Even Harlan in his dissent in *Plessy* gave credence to the idea of White domination.[34]

The legal changes ushered in by the North's victory created a legal formalism that was welcomed as "hegemonic jubilee" by the various Black social classes in the North, South, East and West. However, Klan violence with Constitutional leeway ensured that the content of these legal forms would be the basis of a jubilee of a "certain kind of freedom." The processes of formal legal rationality coupled with Klan activity reduced freed Black social conformity to the prurient and material interests of ruling class factions in both the New South and the corporatism of Northern capital. This point cannot be overstated. Law's ability to force coherent behavior by mass society is not only ideological but, in the first and last instance, is coercive by the use of the gun.[35] Once federal armed legal protection was decreased or withdrawn from the South, then law, legal protection, and race relations were defined by those with the coercive power of the gun—the Klan. Black Codes, Klan law, also known as *lynch law,* tried, judged, imprisoned, and executed Black folk without any pretense of hegemony, of legal formalism, of legitimacy.[36] Of course, this violent legal form coexisted with the Southern formal legal rules system that, at times, gave any individual Black person the due processes of the law.[37] The roller-coaster ride of never knowing which legal form would be applied in an adversarial situation forced African Americans to bear the cross of constant uncertainty within their tenuous material freedom.[38]

Because African Americans have been the doormats of a ruling class that defined itself as "White" and, thereby, mesmerized the broader society of European descent in concrete ways to also see itself as White, a significant amount of struggle to precipitate social change has taken on obvious racial dimensions. As the most exploited class within American political economy, Blacks have strived, in part, to bring about a change on their own behalf. The failure of this striving can only be understood by using the theoretical constructs that I have outlined as tools of analysis. These constructs explicate the reason why law changed its form, but very seldom its content, when addressing the protected interests of Afro-Americans.[39]

The civil rights legislation of the Civil War and Reconstruction era reveals how the law's form, given the insistence of abolitionist and radical congressional leader protests, could seize the time and change law on the ideological level while maintaining/retaining its substantive material content. Federalism, restrained by political and racial conservatism, severely limited the potential of jubilee.[40] In explaining this formal legal change and, thus, indirectly such historical periods, Marx stated that the ruling class, in order to dilute, direct, and co-op lower class or intra-class pressure for social change, at any given time will "recognize the ideas, traditions, and norms of other groups as law in order to ensure the reproduction of the economic system which the (ruling) class benefits from."[41] The new amendments and civil rights laws represented the hopes and dreams of the Black dispossessed, but by conveying these hopes in the guise of legal formality, these hopes were interpreted in a way in which the political economy of industrial capitalism was not threatened. Even though Roscoe Conklin's testimony was rejected by the Supreme Court, the Court, by the late nineteenth century, decided most Constitutional cases on a racial and class level reflecting Conklin's views on the origins of the Fourteenth Amendment, and thus confirming the triumph of industrialized and emerging monopoly capitalism.[42]

In the context of American history, law has been the steam valve that released the tensions and contained the displeasures that the African-American community felt and expressed over its degraded conditions.[43] These displeasures led Black folk to engage not only in civil rights activity, but also in criminal activity, rebellious activity, and, ultimately, in the 1960s, in revolutionary activity. Law had to and did mediate all these forms of racial and class antagonisms.[44] Although accepting, in a much less than substantive manner, the occasionally asserted rights of this racially dispossessed group, law functioned hegemonically to alleviate class tensions within permissible limits dictated by the experience of what the White ruling class knew and knows it can live with.[45] Political progress for Blacks is contained by precise legal parameters, both through ideology and by armed coercion. Civil rights leaders have never quite understood this mediative aspect of the law as they have continued to pay homage to an institution, the U.S. Supreme Court, which in its inner essence cannot go the distance in substantively protecting the interests that those leaders purport to represent.[46] The legal rationale for racial domination in American life forces scholars to explicate the precise relationship of the ideology of race to the ideology of law and its materiality.

Scholars who embraced Marxist legal theory have examined that relationship.[47] Marxist legal theory analysts link class, race, and the law as inextricably locked in the base activity of political economy. Keeping in step with Marxist theorists, critical race theorists also understand that racism is a false idea, but historical circumstance has given *race* a reality based on concrete social relationships institutionalized in the materiality of plantations, courts, judges, law statutes, slave-catchers, night-riders, Jim Crow, and most important, the Constitution itself. In understanding this real basis of the social category of race, Marxists see "law as a constitutive element of race itself."[48] Critical race theorists reject liberal legalism's view that law is distinct from politics and thus has a rationality, a neutrality. Race critics understand that law constructs race in an indeterminate manner. This indeterminacy is clear when one examines the Warren Court's emphasis on "results rule" when determining the facts of racial discrimination, and its predecessor Court's emphasizing "intent rule" when doing the same. Even when today's Court is emphasizing the color-blindness of law, it is really affirming race by refusing to recognize how *de facto* racism still gives a material reality to race and its legal relationships.[49] Marxist legal theory strives to analyze these relationships without falling into either race reductionism or class reductionism.[50]

Consistent with many of the assumptions of critical race theory, a definition of racism is as follows: *Racism,* as an ideological and institutional force, as with law, in its essence "is a distinct, historically determined structure of beliefs, discourses (systems of beliefs) . . . and practices, with its own contradictions and rhythms of development, none of which can be divorced from the economics or politics of that social formation."[51] This definition is consistent with the assumptions in Frederick Douglass's queries that the phenomenal relations of racism and law are superstructural correlates of America's democratic slave economy.

A MATERIALIST CONCEPTION OF RACE

Racism as a total concept promulgates the false view that the social and moral behavior of people who are not of visual European origin is determined by fixed or permanent inherited characteristics deriving from their racial stock that is, as are the characteristics themselves, inferior.

Inversely, those people who are of visual European stock are superior based on the same inherited fixity. This intellectual ruse, grounded in Western pseudo-scientific thought, was succinctly expressed by one Southern planter: "Your fathers and my fathers built this government on two ideas: the first is that the White is the citizen and master race . . . and the second idea is that the negro is the inferior race."[52]

The foremost Marxist thinker on the question of race and class, Dr. John H. McClendon III, explains that the etymology of *Negro* points to both phenotype and genotype. Both were grounded in the social relationship of slave political economy. New World slavery and the demand for labor took on a color or visual designation. This explains why capitalism and race became uniquely intertwined. Capitalism is driven by class relationships, but because of the social and geographic context of colonial development, *race* itself became a "social category." McClendon argues that the material conditions of White over Black within the production of market commodities led to "the reification of African Americans from their status as social beings, or to what can be more simply stated as their reduction from human to property."[53] Finally, McClendon notes that as politics makes for strange bedfellows, one saw the rise in miscegenation, wherein individuals who represented the phenotype of White over Black were indistinguishable from another. Because of individuals such as Sally Hemmings, Homer Plessy, and Walter White, the ideology of White supremacy had to refine itself to include genotype as a mark of social oppression as well as phenotype. The "one drop rule" became an enormous body of case law as individuals tried to prove their Whiteness and therefore claim all the golden opportunities that such a legal definition would grant them.[54]

Race, as defined by law, reflected and was a manifestation of the social relations of colonial political economy. However, there developed a finite number of cases in which race as phenotype would and did create explicit contradictions in White over Black. In the 1806 case of *Hudgins v. Wright,* one can see the role of law in reifying racial identities.[55] In this case, a Virginia court determined that the racial parameters as defined by the law of the womb should set three intergenerationally related Indian women free. The law of the womb changed in English common law by stating that status of children shall follow status of mother. This legal change had to take place to address the widespread miscegenation of White men sexually impregnating enslaved Black and Indian women. Rights of inheritance would turn on their head if the children of these relations would take on the status of the free White fathers as dictated by continental English common law. In the 1857 Alexina Morrison case, Morrison, being of a White genotype, gained her freedom when "Several doctors testified on her behalf that the shape of her hair follicles and the arches of her feet proved her Whiteness."[56] Because she and other women did not have the genotypic or phenotypic characteristics of race, a "flat nose" or a "woolly head of hair,"[57] they were declared White. In the early twentieth century, the *Alice Jones vs. Leonard "Kip" Rhinelander* case in New York City revealed how phenotype and genotype were summed up in the idea of the one drop rule.[58] Having married and during divorce proceedings, Rhinelander argued that he did not know Ms. Jones was Black because her appearance was White. Had he known, the marriage would have never taken place. Alice Jones was unrobed in the courtroom so jurors might discern "a mark" of Blackness on her body.[59] These cases and others that discussed in this book reveal that the law's reification of race reflects real master-and-slave relationships, or the post-slave America of White over Black.[60] Skin color, hair texture, nose and hip structure, and so on compose the "racial stock" that Western science has always failed to objectify. Racism cannot be validated via science, but Blacks as a race are socially, culturally, and materially real, and this reality has been determined by historical circumstance within a set of social relations of production. Therefore, to be Black is a reality, but what is false is how racism confers negative values, volition, and moral prescriptive conditions on Blackness itself. Racism is an ideology expressing and justifying an inequality within hierarchical, juridic, and economic relationships.

This book examines how law and race converge as ideology and structure, and how both have helped to maintain, in a class of people, a material inequality of immense proportions. Their reaction to this social existence may lead Blacks to become the potential locomotive vanguard if and when revolutionary social change occurs in this country. This interpretation of the potential impact of this twin convergence was stated in the 1830s by historian Alexis de Tocqueville: "If ever America undergoes great revolutions, they will be brought about by the presence of the Black race on the soil of the United States; that is today, they will owe their origin, not to the equality, but to the inequality of conditions."[61]

The "inequality of conditions" to which de Tocqueville refers have been shaped by law and racism as they have been intertwined within the historical development of American political economy. Oliver Wendell Holmes' salutations to his singular profession reveal how law is the handmaiden of such political and economic stimuli:

> the felt necessities of the time, the prevalent moral and political theories, intuitions of public policy, avowed or unconscious, even the prejudices which judges share with their fellow men, have a good deal more to do than the syllogism in determining the rules by which men should be governed.[62]

As with law, racism has responded to the felt necessities of time and place, its contours shaped by pseudo-science as well as common prejudices, and ultimately by public policy aimed at achieving economic growth.[63]

In describing the zigzag of how humans govern each other, depending on the historic instance—both public and private—Oliver Wendell Holmes revealed the difficulty in explaining the historical development of any type of social formation. Because this book is concerned with certain dialectical influences on a specified social formation and its historical development, it becomes very important to apply theory to history. In carefully choosing Marx and his legal theory and other major theorists inspired by Marx, I believe that the salient turning points in African-American Constitutional history can be clarified and understood. The critical watersheds within this history are the periods of slavery, the transition era of Civil War and Reconstruction, the rural-agricultural period, the transition era of migration, and the urban-industrial period. Within these temporal junctures, this book attempts to clarify the praxis of law, race, and political economy by using the materialist theory of law outlined here.

There are risks involved in attempting to answer Frederick Douglass' queries by concentrating one's analysis mainly on U.S. Supreme Court decisions vis-a-vis the African American. Isolating cases of the African American as slave, freeman, and citizen could be inadequate for the task at hand. The Court's decision and issues before it are rarely so narrow as to be racially one dimensional.

However, I focus on this legal institution because of its salient position within America's political and social order, which augurs that this is "a nation of laws, not of men." This position affords the Court special opportunities to express hegemonic ideologies that seek to resolve the material contradictions within political economy. Law cases are narratives that explain moments in history and time, thus defining the present. In the words of Alexis de Tocqueville, "Scarcely any political question arises in the United States that is not resolved sooner or later, into a judicial question."[64]

This work demonstrates that the use of Marxist legal theory brings clarity to any specific case and to the variant political, social, and economic questions that are germane to historical circumstance. Many of the great Constitutional controversies (e.g., the formation of the federal system, the institutionalization of judicial review, the meaning of Federalism, the direction of federal policy during the Great Depression, and the questions of law and order since the 1950s) in part involved, in their incongruities, essential questions of law, race, and political economy.

I do not cite or discuss all Supreme Court cases involving people of African descent, nor do I analyze all the changes in American political economy. Some cases and some political and economic changes are minor aberrations or redundancies of critical elements that are examined in other substantive cases.

When including an analysis of dissenting opinions of the Court's justices, this work presumes the idea of competing ideologies. Individual justices, at any particular time, did and do represent and present the emerging ideology of different minor ruling class factions with interests different than those of the leading faction of the ruling social class. At times, we can see in dissenting opinions the germination of a new faction moving from a segment in itself to a segment for itself.[65] At times, the battles over appointments to the high Court mirror these intense struggles within segments of the ruling class.[66]

The problematics of law, race, and political economy via the contours and rhythms of African American history are addressed in previous research.[67] I build on this research and, I believe, by choosing Marxist legal theory as the major intellectual focus for explicating this history, open new lines of dialogue on such an important field of historical inquiry.

In conclusion, the title of this book addresses two political paradigms. By selecting the phrase *Black Marxism,* I am using the word *Black* as an adjective, and therefore, I do not "alter in substance or content that which surrounds its meaning of Marxism in its function as a definitive type of political philosophic viewpoint."[68] Therefore, Black Marxism is not a particularity of regressive nationalism that always inverses classical Marxism by standing it on its own head.[69] *Black Marxism* is nothing more than "Marxism in Ebony" and, therefore, a mere descriptive of the phenotype of the author. The second part of the tile, *American Constitutionalism,* refers to the modern idea that those who hold political power must be limited and restrained in their instrumental use of this power. The procedural guarantees of "procedural regularity, substantive limitations, government by consent, spiritual freedom, free expression, and an open political process"[70] were elements negated in the social existence within the Black experience. This book examines this negation by using Marxist legal theory by a Marxist clothed in Ebony.

ENDNOTES

1. Andrew Fraser, "The Legal Theory We Need Now," *Socialist Review,* no. 40–41 (vol. 8, no. 4–5, July–October 1978), 179.

2. Eugene Genovese, Elizabeth Fox-Genovese, and Harold D. Woodman, *Fruits of Merchant Capital* (New York: Oxford University Press, 1983), 337; see also Colin Sumner, *Reading Ideologies: An Investigation into the Marxist Theory of Ideology and Law* (New York: Academic Press, 1979), 258.

3. Frederick Douglass, "The Constitution and Slavery," *North Star,* March 16, 1849; see also Martin Duberman, *The Anti-Slavery Vanguard* (Princeton: Princeton University Press, 1965), 209–239.

4. Lennox S. Hinds, *Illusions of Justice: Human Rights Violations in the United States* (Iowa City: University of Iowa, 1979).

5. Gordon S. Wood, *The Creation of the American Republic, 1776–1787* (Chapel Hill: University of North Carolina Press, 1969); Russell B. Nye, *Fettered Freedom: Civil Liberties and the Slavery Crisis, 1836–1860* (East Lansing: Michigan State University, 1964); Melvin I. Urofsky, *A March of Liberty: A Constitutional History of the United States* (New York: Oxford University Press, 1988); Jacobus ten Broek, *The Anti-Slavery Origins of the Fourteenth Amendment* (Berkeley: University of California Press, 1951); Dwight L. Dumond, *Antislavery: The Crusade for Freedom in America* (Ann Arbor: University of Michigan Press, 1961); John T. Noonan, Jr., *Persons and Masks of the Law* (New York: Farrar, Straus, and Giroux, 1976); John T. Noonan, Jr., *The Antelope: The Ordeal of the Recaptured Africans in the Administration of James Monroe and John Quincy Adams* (Berkeley: University of California Press, 1977); Bernard Bailyn, *The Ideological Origins of the American Revolution* (Cambridge: The Belknap Press, 1967); Leonard Levy, *The Law of the Commonwealth and Chief Justice Shaw* (Cambridge: Harvard University Press, 1957); George Dargo, *The Roots of the Republic: A New Perspective on Early American Constitutionalism* (New York: Praeger, 1974).

6. Richard Kluger, *Simple Justice* (New York: Vintage Books, 1975); John Phillip Reid, *The Concept of Liberty in the Age of Revolution* (Chicago: University of Chicago Press, 1988); David Waldstreicher, *Slavery's Constitution: From Revolution to Ratification* (New York: Hill and Wang, 2009); Donald L. Robinson, *Slavery in the Structure of American Politics, 1765–1820* (New York: W.W. Norton, 1971); Robert M. Cover, *Justice Accused: Antislavery and the Judicial Process* (New Haven: Yale University Press, 1975); David Brion Davis, *The Problem of Slavery in the Age of Revolution, 1770–1823* (New York: Oxford University Press, 1975); William M. Wiecek, *The Sources of Antislavery Constitutionalism in America, 1760–1848* (New York: Harper Collins Publishers, 1986); Stanley Campbell, *The Slave Catchers: Enforcement of the Fugitive Slave Law, 1850–1860* (Chapel Hill: University of North Carolina Press, 1976); Arthur Zilversmith, *The First Emancipation: The Abolition of Slavery in the North* (Chicago: University of Chicago Press, 1976); A. Legal Higginbottom, *In the Matter of Color: Race and the American Legal Process: The Colonial Period* (New York: Oxford University Press,1978); Harold M. Hyman and William M. Wiecek, *Equal Justice Under Law: Constitutional Development, 1835–1875* (New York: Harper Collins Publishers, 1982); Donald E. Lively and Paul Finkleman, *An Imperfect Union: Slavery, Federalism, and Comity* (Union, N.J., Lawbook Exchange, 2000), Thomas D. Morris, *Free Men All: The Personal Liberty Laws of the North, 1780–1861* (Baltimore: Johns Hopkins Press, 1974); Donald Lively, *The Constitution and Race* (Westport: Praeger, 1992); Alexander Tsesis, We Shall Overcome: *A History of Civil Rights and the Law* (New York: Yale University Press, 2008).

7. Neo-revisionists write across a broad spectrum, from bourgeois theorists to those within the critical legal studies movement to Marxist critics. See James Willard Hurst, *Law and the Conditions of Freedom in the Nineteenth-Century United States* (Madison: University of Wisconsin Press, 1956); Robert Paul Wolf, ed., *The Rule of Law* (New York: Simon and Schuster, 1971); Morton Horowitz, *The Transformation of American Law* (Cambridge: Harvard University Press, 1977); Lawrence M. Friedman, *A History of American Law* (New York: Simon & Schuster, 1985); Kermit Hall, *The Magic Mirror: Law in American History* (Oxford: Oxford University Press, 1989). For a review of critical legal studies writers, see Roberto Mangabeira Unger, "The Critical Legal Studies Movement," *Harvard Law Review* 96 (1983), 560; Mark Tushnet, "Critical Legal Studies: An Introduction to Its Origins and Underpinnings," *Journal of Legal Education* (1986); Tom Denyer, "Toward a Socialist Jurisprudence: A Critique of Instrumental Legality" (unpublished paper, Binghamton, New York, 1979); Charles Lawrence, "The Id, the Ego, and Equal Protection: Reckoning with Unconscious Racism," *Stanford Law Review* 39 (1987): 317; Jose A.

Bracamonte, Richard Delgado, Mari J. Matsuda, Patricia J. Williams, and Harlon L. Dalton, "Minority Critiques of the Critical Legal Studies Movement," *Harvard Civil Rights–Civil Liberties Law Review* (Spring 1987); and see two anthologies on Critical Legal Studies: Kimberle Crenshaw, Neil Gotanda, Gary Peller and Kendall Thomas, *Critical Race Theory: The Key Writings That Formed the Movement* (New York: The New Press, 1995); Richard Delgrado and Jean Stefancic, *Critical Race Theory: The Cutting Edge* (Philadelphia: Temple University Press, 2000). On the Marxist critique of American Law, see Piers Beirne and Richard Quinney, *Marxism and Law* (New York: John Wiley and Sons, 1982); Piers Beirne and Robert Sharlet, *Pashukanis: Selected Writings on Marxism and Law* (New York: Academic Press, 1980); E. P. Thompson, *Whigs and Hunters* (New York: Pantheon Books, 1975); Maureen Cain and Alan Hunt, *Marx and Engels on Law* (New York: Academic Press, 1979); David Sugarman, ed., *Legality, Ideology and the State* (New York: Academic Press, 1983); G. Cohen, *The Labour Theory of Value and the Concept of Exploitation in Marx, Justice and History* (1980); B. Fine, ed., *Capitalism and the Rule of Law* (London: Hutchinson, 1979); David Kairys, ed., *The Politics of Law: A Progressive Critique* (New York: Pantheon Books, 1982); Arnold Peterson, *The Supreme Court: Watch Dog of Capitalism* (Brooklyn: New York Labor News, 1971); Alan Hunt, "Law, State, and Class Struggle," *Marxism Today* (June 1976); Paul Costello, "Racism and Black Oppression in the United States: A Beginning Analysis," *Theoretical Review*, 24 (September–October 1981); Sumner (1979); Antonio Gramsci, *Selections from the Prison NoteBooks* (New York: International Publishers, 1971); E. P. Thompson, Douglas Hay, Peter Linebaugh, John G. Rule, and Cal Winslow, *Albion's Fatal Tree: Crime and Society in Eighteenth-Century England* (London: Pantheon, 1977); Roberto M. Unger, *Knowledge and Politics* (New York: Free Press, 1975); Fraser (1978).

8. See previous citations but especially the essay by Roberto Mangabeira Unger, "The Critical Legal Studies Movement," *Harvard Law Review*, 96 (1983); F. Valdes, J. M. Culp, A. P. Harris, eds., *Crossroads, Directions, and a New Critical Race Theory* (Philadelphia: Temple University Press, 2002).

9. Cain and Hunt (1979); Piers Beirne and Richard Quinney, eds. *Marxism and the Law* (Hoboken: Wiley and Sons, 1982).

10. Unger, "The Critical Legal Studies Movement," 563.

11. Crenshaw, et al., *Critical Race Theory,* xxv.

12. *Relative autonomy* is a major theme of the CLS movement. See essay: Isaac Balbus, "Commodity Form and Legal Form: An Essay on the 'Relative Autonomy' of the Law," *Law and Society Review,* 11 (Winter 1977), 571–588; see also Mark Tushnet, "The American Law of Slavery, 1810–1860: A Study in the Persistence of Legal Autonomy," *Law and Society* (Fall 1975).

13. Karl Klare, "Judicial Deradicalization of the Wagner Act and the Origins of Modern Legal/Consciousness, 1937–1941," *Minnesota Law Review.* 62 (1978): 266.

14. Max Weber, *Economy and Society,* three volumes (1968); or see David Trubek, "Max Weber and the Rise of Capitalism," *Wisconsin Law Review* (1972), 740–745; see also Robert Graptein, "The Failure of Weber's Conception of Legitimacy: Its Causes and Implications," *The Journal of Politics,* 43 (1981): 457.

15. Trubek, 740.

16. David Trubek, "Complexity and Contradiction in the Legal Order: Balbus and the Challenge of Critical Social Thought About Law," *Law and Society* (Winter 1977): 538.

17. Trubek, "Complexity and Contradiction in the Legal Order," 538–539.

18. Isaac Balbus, *The Dialectics of Legal Repression* (New Brunswick: Transaction Books, 1973).

19. Balbus (1973), 6.

20. Balbus (1973), 6.

21. Charles A. Beard, *An Economic Interpretation of the Constitution of the United States* (New York: Macmillan, 1941); Henry Steele Commager, "The Constitution: Was It An Economic Document?" *American Heritage,* 9 (1958); John P. Diggins, "Power and Authority in American History: The Case of Charles A. Beard and His Critics," *American Historical Review,* 86 (1981); Staughton Lynd, "Capitalism, Democrcay, and the U.S. Constitution," *Science and Society,* 27 (1963); Joyce Appleby, *Capitalism and a New Social Order: The Republican Vision of the 1790s* (New York: New York University Press, 1984).

22. Hunt (1976), 179.

23. Sumner(1979), 257.

24. Hunt (1976), 184.

25. See research by A. E. Keir Nash, "Fairness and Formalism in the Trials of Blacks in the State Supreme Courts of the Old South," *Virginia Law Review,* LVI (February 1970); "The Texas Supreme Court and the Trial Rights of Blacks, 1845–1860," *Journal of American History,* LVIII (December 1971).

26. C. J. Arthur, *Critique,* 7 (Winter 1976) 36.

27. Balbus (1973), 6.

28. Harold McDougall, "The Role of the Black Lawyer: A Marxist View," *The Black Law Journal,* vol. 7, no. 1 (1981–1982).

29. McDougall (1981–1982XXXX), 5–6.

30. C. Vann Woodward, *The Origins of the New South, 1877–1913* (Baton Rouge: Lousiana State University Press, 1951); Roger Ranson and Richard Sutch, *One Kind of Freedom: The Economic Consequences of Emancipation* (Cambridge: Cambridge University Press, 1977).

31. Robert McClosky, *American Conservatism in the Age of Enterprise, 1865–1910* (New York: Harper & Row, 1951), 161–162.

32. Loren Miller, *The Petitioners* (New York: Pantheon, 1966), 180.

33. *Civil Rights Cases,* 109 U.S. 3 1883).

34. *Plessy v. Ferguson,* 163 U.S. 537 (1896). In his dissent, Harlan observed the great dominant leadership and intelligence of the "Anglo Saxon" race.

35. Eugene Genovese quoting Mao Tse-tung in "The Hegemonic Function of the Law," in *Roll, Jordon, Roll: The World the Slaves Made* (New York: Vintage, 1972), 12.

36. LeAnn Keith, *The Colfax Massacre: The Untold Story of Black Power, White Terror, and the Death of Reconstruction* (New York: Oxford University Press, 2008); Charles Lane, *The Day That Freedom Died: The Colfax Massacre, The Supreme Court, and the Betrayal of Reconstruction* (New York: Henry Holt and Co., 2008); Allen Trelease, *White Terror: The Ku Klux Klan and Southern Reconstruction* (New York: Harper & Row, 1971).

37. Christopher Waldrep, "Substituting Law for the Lash: Emancipation and Legal Formalism in a Mississippi County Court," *The Journal of American History* (March 1996); and Leon Litwack, *Been in the Storm Too Long: The Aftermath of Slavery* (New York: Knopf, 1971).

38. Ranson and Sutch, 1977; Pete Daniel, *The Shadow of the Plantation: Peonage in the South, 1901–1969* (New York: Oxford University Press, 1973).

39. McDougall (1981–1982), p. 32; see also Balbus (1977), 576.

40. Earl Maltz, "Reconstruction Without Revolution: Republican Civil Rights Theory in the Era of the Fourteenth Amendment," *Houston Law Review,* 24, 2 (March 1987); Michael Les Benedict, "Preserving the Constitution: The Conservative Basis of Radical Reconstruction," *The Journal of American History,* LXI (June 1974).

41. Sumner (1979), 247; see also Hunt (1976), 187; see also McDougall (1981–1982XXXX), 43.

42. Andrew McLaughlin, "The Court, the Corporation, and Conkling," *American Historical Review,* 46 (1940); James F. S. Russell, "The Railroads and the 'Conspiracy Theory' of the Fourteenth Amendment," *Mississippi Valley Historical Review,* 41 (1955); Louis B. Boudin, "Truth and Fiction about the Fourteenth Amendment," *New York University Law Quarterly Review,* 16 (1938).

43. See McDougall (1981–1982), for an excellent overview delineating this theme.

44. See Balbus (1973), which gives the reader a theory of the mediated aspects of law and criminal/rebellious activity.

45. *Brown II* dictum "With All Deliberate Speed" is a confirmation of this point. A constitutional right recognized but denied immediate implementation because of the sensibilities of Southern Whites, who were given time to adapt to a new set of social relations/race relations.

46. See Lewis Steele, "Nine Men in Black Who Think White," first published in *New York Times Magazine* and reprinted in *Philadelphia* Tribune, February 8, 2000, 2K; see also Melvin Wulf's analysis in his essay "Purge at NAACP," in *Commonweal* (December 20, 1968): 403–404.

47. See endnote 7.

48. Crenshaw et al. (1995), xxv.

49. Crenshaw et al. (1995), xxvii.

50. Crenshaw et al. (1995), xxiv.

51. Paul Costello, "Racism and Black Oppression in the United States: A Beginning Analysis," *Theoretical Review,* 24 (September–October 1981), 11; see also John Gabriel and Gideon Ben-Tovim, "Marxism and the Concept of

Racism," *Economy and Society,* 7, 2 (May 1978); Dr. Marios Nikolinakos, "Notes on an Economic Theory of Racism," RACE (London: Institute of Race Relations, 1974).

52. Stated by William L. Yancy, U.S. Congressman from Alabama; served as a senator in the Confederate States of America's congress. Quoted in Ronald Walters, *White Nationalism, Black Interests: Conservative Public Policy and the Black Community* (Detroit: Wayne State University Press, 2003), 23.

53. John H. McClendon III, "Black/Blackness: Philosophical Considerations," in Carol Boyce Davies, ed., *Encyclopedia of the African Diaspora,* vol. 1 (2008), 202.

54. Ian Haney Lopez, *White by Law: The Legal Construction of Race* (New York: New York University Press, 1996). Professor Haney examines a wide variety of lawsuits of plaintiffs claiming "Whiteness" under the legislation—Naturalization Act of 1790. See also Bliss Broyard's biography of her father, *One Drop: My Father's Hidden Life—A Story of Race and Family Secrets* (New York: Little, Brown and Company, 2007); Scott L. Malcoson, *One Drop of Blood: The American Misadventure of Race* (New York: Farrar Straus Girous, 2000); for an excellent study on this topic, see Ariel Gross, *What Blood Won't Tell: A History of Race on Trial in America* (Cambridge: Harvard University Press, 2008)

55. Richard Delgado and Jean Stefancic, *Critical Race Theory: An Introduction* (New York: New York University Press, 2001), 92.

56. Gross (2008), 2.

57. Gross (2008), 193.

58. Earl Lewis and Heidi Ardizzone, *Love on Trial: An American Scandal in Black and White* (New York: W.W. Norton & Co., 2001); Gross, (2008); Ian Haney Lopez, *White by Law: The Legal Construction of Race by Law,* 10th ed. (New York: New York University Press, 2006).

59. Lewis and Ardizzone (2001).

60. Rayford Logan, *Betrayal of the Negro: From Rutherford B. Hayes to Woodrow Wilson* (London: Collier Books, 1969).

61. Alexis de Tocqueville, *Democracy in America* (New York: The Colonial Press, 1900), 264.

62. Oliver Wendell Holmes, "The Path of the Law," *Harvard Law Review,* 10 (1897), 457; see also O. W. Holmes, *The Common Law* (New York: Little, Brown Publishers, 1881), 1.

63. Nikolinakos (1974).

64. Alexis de Tocqueville, *Democracy in America,* as quoted in Kermit L. Hall, *The Magic Mirror: Law in American History* (New York: Oxford University Press, 1989), 86.

65. Genovese (1972), 27.

66. Glendon A. Schubert, *Judicial Mind: The Attitudes and Ideologies of Supreme Court Justices, 1946–1965* (Evanston: Northwestern University Press, 1965); Karl A. Lamb, "The Opposition Party as Secret Agent: Republicans and the Court Fight, 1937," *Papers of the Michigan Academy of Science, Arts, and Letters,* 46 (1961).

67. Fraser (1978), 147.

68. John H. McClendon, III, "Marxism in Ebony Contra Black Marxism: Categorical Implications," *ProudFlesh: Journal of Culture, Politics, and Consciousness,* ISSN 1543–0855, Issue 6 (2007).

69. John H. McClendon, III, "On the Nature of Whiteness and the Ontology of Race: Toward an Dialectic Materialist Analysis," in George Yancy, ed., *What White Looks Like: African American Philosophers, or the Whiteness Question* (New York: Routledge, 2004); John H. McClendon, III, "Act Your Age and Not Your Color: Blackness as Material Conditions, Presumptive Context, and Social Category," in George Yancy, ed., *White on White, Black on Black* (Lanham, Maryland: Roman and Littlefield Publishers, 2005).

70. George Dargo, *Roots of the Republic: A New Perspective in Early American Constitutionalism* (New York: Praeger Publishing, 1971); see the influence of Native Americans on the U.S. Constitution in Bruce E. Johnson, *Forgotten Founders: Ben Franklin, the Iroquois, and the Rationale for the American Revolution* (Cambridge: Harvard Common Press, 1982).

CHAPTER I

The Colonial Background

*The discovery of gold and silver in America, the extirpation, enslavement . . . of the aboriginal . . .
the turning of Africa into a warren for the hunting of Black skins, signalized the rosy dawn of the
era of capitalist accumulations . . . of primitive accumulation . . . but also the looting of . . . non-
European peoples and the fostering of a new system of slavery to exploit their labor.*

—KARL MARX[1]

Caio Prado Junior once stated that New World slavery was a radical departure from all previous forms of exploitative servile laboring systems. Prado suggested that slavery in the Americas
"derived from an order of events that was inaugurated in the 15th century" with the maritime
colonization and the establishment of new social order in lands discovered.[2] This colonization
and new sets of social relationships of White over Black led to four major developments,
according to Eric Williams. First, the rise of a political economy based almost solely on the
exploitation of African labor led to the rationalizing ideology of White racism. Second, this
racially based political economy, producing commodities for the world market, led to the primitive accumulation of capital that became the basis for the rise of the European Industrial
Revolution. Third, merchant–capitalists who became leaders in the abolitionist movement had
an economic incentive to proclaim the "rights of men" ideas as applicable to the servile class.
Fourth, abolitionist advocates, as merchant-capitalists, understood the declination of slave-
based economies as enhancing future market growth.[3] However, if abolition was achieved, it
would "end slavery but not free the Negro."[4] Racialism took on a life of its own and became
an autonomous idea which "ran like a fault line . . . appearing in . . . legislative enactments,
common law" and case law.[5] This chapter examines how the superstructure of racial ideology

and law became a clear manifestation of class domination and exploitation during the colonial period of American settlement.

The juridical and racialist concepts that "a slave cannot be a White man, and every man of color was descendant of a slave"[6] had its origins and development within the changing world economy between the sixteenth and nineteenth centuries. It was during this phase of human development that one saw the rise of nation–state formations in Western Europe, the concomitant evolving of science and technology, and the entrepreneurial application of these social and cultural phenomena which signaled the unfolding and maturation of the mercantilist clarion of capitalist development.[7] The discovery, enslavement, and conquest, from the sixteenth century onward, of "New World" lands and people helped solidify merchant capital and the new nation–state bureaucracies; the relationship among science and technology and political power greatly accelerated the "primitive accumulation of capital," all of which became the preconditioned sine qua non for the rise of merchant capitalism.[8]

The political and economic enclosure of the geographic regions of both the Old and New Worlds created a world market, with the Old World as reinvigorated finance and importing commodities centers and the New World as exploited, exporting latifundia-based commodities producing peripheries.[9] The mercantile capitalist interests of the European metropoles directed and controlled the world marketplace, which entrenched their political economies to the detriment of the exploited aborigine populations of the West Indies, the indigenous people of the East Indies, and the native inhabitants in Africa or the Diaspora.

This process of political and economic domination and empire building revolved to a large extent around the trans-Atlantic slave trade and slave production of agricultural commodities on New World plantations for the ever-growing international consumer market system. Slave commodity production accelerated the growth of wealth and power among the merchant–capitalists of Western Europe. The slave trade was initially centered in Iberia and the Mediterranean, but as the New World lands were "legally claimed,"[10] the need to have at one's disposal the labor power required to mine, plant, and harvest these resources became problematic. The Spanish and Portuguese merchant adventurers—after their *conquistas* in Mexico, Peru, and Brazil—found their labor-problem solution in the bodies, feet, backs, and hands of the former citizens of the vanquished Aztec, Mayan, and Inca empires (Brazil) and Carib people. When, through death and disease, this workforce decreased to harmful productive levels, the Iberians redirected the already established African slave trade from the peninsular region to their plantation colonies in the New World.[11]

The high mortality rate of Native-American populations led to Africans becoming, through a torturous process that differed from one region to another, the fundamental and sole laboring base for the cultivation, production, and exportation of sugar, coffee, tobacco, rice, indigo, and ultimately "King" Cotton. It was the control over these staples that led England, by military force, to establish colonial domination first in Barbados and Jamaica, and later with the thirteen British colonies in North America. The enslavement of Africans in these colonies developed in direct proportion to the laboring needs that each had in juxtaposition to the correlative political and economic changes that took place during the seventeenth and eighteenth centuries. The legal and racialist ideological rationale of African enslavement was a history-specific response to the developing necessities of colonial political economy. This rationale, both moral and legal, was expressed by Bishop La Casas when he advocated, in 1517, the transportation of Africans to the New World so that the "poor indio" could be saved.[12] The irony, of course, was that the poor indio was not saved, whereas the transportation still occurred. The formal legal contractual basis for the trans-Atlantic slave came in the guise of the *asiento,* which was issued by Spain as a legal contract to slavers who could then import Africans into the Spanish possessions in the New World.[13] The Dutch, French, Portuguese, and then the British dominated the transportation of "Black Gold" across the Middle Passage over the next several hundred years. Africans, as commerce of labor and worth their weight in gold, became "things" contested in maritime courts as insured owners sued to collect on their lost property at sea. Slave transportation on the high seas was a high-risk venture, and a whole body of law developed surrounding the assumption of risk.[14]

The commodification of Africans as articles of commerce with legal imprimatur is revealed by the infamous *Zong* case, known in maritime law as *Gregson v. Gilbert,* 1782. This case demonstrates that slaves as things were owned by juridic subjects. The facts of the case are striking. The slave ship *Zong*, under the captaincy of Luke Collingwood, embarked from West Africa to Jamaica on September 6, 1781. In chains were 470 slaves. Eight weeks into the voyage, a viral epidemic took the lives of sixty Africans and sixteen crew members. Knowing he was running low on water, Captain Collingwood, over the objections of his chief mate James Kelsa, decided to throw overboard the weakened and sick slaves. Collingwood understood that maritime insurance law would protect his insurers if slaves were lost when thrown into the sea because of maritime necessity. Collingwood died before the *Zong* returned to London and thus did not witness the adversarial litigation between Gregson, owner of the *Zong*, and Gilbert, the insurance underwriter. Gilbert refused to pay the thirty pounds per slave loss that Gregson was claiming. The initial trial jury found for the plaintiff, Gregson, but Gilbert appealed to a three-judge panel, which included Lord Justice Mansfield.[15] The panel recommended a new trial, but the historical record is silent as to the resolution of this case. British abolitionists, Black and White, demanded that a charge of murder should be added to the litigation; however, Gilbert's attorney rejected this possibility by demurring that Africans were property and therefore could not be murdered, contending it would be "madness" to think otherwise.[16] The legal commodification of humans as issues of commerce, profit, and fault that accrued to monetary damages revealed law's own internal, logical structure, but also how that structure was contoured by racialism grounded in the needs of political economy.

Africans were first commerced into the English colony of Jamestown, Virginia, in 1619. They became an adjunct labor segment to an already existing, quasi-free laboring system that up to then included a small number of coerced Indians and the mainstay of imported lower-class, disinherited Europeans under contracts of indentured servitude.[17] By the late seventeenth century, the commercial importation of Africans into Virginia and other North American colonies became part and parcel of a worldwide integrated system of ordering and mastering African labor.[18] Toward the late seventeenth century, the tremendous growth and market demand for varied agricultural staples forced the settler planter to increase the size of his African labor force while ensuring that legal control over them would be maintained. The need to tighten up the juridic status of Africans revolved around the differing types of social status that defined Africans. Some were free yeomen, some indentured servants, and some were slaves. However, by the latter decades of the seventeenth century, the status of most Africans had deteriorated to the condition of *durante vita* slavery, or slavery for life.[19] The reasons for this were threefold. First, the demands of the international marketplace led to the colonial economy changing from small units of agricultural production, which had as their labor source both White and Black bonded servants, to highly capitalized, labor-intensive, large-scale plantation units of production in which racial slavery became the major labor source. Second, this economic change corresponded with a severe labor shortage in the availability and thus the cost of White bonded servants. This problem stemmed from the internecine European wars that restricted the immigration of indentured servants, the leveling off of England's population growth, and the widespread rumors that servants were treated harshly and that the promises of "bounty" in the New World were false.[20] Third, in response to such bad treatment and lack of acquiring the bounty of land ownership, a series of popular uprisings occurred in late seventeenth-century Virginia by the class camaraderie of both White and Black bonded servants and slaves that forced the colonial ruling elite to rethink their political and economic class and racial ordering and thus the maintenance of their class domination within that political economy.[21] The rise of an exclusive laboring system based on human beings of African origin was intricately tied to these three factors.

The integration of all New World colonies into the world market system led to the development of similar types of plantation production units with the interchange of ideas, methods, technology and a general way of doing business and marketing for the bourgeois consumer markets of Europe. Beginning in the Mediterranean and moving to the Sal Islands of North Africa and then to the New World, the use of an interracial labor force and new technologies of producing "sweetness" led to the "westward movement of sugar."[22] For the North American colonists, their European brethren in the English Caribbean and Latin America had previously developed large-scale units of staple production using the gang labor of African slaves. With this development, the knowledge and ways of organizing the labor of Africans became well-known throughout New World colonial societies.[23]

The importance of African labor for this development was stated by one planter as follows: "[Y]ou know very well how one shall mayntayne 20 moores cheaper than one English servant."[24] Colonial America, both the upper Northern and lower Southern colonies, became integrated into what one historian has labeled the South Atlantic system that "centered on the production of tropical staples in Brazil, the Caribbean mainland and islands, and southern North America. The system reached to Africa for labor, to Europe for managerial staff and commercial direction, to northern North America for timber, food and shipping."[25] The rise of American slavery and the law of slavery revolved around this historic process of worldwide integration of commodity production and exchange and new social relationships of race and class.

The decline in the immigration of White bonded servants was resolved by the Peace of Utrecht, which gave Europe a civil détente for the first time in several decades.[26] This led to the noninterrupted flow of new immigrants who, most importantly, had better artisan skills and abilities than the earlier "Newgaters" and had better rights protection because of several pieces of new legislation passed by crown. This legislation was aimed at improving the overall condition and opportunities of its White bonded subjects.[27]

These events, which speeded up the material improvement in the lives of poor Whites, paralleled the rapid debasement and eventual incarceration of Africans as slaves. The poor Whites gradually moved into managerial and interstitial laboring positions, while their once working-class Black cohorts' status remained within bonded servitude or lapsed into *durante vita,* or slavery for one's entire lifetime. The period from the 1640s through the 1670s witnessed these changes in the legal, political, and social stratification within colonial society.[28]

A series of cases concerning slave and servant resistance reveals the confluence of law, race, and political economy. The cases that represent the watershed in race relations during the mid-1640s concerned Black and White servants in Virginia running away or taking flight from the exploited conditions of the plantations. Once these interracial runaways were captured, their unequal treatment demonstrated that the material conditions of the colonies were moderated by an emerging law of race. A legal turning point was witnessed in 1640 when Virginia's General Court sentenced the runaway but recaptured African servant John Punch to *durante vita* slavery. His two White conspirators, a Dutchman and a Scot, were given additional time to serve their master and the colony.[29] This case is important because it demonstrates that early America's class system was not racially specific; however, by the time of this case, the dual legal treatment of Blacks and Whites began to appear. All three class resisters were given their day in court with the formal legal procedures due each of them. However, planters used the courts as an instrument of coercion and punishment to divide and control their interracial working class by giving the Dutchman and the Scot the carrot of leniency while giving John Punch the coercive sanction of the stick. The division of the exploited class along the line of race had begun. Prior to his taking flight, Punch was a servant, but his severe punishment clearly reveals that law, which had determined Punch's prior servant status, was working both with formal legal equality and, at times of resistance, as an instrument of class power and incipient White privilege.[30] Because racialism was not culturally solidified, a court's discretion could lead to case law favoring freedom or slavery.[31]

The biography of Anthony Johnson is also instructive. He arrived in Virginia in 1621 and labored in a class system of exploitation for twenty years before gaining his, his wife's, and his children's freedom. Because of his legal status as a free man, he was able to enter into contractual relations[32] and, by hard work and perseverance, acquired 250 acres of land, livestock, hired servants, and slaves. Formal legal equality and the relative autonomy of the law from political economy permitted him to elevate out of the depth of despair while others such as John Punch were sinking into the abyss of slavery. Judge-made law was used as an autonomous instrument in a discretionary and whimsical manner. The law was reflecting and shaping John Punch's social reality, but the law's own internal autonomy shaped Johnson's reality at polar opposites. This anomaly of Black freedom and Black slavery was resolved by the mid-1660s for the vast majority of Africans. Johnson's own children could not inherit his wealth because by the late 1660s, law had responded to changes in social relations that by that time, began to prohibit Black opportunity per se.[33] As slave law developed during this period, one can see an all-inclusive web of coercion: all-inclusive in reference to Whites and Blacks within the same social class. The ruling elite planters had to divide and conquer this mass of labor on the basis of race because that was clearly the most salient line of delineation.[34] Like the Indian, the African was both militarily defeated, politically powerless, and marked by cultural and physical differences. Indian slavery and African slavery were already a part of New World colonial political economy in the Caribbean, and American colonists were cognizant of this fact.[35] Law used as an instrument to solidify this neoracial division appeared in a wide variety of statutes by the late seventeenth century. These laws forbade Blacks from carrying arms, owning boats, moving without a pass, congregating with Whites in drinking establishments, wearing lace clothing, intermarrying with Whites, and so on. One such law in Virginia is instructive. The 1662 law's declaration was that "if any Christian shall commit fornication with a negro man or woman, hee or shee soe offending" will pay twice the fine as if the transracial variable was not present.[36] This statute and others that quickly followed explicitly condemned and punished White women who sought to satisfy "lascivious and lust full desires" by intermarrying with Negroes or slaves.[37] These statutes are very important, because they reveal the camaraderie of a social laboring class where race is of no great importance. A class that socializes together can make revolution together. These statutes were passed by a planter class that recognized the social and sexual and, therefore, the political implications when class subsumes race.[38]

The major change in English common law took place in this decade. Breaking with English common law heritage, most colonies required that status of children must follow status of mother via the "law of the womb."[39] The common law tradition of England required the child's status to follow that of the father. This tradition could not be maintained if colonial society was moving toward a race-based hierarchical social structure. Sexual relations between White men and Black women and their offspring would certainly affect a hierarchy based on racial exclusion and color. Interracial sex was severely punished, and any transgressors, male or female, were punished harshly.

These legal changes, coupled with the growth of plantation economy and the domination by large planters, led to a series of interracial and class-related resistance movements that culminated in Nathaniel Bacon's Rebellion in 1676 Virginia.[40] This major act of resistance was brought on by tight restrictions on land availability preventing opportunities by the landless and marginal freeman. Virginia's planter class restricted land to maintain economic stability and steady growth without the possible disruption of an Indian war that would be caused by further White land aggrandizement.[41]

To maintain social order, the ruling planter class by the earlier 1660s had decided to divide and conquer the "giddy multitudes" of Black slaves, Black and White freemen, Black and White servants, and small Black and White farmers.[42] Bacon's Rebellion was a confirmation that the legal and political changes being made by the large planters were in their class interests and now, racial interests as well.[43] The planter class defeated the giddy multitudes by military decisiveness and the use of law to ensure the separation of these once-exploited compatriots. This fateful decision of separation was based on race and color. The color line would henceforth determine which class of persons would be free or quasi-free and which class of persons would be slave. The ideology of color or social race was to determine not only Virginia's colonial identity, but eventually the national identity of America as well.[44] Each colony, from the northernmost part of New England to the middle region and on to the South, made similar decisions concerning race and class in their own experimental and experiential way. The outcome of these decisions was quite the same: White liberty and Black enslavement.[45]

The molding of a cultural consciousness of race was the decisive solution to a social order being torn asunder by the periodic rebellions and insurrections of a collectivity of White landless freemen, indentured Blacks and Whites alike, and slaves. The extension of liberal legal privileges to Europe's emigrating poor, while excluding the Native American Indian and the African slave, led to what one historian described as the *American paradox*. Edmund Morgan noted that "the rise of liberty and equality in this country was accompanied by the rise of slavery" and "such contradictory developments were taking place simultaneously over a long period of our history, from the seventeenth century to the nineteenth."[46] Liberty and inequality became essential criteria of American law as it succumbed to the demands of this new agricultural-intensive and exporting economy. The codification of a racialist ideology within law occurred between the late seventeenth and the early eighteenth centuries.

Most historians agree now that this process began as early as the 1640s, when certain court cases indicated that Africans had already been singled out for special discriminatory treatment. Even though the racial composition of the laboring force was mixed at this time, it appears that some Africans, unlike Europeans, were serving their masters for life's entirety. This lifetime servitude was transmitted to the status of "his assigns for the time of his natural life here or elsewhere."[47] Africans were also prohibited by law from holding arms, and it seems ostensibly that Africans per se, but especially children, were valuated as servants much more than Europeans, and that African women worked in the fields and as such became taxable. Both of these last two indices strongly suggest that Africans, irrespective of gender, were expected to perform the hot, heavy, and backbreaking toil of field labor and, coupled with lifetime service, one could readily understand why the inventories of estates valued their Africans higher than their European indentures.[48]

As the importation of African labor reached proportions higher, in certain colonies, than European labor, the artifices of law began to control, discipline, and domesticate the new racial slave class. The statutes and codes concerning the enslavement of Africans differed little from one colony to the next. The common characteristics of this legislation were as follows: (1) being visibly African was tantamount to the status of slavery; (2) this enslavement was to be *durante vita*—for the lifetime of the individual; (3) this life servitude was inherited through the mother and to all her progeny—*partus sequitur ventrem*; (4) Christian conversion would not or could not change this heritable status; (5) the African as slave was to be either chattel (e.g., land, buildings) or personality (e.g., property akin to horses, wagons, and farming implements), depending on the case in controversy; and (6) slaves resisting their masters could be killed, and the master could not be charged with a felony because no man would intentionally "destroy his owne estate."[49]

By the late 1760s, each colony from Maine to Georgia had slave codes that embodied all or several of these characteristics. Virginia's law of 1660, which dealt with the problem and punishment of servants for running away, referred to "negroes who are incapable of making satisfaction by addition of time"[50] because they were presumably already serving *durante vita.* Maryland's law of 1663 used the words *durante vita* in reference to the length of African servitude. Virginia's law of 1669 removed the murder of a slave by the master as a felonious act on the entrepreneurial premise that "it cannot be presumed that prepense malice, which alone makes murther [*sic*] felony, should induce any man to destroy his own estate."[51] Because many English planters from Barbados arrived in the Carolinas with both their spirit of enterprise as well as their slaves, the *Fundamental Constitutions of Carolinas* assured that "Every Freeman of the Carolina shall have absolute power and authority over Negro slaves, of what opinion or Religion soever."[52] In Georgia, there were some incipient capitalist assumptions about the advantages of free White yeoman labor over slave labor and thus the initial prohibitions against the importation of slaves, but Georgia rapidly fell in line with the viability and the establishment of slavery within fifteen years of its founding.[53]

Although slavery in New England and the middle colonies did not have the latifundia base and therefore the need to import the massive number of Africans slaves, both areas developed African slavery and slave law. Slavery in these areas developed in the interstices of such laboring sectors as "household servants . . . artisans . . . Bakers, ropemakers, brewers, shipwrights . . . sailmakers . . . and ferrymen."[54] The exception to such laboring diversification was the Narragansett area of Rhode Island, where African slaves in gangs of up to forty worked on large landed estates that produced dairy products, raised cattle or sheep, and yielded some tobacco.[55]

In New York, the Duke's Laws of 1664 gave slavery the sanction of law, and because his power extended into the Delaware region of Pennsylvania, slavery became *de jure* there also. Slavery continued in these areas until William Penn and his religious cohorts, the Quakers, arrived in 1688.[56]

Even though there appeared to be opposition to slavery of the abolitionist sort in Pennsylvania and throughout the New England area, slavery entrenched itself, and some of the harshest legal repercussions for slave resistance exhibited themselves in these regions.[57] New York applied the hangman's noose, the axe for castration and limbs, and rack and quartering of corpses for activities of the insurrection type.[58] The slave codes of the northern colonies were also aimed at social control of African slaves. Laws were passed that restricted both slaves and free Africans from military service, from violating curfew, and from "trucking" in liquor, armaments, certain fine cloth, and other commodities reserved for elite consumption.[59] Massachusetts passed laws forcing free Blacks into stevedore service on state highways, streets, and other public services, whereas Pennsylvania restricted slaves from "hiring-out" their extra time, which resulted in preventing them from accumulating wages.[60]

These legal statutes were aimed at maintaining the proper relationship between the planter or business elites and the coerced labor of Africans. The hegemonic powers of the legal system reflected the colonial ruling class's attempt to stabilize an ever-growing rebellious laboring force. To stabilize this labor force, the statutes concentrated on segmenting it along racial lines, and prohibiting working-class contact in the social arena. Virginia and Georgia passed laws prohibiting social camaraderie in terms of buying and selling of liquor to Africans and fraternizing in taverns or other public places of entertainment.[61] South Carolina's statutes punished slaves found guilty of stealing or lying with the cutting off of an ear.[62] All thirteen colonies legally prohibited slaves from owning weaponry and intermarrying with Whites, and most southern colonies provided legal provisions that required the constant surveillance and policing of slaves. South Carolina coerced non-slaveholding Whites, by penalty of law, to ride slave patrols as many as twelve months without pay.[63]

Statutes also placed severe liabilities on quasi-free Blacks. In New Jersey and New York, free Blacks were prohibited from owning real property, whereas in Virginia and South Carolina, they were obliged to leave the state on being manumitted.[64] In Pennsylvania and Delaware, a free Black could be coerced into laboring as an "apprentice" to a White master if found "loitering or misspending his or her time."[65] However, in Connecticut, the life of Venture Smith reveals how the social system was being closed off to Blacks. The internal dynamics of legal formality created small, autonomous "due process spaces" in which individual Blacks could use the law to contradict the social reality of Black slavery. Venture Smith was born in Guinea in 1729 and was enslaved via a purchased transaction for "four gallons of rum and a piece of calico." After toiling for many years as a slave in Connecticut, Smith was able to purchase his freedom after saving money from being "hired out" by his master. The mere fact that many slaves were able to accomplish their freedom through such contractual "hiring out" demonstrates that the law has an internal logic and autonomy, and at any given time, it will be applied in any individual case. The legitimacy of the law requires that it do so. Law as ideology cannot maintain its legitimacy if it is subsumed under the ideology of race at all times. Venture Smith's eventual freedom ensured that at least one Black man, and some others, would see the law as working in his own interests. Venture Smith eventually paid for his wife Meg's freedom and for that of their children, Solomon, Cuff, and Hannah. Using contract law[66] and its protection, Smith worked hard and acquired a seventy-six acre farm and several slaves himself. Capitalist–slave relationships reflected White over Black, but not in the absolute. The law assured that any racial absolutism would be moderated by the law's own autonomous formal rules. White beliefs in the law's legitimacy and, therefore, its hegemony revolved around the lives and good fortunes of Anthony Johnson, Venture Smith, and others. It was difficult to see the immorality of the law of slavery when one could see that the ideology of race, which was the locomotion of slave law, had a constant check whenever law balanced the interests of individual Blacks and the interests of those who dominated political economy.

On the eve of the American Revolution, the political economy of all the colonies was cemented by racialism, which helped create a society of White against Black and White over Black, and therefore Black under an iron fist of authority and domination. The economic foundation of colonial America, politically controlled by an ever-emerging entrepreneurial elite, produced a juridical world that reflected the realities, needs, and interests of this elite. The rationalization and justification for the legalization of America's capitalist-slave mode of production revolved around the idea of race. The solidification and thus the hegemonic function of racialism in an intellectually formal sense had to await the post–American Revolutionary era and its aftermath.[67]

ENDNOTES

1. Karl Marx, *Capita: A Critical Analysis of Capitalist Production,* vol. 1 (Moscow: 1959), 751.
2. Laura Foner and Eugene Genovese, *Slavery in the New World* (Englewood Cliffs: Prentice Hall, 1969), ix.
3. Eric Williams, *Capitalism and Slavery* (New York: Capricorn Books, 1944).
4. Frank Tannenbaum, *Slave and Citizen* (New York: Knopf, 1947).
5. Kermit Hall, *The Magic Mirror: Law in American History* (New York: Oxford University Press, 1989), 132.
6. Oscar and Mary Handlin, "Origins of Southern Labor System," *William and Mary Quarterly* 7, no. 1 (January 1950), 217; see also Helen Catterall, *Judicial Cases II* 93, 269, 358.
7. Eugene Genovese, *Fruits of Merchant Capital: Slavery and Bourgeois Property in the Rise and Expansion of Capitalism* (London: Oxford University Press, 1983).
8. Tamas Szentes, *The Transformation of the World Economy* (London: Zed Books, Ltd., 1988). See Chapter 3, "Primitive Capital Accumulation," 36.
9. Harold Baron, "Demand for Black Labor: Historical Notes on the Political Economy of Racism," *Radical America*, vol. 5, no. 2 (March–April 1971), 2–3; Immanuel Wallerstein, *The Modern World-System: Capitalist Agriculture and the Origins of the European World-Economy in the Sixteenth Century* (New York: Academic Press, 1974).
10. Alan Watson, *Slave Law in the Americas* (Athens: The University of Georgia Press, 1989). See also Edmund Morgan, "The Labor Problem at Jamestown," in *Interpreting Colonial America,* ed. James Kirby Martin (New York: Harper & Row, 1973).
11. Philip D. Curtin, "The Slave Trade and the Atlantic Basin: Intercontinental Perspectives," in *Key Issues in the Afro-American Experience,* vol. 1, ed. Nathan Huggins, Martin Kilson, and Daniel M. Fox (New York: Harcourt

Brace Jovanovich, Inc., 1971), 74–95. Margit Mayer and Margaret A. Fey, "The Formation of the American Nation State," *Kapitialiste: Working Paper on the Capitalist State,* no. 6 (Fall, 1977) 40–43.

12. Robin Blackburn, *The Making of New World Slavery* (London: Verso, 1997); Lewis Hanks, *The Spanish Struggle for Justice: In the Conquest of America* (Philadelphia: University of Pennsylvania, 1949); Charles Gibson, *Spain in America* (New York: Harper & Row, 1966); Colin Palmer, *Slaves of the White God in Mexico, 1570–1650* (Cambridge: Harvard University Press, 1976).

13. A. Leon Higginbotham, *In the Matter of Color* (New York: Oxford University Press, 1978), 63; Elizabeth Donnan, *Documents Illustrative of the History of the Slave Trade* (Washington, 1933); Joseph Miller, *Way of Death: Merchant Capitalism and the Angolan Slave Trade, 1730–1830* (Madison: University of Wisconsin Press, 1988)

14. James Walvin, *Black Ivory: A History of British Slavery* (New York: Harper Collins, 1992); Colin Palmer, *Human Cargoes: The British Slave Trade to Spanish America, 1700–1739* (Urbana: University of Illinois Press, 1981); Malik Simba, "The *Zong* Case," in *The Historical Encyclopedia of World Slavery,* vol. II, ed. Junius Rodriguez (Oxford: England, ABC-CLIO Press, 1997).

15. Higginbotham, *In the Matter Of Color,* see Part III, "The English Experience with Slavery," 313–370; see also James Walvin, *Black Ivory,* "Murdering Men," 10–20 (best analysis concerning the *Zong* case).

16. Walvin, "Murdering Men."

17. T. H. Breen, *Myne Owne Ground: Race and Freedom on Virginia's Eastern Shore, 1640–1676* (New York: Oxford University Press, 1980); see also Philip D. Curtain, "The Slave Trade and the Atlantic Basin."

18. T. H. Breen, "A Changing Labor Force and Race Relations in Virginia, 1660–1710," *Journal of Social History* 7 (1975), 3–25.

19. See the debate between Carl Degler and Oscar and Mary Handlin. Oscar and Mary Handlin, "Origins of the Southern Labor System," *William and Mary Quarterly,* 3rd Series, VII (1950), 199–222; Carl Degler, "Slavery and the Genesis of American Race Prejudice," *Society for the Comparative Study of Society and History* (The Hague: 1960), 49–66; Winthrop Jordan, *White Over Black: American Attitudes Toward the Negro, 1550–1812* (Chapel Hill: NC, 1968).

20. Eric Williams, *Capitalism and Slavery,* 16; see also Edmund Morgan, "The Laboring Problem at Jamestown, 1607–18," in *Interpreting Colonial America: Selected Readings,* ed. James Kirby Martin (New York: Harper and Row, 1973), 20–36.

21. Theodore Allen, "They Would Have Destroyed Me: Slavery and the Origins of Racism," *Radical America* 9, Issue 3 (1975), 41–63.

22. Stuart Schwartz, *Sugar Plantations in the Formations of Brazilian Society, Bahia, 1550–1835* (Cambridge: Cambridge University Press, 1985); Phillip Curtin, "The Slave Trade and the Atlantic Basin." I use this term to describe Professor Curtin's thesis.

23. Curtin, 77.

24. Dan Lacy, *The White Use of Blacks in America: 350 Years of Law and Violence, Attitudes and Etiquette, Politics and Change* (New York: McGraw-Hill, 1972), 13.

25. Curtin, 74–75. See also Paul Gilroy, *Black Atlantic: Modernity and Double Consciousness* (London, 1991); James Walvin, *Making of the Black Atlantic: Britain and the African Diaspora* (London: Cassell, 2000), 10–11.

26. Kimberly Henke Breuer, "Treaty of Utrecht, 1713," *The Historical Encyclopedia of World Slavery* (Oxford: ABC–CLIO Publishers, 1997), 667.

27. Marcus Jernegan, "The Economic and Social Influence of the Indentured Servant," in *The Underside of American History,* ed. James Kirby Martin (New York: Harcourt Brace Jovanovich, Inc., 1971), 63. See also Theodore Allen, "They Would Have Destroyed Me: Slavery and the Origins of Racism," 56.

28. Theodore Allen, 56.

29. Winthrop Jordan, Carl Degler, and Oscar and Mary Handlin discuss this case in their research. See citations in footnote 19.

30. T. H. Breen, "A Changing Labor and Race Relations in Virginia, 1660–1710," *Journal of Social History* 7, no. 1 (Fall 1973), 12–13.

31. Autonomy of law cases are analyzed with the Degler-Handlin debates.

32. Steve C. Ferguson III, "Social Contract as Bourgeois Ideology," *Cultural Logic,* ISSN 1097-3087.

33. Gary Nash, et al., *The American People* (New York: Pearson Educational, 2008), 63. The John Punch case is discussed in Leon Higginbotham, 27–28; On Black slave owners in the changing class to race- and class-based

Colonial America, see Carter G. Woodson, *Free Negro Owners of Slaves in the United States in 1830* (Washington, DC: Associated Publishers, 1925); Larry Koeger, *Black Slave Owners: Free Black Slave Masters in South Carolina, 1790–1860* (Jefferson, NC: McFarland Publishers, 1985); Loren Schweninger, "John Carruthers Stanly and the Anomaly of Black Slaveholding," *North Carolina Historical Review* 67 (April 1990); Michael Johnson and James L. Roark, *Black Masters: A Free Family of Color in the Old South* (New York: Norton, 1984).

34. Theodore Allen, "They Would Have Destroyed Me," 58. This is Professor Allen's thesis.

35. Winthrop Jordan, *White Over Black: American Attitudes Toward the Negro, 1550–1812* (Chapel Hill: University of North Carolina Press, 1968).

36. Winthrop Jordan, "Modern Tensions and the Origins of American Slavery" in Jordan's *White Over Black: American Attitudes Toward the Negro, 1550–1812* (Chapel Hill: University of North Carolina Press, 1968), 19.

37. Winthrop Jordan, "Modern Tensions," 20.

38. In sum, this is the objective conclusions of most scholars of American slavery today.

39. Jordan, p. 19; note in Leon Higginbotham, 43, 1662, Act XII: "Children got by an Englishman upon a Negro woman shall be bond or free according to the condition of the mothers, and if any Christian shall commit fornication with a Negro man or woman, he shall pay double the fines of a former act."

40. Jordan, 20; for best analysis, see Theodore Allen's essay cited at note 21.

41. Theodore Allen, 54.

42. T. H. Breen's and Theodore Allen's research take this analytical approach.

43. T. H. Breen, "A Changing Labor Force and Race Relations in Virginia, 1660–1710," *The Journal of Social History* 7, no. 1 (Autumn 1973); Theodore Allen, "They Would Have Destroyed Me: Slavery and the Origins of Racism," *Radical America* 9, Issue 3 (1975).

44. Edmund Morgan, "Slavery and Freedom: The American Paradox," *The Journal of American History.*

45. T. H. Breen, 3 (1980).

46. Edmund Morgan, "Slavery and Freedom: The American Paradox," 5–6.

47. Higginbotham, *In the Matter of Color,* attempts to explain this point by examining race and law and national identity in this masterful study of the colonial law and society.

48. Carl Degler, "Slavery and the Genesis of American Race Prejudice" (Netherlands: Society for the Comparative Study of Society and History, 1960), 59.

49. Winthrop Jordan, "Unthinking Decision: Enslavement of Negroes in America to 1700," in *White Over Black*, 35.

50. Higginbotham, 34–35.

51. Higginbotham, 36.

52. Higginbotham, 163.

53. Higginbotham, 216–217.

54. Donald Wright, *African Americans in the Colonial Era: From African Origins Through the American Revolution* (Arlington Heights IL: Harlan Davidson, Inc., 1990), 74.

55. August Meier and Elliott Rudwick, *From Plantation to Ghetto: An Interpretive History of the American Negro* (New York: Hill and Wang 1996), 41. See also Edgar J. McManus, *Black Bondage in the North* (Syracuse: Syracuse University Press, 1973), 7.

56. Higginbotham, "Pennsylvania: The Quaker and German Liberal Influence," 267–312.

57. McManus, 122–123.

58. Jordan, *White Over Black,* 154. Higginbotham, "New York: From Half-Freedom to Slavery," especially 118–119.

59. McManus, 80–81.

60. Higginbotham, 174.

61. Higginbotham, 172.

62. Higginbotham, 177.

63. Higginbotham, "South Carolina: White Minority/Black Majority," 151–215.

64. For Virginia, see Higginbotham, 47–50. For South Carolina, see Higginbotham, 175–176.

65. See Higginbotham on loitering, 269, 309.

66. Refer to the Steve Ferguson III essay on "Bourgeois Contractualism."

67. Donald Robinson, *Slavery in the Structure of American Politics,* 1765–1820 (New York: Harcourt Brace, 1970).

CHAPTER 2

Ideology, the American Revolution, and Constitutional Slavery

Neither Marx nor I have ever asserted more than this. . . . The economic situation is the basis, but the various elements of the superstructure-political forms of the class struggle and its results, such as constitutions established by the victorious class . . . juridical forms . . . the brains of the participants, political, legal, philosophical theories, religious views . . . exercise {s} their influence . . . {and} determines their forms in particular. . . . There is an interaction of all these elements in which . . . the economic movement {will} assert itself.[1]

—FREDERICK ENGELS, *LETTER TO BLOCH* (SEPTEMBER 21, 1890)

Engels' explanation on the locomotion of history not only clarifies an aspect of the stereotype of Marx as an economic reductionist, but also gives us an insight into the multiple dynamics of forces that created the American nation state. Ideas of the enlightenment, Christian faith, economic self-interests, class interests, civic virtue, legal theories, and theories of human nature were all driving forces of the American Revolution and were present at the Constitutional Convention.

However, under a close examination of these "various elements of the superstructure," one can ultimately see they manifested themselves into this period's dramatic and traumatic changes and produced a nation whose government responsibilities were to protect the propertied class "from popular uprisings, from fiscal uncertainty and irregularities in trade and currency, from trade barriers between states, from economic competition . . . and from attacks by the poor on property and on creditors."[2]

In 1776, the men of the revolutionary faith, through their singular protagonist, Thomas Jefferson, declared their rationalization and justification for striking for their freedom against their sovereign, King George III of England. The American revolutionaries used the enlightened natural rights theory of the late eighteenth century as their ideological vehicle of exoneration.

Jefferson, in haranguing the English king, used the right of revolution theory when he asserted that "when a long train of abuses and usurpations is . . . designed to reduce them (the people) under absolute despotism, it is their right, it is their duty to throw off such government." The blame for the breakdown in law and order, the faithful rebels rationalized, was thus due to an abusive usurper who had denied man's inalienable right to life, liberty, and happiness in a compact government created of, by, and for the people. Interestingly, in an earlier draft, Jefferson blamed George III for pirating "innocent Africans" via the slave trade and then incited those very slaves to wage war against the liberties of the colonists. This version was debated and "cut out by the Continental Congress."[3] These novel political concepts rejected the feudalist beliefs in caste and "blood" privilege, unitarian religious consciousness, and authoritarian social structure.[4]

The forceful ideals expressed in the *Declaration of Independence* were, in part, derived from John Locke's *Second Treatise*. Much has been made of Jefferson's phrase "the inalienable rights of life, liberty, and the pursuit of happiness," which, some have argued, was a repudiation of Locke's emphasis on estate in his original phrase—life, liberty, and property.[5] To understand this semantic dilemma, one must grasp the fact that in order to correctly decipher the meaning of social consciousness as expressed by ideas in action, one must judge the meaning of these ideas within the appropriate space and time in which they were expressed. Jefferson was truly an enlightened colonial aristocrat whose consciousness was molded by the most progressive worldview of the eighteenth century, as explicated by such enlightened philosophers as Locke, Milton, Coke, Sidney, Harrington, Hobbes, Rosseau, and others.[6] For these ideologues, the basis of liberty and, thus, happiness was premised on a man's property. The more property he acquired, the more liberty and happiness he would accrue. Government, by consent, was created for the protection of property so that man's other liberties could be actualized. The contemporary *De Felice's Encyclopedie* best stated this complementary (symbiotic) relationship when it asserted the following: "Despoil a man of all his rights of property, and I defy you to find in him any vestiges of liberty; on the other hand, imagine a man who has been deprived of all kinds of liberty, and I challenge you to say that there remains to him in reality any right of property."[7] Jefferson's semantic changes must be understood in this light. His paraphrasing of Locke was consistent with the contemporary dominant view that a man's private property and what he did with it to enhance his liberty were salient features of life, and government's duty was to ensure that all propertied men would be treated equally before the bar of justice administered by justices as officers of the State.[8]

Equality as expressed in the phrase "all men are created equal" must be understood as a philosophized abstraction whose real meaning is clarified by the widespread social inequality in colonial and post-colonial America. Jefferson, being a man of his times, was expressing the then novel and advanced idea about equality as expressed by his philosophical coeval, DeLolme, that "To live in a state where the laws are equal for all and sure to be executed, is to be free."[9] Jefferson merely exhorted that in America, all men (White men) should be given the equality of due process before the courts of justice. He was not suggesting that this due process equality would have or should have a sociological leveling effect on such a racially and class-stratified society as was the new republic. British and American essayists recognized the contradictions of equality within these American social relationships and their spokesperson's pronouncements of "equality." Thomas Day noted, "If there be an object truly ridiculous in nature, it is an American patriot, signing resolutions of independency with the one hand, and with the other brandishing a whip over his affrighted slaves," and Dr. Samuel Johnson echoed, "How is it that we hear the loudest yelps for liberty among the drivers of negroes."[10] Colonial elites, of which Jefferson was arguably foremost, believed that "some men are born booted and spurred, while *others* are born with saddles on their backs." The process of riding and of being ridden does both groups physical as well as psychological good. Jefferson, as his *Notes on Virginia* revealed, did not believe that Africans and others of the "giddy multitudes" were the moral, political, or intellectual equal of Whites of aristocratic status. Jefferson remained an aristocrat and slaveholder until his death. In attempting to exonerate and therefore legitimize their armed struggle, Jefferson and his insurgent colleagues put forth a broad ideological fabrication that rationalized and justified the events of their day.[11]

The post-Revolutionary society of the founding fathers was wrought with deep class and racial hierarchical divisions. The periodic class and racial rebellions were symptomatic of these divisions. The rhetoric of propaganda—liberty, equality, and the pursuit of happiness—were sorely devoid of what today we assume are their intrinsic definitions. What those words and phrases meant at the turn of the eighteenth century was circumscribed by the political economy of slavery and merchant capital. Looking back on this period, one noted contemporary, Alexander Hamilton, reflected, "It was certainly true that nothing like an equality of property existed; that an inequality would exist as long as liberty existed, and that it would unavoidably result from that very liberty itself."[12]

The Declaration of Independence addressed such ideas, as liberty and equality in the context of vindicating revolution. The men who structured the Constitution had to address these ideas, however ideological, within a realistic, mature, and workable form of government that, unlike the Articles of Confederation, could resolve the problematic exigencies of the infant nation-state. The deliberate judgment of the different ruling elite factions, that is, merchants, manufacturers, slaveholding planters, bankers, and lawyers that met in Philadelphia in 1787 for four long, hot, summer months ultimately led to the ratification and implementation of the Constitution by all thirteen colonies. This new federalized government reflected a consensus by these factions that government's modus operandi should be to secure the protection of private property and further national and regional economic growth.[13] The new government should also maintain social and political order through the rule of law by balancing, via the art of political compromise, not only the conflicting interests within a factious elite but equally as important the antagonistic interests of these elites and the oppressed social classes.[14]

The political compromises between various sectors of the ruling elite at the Constitutional Convention led to a series of concessions that established a class, gender, and racial polity grounded on basic political structures and principles. The concessions revolved around regional interests whose ruling classes sought to use the convention to argue and gain protection for their class interests as the new government was formed. These divergences of interest were referred to as "the line of discrimination" by James Madison,[15] a reference to northern versus southern regional interests based on slavery and its implications. The principles embodied in the Constitution recognized these interests and thereby forced elites on both sides of "the line of discrimination" to assert their interests as classes in and for themselves. The incipient nationalism of the newfound nation-state was already being tempered by the divergences and contradictions within its own sectionalized political economy.

Compromises over Constitutional political principles and structures would mollify the tensions of interests that could have but did not wreck the great "democratic" experiment at birth. The most salient of these principles were federalism, separation of powers with checks and balances, popular elections, military clauses, and, in latency and most importantly, judicial review.

Federalism is the division of enumerated powers between the central government and the states and is codified in the Tenth Amendment,[16] which delegates to the central government the power to regulate foreign policy and interstate commerce and to provide for and maintain public order. Federalism secured a bifurcated political structure by which the southern region could further solidify African slavery without any interference from federal power.[17] For some historians, "the main beneficiaries (of federalism) throughout American history have been the southern whites, who have been given the freedom to oppress Negroes, first as slaves and later as an oppressed class.[18]

The military clauses of the Constitution gave the federal government the responsibility of maintaining "republican" forms of government within the states and the power to suppress class revolts—for example, the Whiskey Rebellion, Fries's Rebellion, and slave resistance movements such as the Prosser, Vesey, and Turner rebellions that threatened this peculiar republican form based on White over Black and a hierarchical social class structure. It could do this, in part, by nationalizing state militias.[19] Of course, both federal and state militias were used to continually repress and destroy remaining Native American Indian resistance, especially when both Blacks and Indians bonded as Seminoles to resist the onslaught of White domination.[20]

One compromise at the 1787 Constitutional Convention that explicitly involved the issue of race was the question of representation. To mollify the South's fears and regional interests, the convention permitted the planters to have each slave count as three-fifths of each White man in each state in determining that state's representation in the House. In return, northern delegates received the benefit of having these same proportionate slaves counted in the direct taxation of states according to population. One scholar has argued that the three-fifths clause and its effect on the electoral college helped Thomas Jefferson attain the presidency in 1800.[21]

James Madison's writings in the *Federalist,* No. 54, clarified this compromise by stating in "real politick" that "the Federal Constitution . . . views them [slaves] in the mixed character of persons and of property. . . . Let the compromising expedient of the Constitution be mutually adopted, which regards them as inhabitants, but debased by servitude below the equal level of free inhabitants, which regards the slave as divested of three-fifths of the man."[22] Madison was referring to Article 1, Section 2, of the Constitution, which states that individual state representation in the House would be "determined by adding to the whole number of free persons . . . excluding Indians not taxed, three fifths of all other persons."[23] This clause, the key agreement within the great compromise, was the material and substantive driving force that created the "new republic." The clause reflected a realization by all conventioneers, those from large and small states,

North and South, quasi-industrial and agrarian, that however their material basis and social structure differed, they were all in consensus on the idea of race. The natural rights ideology of liberty, individualism, and equality would be contoured and subsumed to the symmetric form of a racist republicanism political structure so aptly questioned by Alexis de Tocqueville in his *Democracy in America* and by British critics. Sectionalism along the lines of regional interests with slavery versus those in the process of eliminating it was assessed crudely when Patrick Henry said the South's basic fear was that the North will "take their niggers from them."[24]

James Madison's denotation of lines of interest was reflected in the 1790 census, which indicated that there were "1,900,976 whites and 27,112 free Negroes in the northern states, as against 1,271,488 whites and 32,354 free Negroes in the southern states. There were, however, only 40,364 slaves in the North and 657,533 in the South."[25] The lack of a "Black presence" in the North and the necessity of Black slave labor in the South led to the ideology of natural rights being tiered by race and class and, therefore, compromised and not applied in the new republic. Madison's words spoke volumes when he wrote that the convention compromises were argued "[by] different interests not by their difference of size, but by other circumstances; the most material of which resulted partly from climate, but principally from the effects of their having or not having slaves."[26] Madison noted this on June 29-30, and by July 14, two days after the adoption of the infamous three-fifths compromise, he could firmly state that the "institution of slavery and its consequences formed the line of discrimination" between regional ruling class factions at the convention.[27] The reference to the infamous three-fifths compromise explicitly revealed these intraclass conflicts revolved around the issues of power and representation in the newly formed bicameral "State" apparatus. For Staughton Lynd, the noted historian of American Constitutionalism, the July 12, 1787, three-fifths compromise can only be understood by perceiving it as the flipside of the Continental Congress (which was meeting at the same time) passage, on July 13, of the anti-slavery provision in the Northwest Ordinance. This provision outlawed slavery in the Northwest territories and thus supported the commitment of the Founding Fathers to the ideals of quasi-antislavery, while the three-fifths compromise represented a refutation of the same.[28]

Northerners were pleased that the Northwest Ordinance supported, in part, the ideals of the Revolution, and the South was pleased because of what they believed was to be a rosy future and the fact that the same Ordinance required fugitive slaves to be returned to their owners if they escaped to freedom.[29]

The fugitive slave clause in the Ordinance was rewritten and included by the Constitutionalists as Art. IV, Sect. 2, which stated that "No person held to Service or Labour in one State . . . escaping into another, shall be discharged from such Service or Labour, but shall be delivered up on Claim of the Party to whom such Service or Labour may be due."[30] This clause in the Constitution was a mere addendum to the other great issue of race, law, and political economy that faced the Philadelphia delegates: "the importation of African slaves into the new republic." The Constitutional delegates drafted Art. 1, Sec. 9, which stated that the "Migration or Importation of such Persons as any of the States now existing shall think proper to admit, shall not be prohibited by the Congress prior to the year one thousand eight hundred and eight; but a tax or duty may be imposed on such Importation, not exceeding ten dollars for each Person. . . . No Capitation, or other direct, Tax shall be laid, unless in Proportion to the Census or Enumeration herein before directed to be taken."[31] This clause protected southern interests by restricting Congress from using its taxing power to the detriment of the institution of slavery.[32] Southerners saw the years before 1808 as time to resupply and fully supply their needs for slaves, and understood that the 1808 date was not a fixed time and did not preclude the slave trade from continuing after that date.[33]

The slave trade ban compromise and its correlative fugitive slave clause became the final disposition of the question of slavery for the Philadelphia delegates. Both sides were pleased and understood that their ideological and material interests were protected by law and authority. Each side judged their final work, the United States Constitution, from their own biased particularities. Both knew objectively that, on the issue of race, law, and political economy, the document was clearly a quid pro quo. As one delegate put it, the economic interests of the North to commerce the South's cash-crop commodities on the domestic and international market would temper their antislavery sentiment,[34] and the possible slave trade ban of 1808 would mean very little to states like South Carolina, which imported more than 40,000 slaves between 1803 and 1808.[35] The fugitive slave clause meant little to northern "liberals" who certainly did not want to see an increase in their Black population via the allure of "freedomland."

The "fig leaves of circumlocution"[36] that hid the social stratification in elegant verbiage went as such: "[I]n order to establish justice, insure domestic Tranquility, provide for the common defence, promote the general Welfare, and secure the Blessings of Liberty to ourselves and our Posterity."[37] What, at this moment in time, was defined as *common, general,* and *our Posterity* included no more than the propertied classes and their descendants who could maintain that material inheritance.

On the racial level, even though fifteen of the Constitutional delegates were slaveholders with their property specifically protected by the "great document," "neither the word *slave,* nor *black* nor *Negro* nor *African* nor *colored*"[38] was written into that sacred document. The Constitution, being, in part, ideological, would have been gravely damaged as an ideological fig leaf if such words were juxtaposed alongside of the natural rights ideals. Referring to Africans in euphemistic phrases such as *persons,* to their resistance as *held to labor,* or to their inhuman commerce as *migration* or *importation,* the Constitution offered an ideological construct, immersed within one euphemism after another, that established "the American bourgeoisie as the first dominate class to deny the existence of necessary separation between itself and the dominated class."[39] The euphemistic fig-leaves that hid the class biases and racism within this "liberal" document were essentially semantic legalese immersed in an ideological glue.[40]

The formulation of a Supreme Court, with its power of judicial review extending to all cases "arising under this Constitution, the Laws of the U.S., and Treaties" and amended in 1789 to provide for establishment of a series of inferior federal courts with rights of appeal from state court case controversies led to the institutionalization of "law" as the driving force that diffused class conflicts while maintaining the jurisprudential support for entrepreneurial growth.[41] The Supreme Court with its class justice and justices of class,[42] through its quasi-explicit function of Constitutional interpretation, would referee a wide variety of cases involving conflict of interests and resolved most of them via the ideas of federalism in support of American slavery.

The utter facade of universalizing class interests in such abstract concepts as fairness, obligation, equity, and due process was and is best demonstrated by how law, using as its rationalizing basis the ideology of racism or federalism, became the major Draconian altar under which slavery was nurtured and its legacy of discrimination and racial intolerance given full credence. This intolerance could be seen in the 1790 Naturalization Act restricting naturalization to "Whites."[43] The Act of 1790 assured new European immigrants that their socially defined status as "Whites" would give them an advantage as they worked hard to climb the class ladder of success. The molding of immigrant working class racist consciousness led to intraclass hostility and conflict between free White labor and their working-class competitors within the slave class.[44]

John Adams noted that this hostility helped the abolition of slavery in Massachusetts. Adams believed that White labor hastened abolition by threatening that if the slave labor's occupational protective statutes were not repealed, they would repeal them through a popular and violent mandate.[45] Ultimately, the aim of White labor was to have all Africans removed or prevented from entering northern states.[46]

Even though the North's African population, free and slave, never totaled more than four percent, two points seem important to note. First, the fact that African slaves were important to this area's ruling classes is indisputable. However, one cannot say, with historical certainty, that the "peculiar institution" itself was as important. This distinction must be made because even though African slave usage varied from one northern region to another, slavery never institutionalized as a fulcrum of economy in any particular region. Because of the limits of slavery in the North, abolition came to this region first and thereby created a conflict between the law of bourgeois freedom in the North and the law of slavery in the South. Many of the states involved in this first emancipation did so with compensation to the owners of slaves.[47]

The case that set in motion this northern abolition was the 1783 Quock Walker case, also referred to as *Commonwealth v. Jennison*.[48] The age of revolutionary thinking about the rights of man led many Massachusetts towns to complain about the absence of an anti-slavery clause in the state's constitution. Responding, the legislature passed a new constitution, Declaration of Rights, with the phrase "all men are born free and equal, and have certain natural, essential, and unalienated rights."[49] This legal change was ideological but also material because merchant capital had already turned to White immigrant labor to meet its labor power needs. In this context, Quaco (also known as Quo or Quock)[50] pursued his freedom. Walker escaped from Nathaniel Jennison and fled to the nearby farm of Seth and John Caldwell, whose deceased brother was Walker's past owner. The widow married Nathaniel Jennison, so technically Walker was her property and became the property of her new husband, Jennison. Jennison, along with several friends, accosted Walker, beat him severely, and returned him to enslavement. The Caldwells, in turn, hired the noted lawyer Levi Lincoln to be Walker's lawyer when he filed assault and battery charges against Jennison. The first case, *Quock Walker v. Jennison*, 1781, was decided in Walker's favor, and the jury awarded him monetary damages and declared he was a "freeman." A vengeful Jennison then sued the Caldwells, claiming they had seduced Walker from his obligatory service as his slave, and the second jury in *Jennison v. Caldwell* found in favor of Jennison and awarded him monetary damages. The third and last case, *Commonwealth v. Jennison,* occurred in 1783 when state authorities indicted Jennison for assault and battery against Walker. The state's attorney general, Robert

Paine, declared that a free citizen of Massachusetts had been unlawfully attacked. Paine claimed that Walker's free status was based on a verbal contract of manumission made to him by his deceased master and renewed by his widow. Chief Justice William Cushing, rejecting proslavery arguments from Jennison's lawyer, referred to the Declaration of Rights and the American Revolution and said that a freeman was attacked who had "rights and privileges wholly incompatible and repugnant to its [slavery] existence."[51] Almost at the same time as the Walker case proceeded through the formal legal system, Elizabeth Freeman sued for her freedom under the new constitution. She initiated this suit after her master, who was a mistress (master John Ashley's wife), threatened both Elisabeth and her sister with bodily harm. A Sheffield, Massachusetts, jury found in favor of freedom for Freeman with monetary damages.

Natural rights, Enlightenment thinking, Christian faith, little economic need, and the Revolution all dovetailed into northern states abolishing slavery between these cases and the 1820s. The northernmost New England states—Massachusetts (1783), Connecticut (1784), Rhode Island (1784), Vermont (1777), and New Hampshire (1783)—removed their formal legal sanction to slavery during these years. The Mid-Atlantic states—Pennsylvania (1780), New York (1799), and New Jersey (1804)—removed their formal legal sanction to slavery in the years to follow. The process and length of abolition varied from state to state, depending on how great the integration of slave labor was into each state's political economy.[52] For example, both New York and New Jersey, with substantial slave populations, created gradual emancipation laws.[53] In New York, male slaves would be freed anytime after age twenty-eight and females slaves after age twenty-five. In New Jersey, the age criterion was twenty-five years for males and twenty-one years for females. This slow and gradual emancipation would permit slavery to die a natural death over the next several decades.[54]

Abolitionism in the North, no matter how hypocritical and, thus, in the interests of the owners, helped solidify the line of discrimination between two American political economies distinguished, according to James Madison, by "slavery and its consequences."[55] These consequences within the North were stated eloquently by Senator Smith of South Carolina, who observed, "Whilst it was their interest to hold slaves, so long they kept them. Whenever the interest coupled with it ceased, slavery ceased, but not before. After the war, trade revived, especially in the Eastern States; it was found that a negro capital must give way to a commercial capital which was infinitely more profitable."[56] Ironically, the Supreme Court initially addressed this northern humanitarian victory not as it appeared in the North, but rather as this libertarianism appeared in its southern form. Unlike the North, the South confronted the contradiction between liberty and slavery by proposing, debating, and ultimately rejecting abolitionist legislation.[57] However, southern antislavery sentiment reappeared in a body of cases known as *freedom lawsuits*.[58] These cases were legal actions litigated by those held in slavery in hopes of obtaining a court order freeing them from bondage.

The backdrop to these cases was the American Revolution and the rights of man rhetoric that pervaded mass consciousness, especially in the upper South. The air of revolutionary idealism helped create a consciousness toward freedom, thus setting the stage for a receptive climate once these cases were initiated and received by the bar of justice. The concurrent decrease in the actual need for slavery in Virginia and Maryland, given soil depletion and the change to less labor-intensive agricultural production, also spurred a benign view toward the sentiments of antislavery.

By 1772, Native Americans living in Virginia began to initiate lawsuits claiming their freedom based on a 1705 statute outlawing Indian slavery. This activity became a crossover tactic when, in Maryland, slaves of African and European heritage filed suits claiming their freedom based on the civil law doctrine *partus sequitur ventrem*—freedom "on the ground of descent from free white maternal ancestors."[59]

The legal basis for the Maryland cases rested on a 1663 statute that enslaved children of marriage between White female servants and African slaves. The so-called *law of the womb*[60] took precedence. The freedom lawsuits were, in part, based on this legislative law of the womb statute, which said that children followed the status of mother, in contradistinction to English common law, in which status of child followed the status of the father. Using this ironic legal loophole, by the late eighteenth century, slaves began to sue and claimed their freedom by arguing descent from a free, White maternal ancestor. Southern courts between 1770s and 1813 became quite receptive to ruling in favor of the slave plaintiffs.[61] What is more remarkable is that these courts accepted and applied broad rules of legal evidence that favored the slave litigant. Slaves, being illiterate and with little genealogical documentation, relied on community reputation or hearsay evidence to prove the fact of having White maternal ancestry.[62] Traditionally, rules of evidence were seen as synonymous with facts that could be validated either by direct witness or written documentation, whereas hearsay was too arbitrary to be substantiated. In accepting hearsay evidence, the courts' attitude was *in favorem libertatis,* and this permitted plaintiffs to claim the pedigree of "race, appearance, and status of his or her ancestors."[63]

Freedom lawsuits found their breath of life wedged between the changing economic condition in Virginia and Maryland. By the 1790s, the upper South states were experiencing deteriorating soils because of years of tobacco and indigo production. Robbed of their nutritious soils by this type of cash-crop production, these states were in transition to less labor (slave) intensive crops such as corn and wheat. It is clear that these states, lacking the economic necessity of maintaining large slave-labor populations, could afford the luxury of revolutionary liberal legalism as expressed in the resolution of freedom lawsuits. However, formal legal rationalism is predicated on due process for the individual, not for classes. Maryland and Virginia's slave class as a whole could not seek juridical relief from American revolutionaries even as they compared their colonial relationship with Great Britain as "enslavement." British imperial enslavement of American Whites was resolved through force of arms that validated "rights of man" legalities. Hope and freedom were extended to individuals in these lawsuits and not to the entire Black slave class who, ironically, would be continually oppressed through force of "revolutionary arms" of the founding fathers.

This obvious contradiction between revolutionary rights and the violation of these rights in due procedural cases that selected freedom for some and slavery for others was resolved in 1813 by the U.S. Supreme Court in the case of *Mima Queen v. Hepburn.* Chief Justice John Marshall ruled that hearsay evidence is incompetent to establish any specific fact,[64] especially in cases concerning the pedigree of humans who are White as opposed to Black. Marshall's ruling truly reflected the solidification of the *quid pro quo* between political economies demarcated by the lines of discrimination. This case was a clear indication that a new proposition had settled into the national consciousness via the altar of Supreme Court law. That proposition stated the importance of property rights in humankind and a reiteration of the Constitutional principle that slavery would be a protected fulcrum in the new political structure of the infant Republic.

Mima Queen v. Hepburn represented the convergence of law and racism as superstructural responses to a democracy based on northern capitalist and southern slave economies. The case indicated that law would function to monitor the interracial basis of "obedience and deference," legitimizing the power of a racist state apparatus and "constantly re-create(ing) the structure of white authority which arose from property and in turn protected its interests."[65]

The praxis of racist lawmaking was instrumentalist, totalitarian, and constitutive in contouring class power and social formation and articulating class interests during the early years of the new Republic. Using its newly claimed powers of judicial review,[66] the Supreme Court functioned to mediate interclass, intraclass, and most importantly, interracial antagonism. The Court, under the considerable influence of John Marshall, in formulating legal rules, was functioning educatively, repressively, ideologically, and facilitatively in structuring a Constitutional social and political order. This order had, within it, disputes that needed to be resolved between regional elites, masters and slaves, men and women, free labor and slave or quasi-free Black labor, and federal and state spheres of authority. Indeed, in mediating the crises generated by antagonistic sets of social relations grounded in a contradictory and segmented political economy, the praxis of Constitutionalism would reveal itself as a hegemonic process in which certain classes rationalized and justified their vision, control, and direction of society by the ideology of race, concretized in class and racial exploitation. Coercive class and racial domination, legitimized by the rule of law and not universal freedom, became the bedrock of the American Republic at the beginning of the nineteenth century.

ENDNOTES

1. Frederich Engels, "Letter to Block, 9/21/1890," in *Marx and Engels on Law*, eds. Mauren M. Cain and Alan Hunt (London: Academic Press, 1979).
2. Michael Parenti, "The Constitution as an Elite Document," in *The United States Constitution*, eds. Bertell Ollman and Jonathan Birnbaum (New York: New York University Press, 1990), 156.
3. "Declaration of Independence," in *The Civil Rights Record: Black Americans and the Law, 1849–1970*, ed. Richard Bardolph (New York: Thomas Y. Crowell Company, 1970), 5; David Walstreicher, *Slavery's Constitution: From Revolution to Ratification* (New York: Hill and Wang, 2009), 46.
4. George Dargo, "Introduction," *Roots of the Republic: A New Perspective on Early American Constitutionalism* (New York: Praeger, 1974).
5. Stanley Katz, "Thomas Jefferson and the Right of Property in Revolutionary America," special issue, "1776: The Revolution in Social Thought," *Journal of Law and Economics* 19, no. 3 (October 1976).
6. Daniel J. Boostin, *The Genius of American Politics* (Chicago, The University of Chicago Press), 97; Gordon Wood, *The Creation of the American Republic, 1776–1787* (Chapel Hill: Omohundra Institute of Early American History and Culture at Williamsburg, Virginia, University of North Carolina Press, 1998), 8, 9, 16, 31, 59; R. M. MacIver, "European Doctrines and the Constitution," in *The Constitution Reconsidered*, ed. Conyer Read (New York: Columbia University Press, 1938), 51–56.
7. Gaetano Salvemini, "The Concept of Democracy and Liberty in the Eighteenth Century," in *The Constitution Reconsidered*, ed. Conyer Read (New York: Columbia University Press, 1938), 114.
8. Salvemini, 113.
9. Salvemini, 113.

10. Thomas Day, quoted in *The Declaration of Independence: A Global History*, ed. David Armitage (Cambridge: Harvard University Press, 2007), 267; Dr. Samuel Johnson, quoted in *In the Matter of Color: Race and the American Legal Process: The Colonial Period,* ed. Leon Higginbotham (Oxford, Oxford University Press: 1978), 377.

11. Gary Wills, *Inventing America: Jefferson's Declaration of Independence* (Garden City: Doubleday and Co, Inc., 1978); see also Bernard Bailyn, *The Ideological Origins of the American Revolution* (Cambridge: Belnap Press of Harvard University Press, 1967); Gordon Wood, *The Creation of the American Republic* (Chapel Hill: University of North Carolina Press, 1969); John Chester Miller, *The Wolf by the Ears: Thomas Jefferson and Slavery* (New York: 1977); Robert McColley, *Slavery and Jefferson Virginia* (Urbana: University of Illinois Press, 1964).

12. Charles Redenius, *The American Ideal of Equality from Jefferson's Declaration to the Burger Court* (Port Washington: Kennikat Press, 1981), 19, 20–21.

13. Juliet E. K. Walker, "Wither Liberty, Equality or Legality: Slavery, Race, Property in 1787," *New York Law School Journal of Human Rights* 299 (1988–1989).

14. See such excellent studies as Francis N. Stites, *Private Interest and Public Gain: The Dartmouth College Case, 1819* (1972); C. Peter Magrath, *Yazoo: Law and Politics in the New Republic: The Case of Fletcher v. Peck* (1966); Samuel J. Knofsky, *John Marshall and Alexander Hamilton: Architects of the Constitution* (1974); Donald L. Robinson, *Slavery and the Struggle for American Politics, 1786–1820* (1971); see also Staughton Lynd, *Class Conflict, Slavery, and the United State Constitution* (New York: Cambridge University Press, 2009).

15. Staughton Lynd, *Class, Conflict, Slavery and the United States Constitution* (New York: Cambridge University Press, 2009), 19.

16. Tenth Amendment reads: "The powers not delegated to the United States by the Constitution, nor prohibited by it to the States, are reserved to the States respectively, or to the people." (1791).

17. Federalism and its importance of slavery is discussed in the following scholarship. Paul Finkleman, *Slavery and the Constitutional Convention: Making a Covenant with Death;* in *Beyond Confederation: Origins of the Constitution and American National Identity,* eds. Richard Beeman, S. Botein, and E. C. Carter III (Chapel Hill: University of North Carolina Press, 1987); Paul Finkleman, *Slavery and the Founders* (M. E. Sharpe, 2001); see also Donald L. Robinson, *Slavery in the Structure of American Politics, 1765–1820* (Chapel Hill: University of North Carolina Press, 1970).

18. William H. Riker, *Federalism: Origin, Operation, Significance* (Boston: Little, Brown, and Company, 1964), 152–153.

19. "The Law of Black Suppression," in *Black Resistance/White Law,* ed. Mary Berry (New York: Appleton-Century-Crofts 1971), 7–17.

20. "The Seminole Wars as a Black Freedom Movement," in *Black Resistance/White Law,* ed. Berry, 20–66.

21. Professor Wills argues that this compromise led to the election of Jefferson to the presidency in 1800. Gary Wills, *Negro President: Jefferson and the Slave Power* (New York: Houghton Mifflin Co., 2003).

22. David Waldstreicher, *Slavery's Constitution: From Revolution to Ratification* (New York: Hill and Wang, 2009), 139.

23. United States Constitution, Article I Section 2. Forrest McDonald and Ellen Shapiro McDonald, *Confederation and Constitution* (New York: Harper Torchbooks, 1968).

24. Alexis de Tocqueville, "The prejudice or race appears to be stronger in the states that have abolished slavery." Cited in *North of Slavery: The Negro in the Free States, 1790–1860,* ed. Leon Litwack (Chicago: University of Chicago Press, 1961), 65. Patrick Henry, quoted in *Slavery's Constitution: From Revolution to Ratification*, 143. See also Roger A. Bruins, *Am I Not a Man and a Brother: The Antislavery Crusade of Revolutionary America, 1688–1788* (New York: Chelsea, 1977).

25. Leron Miller, *The Petitioners: The Story of the Supreme Court of the United States and the Negro* (New York: Pantheon Books, 1966), 19.

26. David Waldstreicher, *Slavery's Constitution: From Revolution to Ratification* (New York: Hill and Wang, 2009), 81.

27. Staughton Lynd, "The Compromise of 1787," *Class Conflict, Slavery and the United States Constitution* (New York: Cambridge University Press, 2009), 201.

28. Staughton Lynd, 212–213.

29. David Waldstreicher, *Slavery's Constitution*, 87–89.

30. United States Constitution, Article IV, Section 2. Forrest McDonald and Ellen Shapiro McDonald, *Confederation and Constitution* (New York: Harper Torchbooks, 1968).

31. United States Constitution, Article I, Section 9. McDonald and McDonald.

32. David Waldsteicher, 6–7, 89–90.

33. Paul Finkleman argues this point in a wide variety of excellent research. See *Slavery and the Founders: Race and Liberty in the Age of Jefferson* (M. E. Sharpe, 2001); *An Imperfect Union: Slavery, Federalism, and Comity* (Chapel Hill: University of North Carolina Press, 1981); "The Founders and Slavery: Little Ventured, Little Gained," *Yale Journal of Law and the Humanities* 13 (2001), 413–448; "The Roots of the Problem: How the Proslavery Constitution Shaped American Race Relations," *Barry Law Review* 4 (2003), 1–19.

34. David Waldstreicher, 94–95. Maryland's representative Luther Martin's observation. See Anne Farrow, Joel Lang, and Jenifer Frank, *Complicity: How the North Promoted, Prolonged, and Profited from Slavery* (New York: Random House, 2005).

35. "Constitutional Convention: A Covenant with Death," in *Beyond Confederation: Origins of American National Identity,* eds. Richard Beeman, Stepin Botein, Edward Carter, III (Chapel Hill: University of North Carolina Press, 1987); Paul Finkleman, Video lecture before the Detroit African American Historical Museum (no date); see also Donald L. Robinson, *Slavery in the Structure of American Politics* (1970).

36. Charles Miller, "Constitutional Law and the Rhetoric of Race," *Perspectives in American History*. Professor Miller uses this concept to demonstrate "remarkable series of euphemisms" or fig-leaves that hid the real intent and meaning of constitutional rhetoric. 154. See pages 154–155, where he discusses why the pro-slavery Constitution uses the word *slave* only when it is "forthright" in prohibiting the institution, but rhetorically silent when the document supports slavery outright.

37. United States Constitution, *Preamble.*

38. Charles Miller, 154–155.

39. Andrew Fraser. "The Legal Theory We Need Now," *Socialist Review,* 40–41 (July-October, 1978), 179.

40. This is Charles Miller's thesis in his essay, "Constitutional Law and the Rhetoric of Race."

41. See Chapter 5, "The Active State and the Mixed Economy, 1789–1861," in Kemit L. Hall, *The Magic Mirror: Law in American History* (New York: Oxford University Press, 1989), 88–105. See also in same book, Chapter 6, "Common Law, the Economy and the Onward Spirit of the Age: 1789–1861," 106–128.

42. Colin Sumner, *Reading Ideologies: An Investigation into the Marxist Theory of Ideology and Law* (London: Academic Press, 1979), 270–285. See also Arnold Peterson, *The Supreme Court: Watchdog of American Capitalism* (1971).

43. Ian F. Haney Lopez, *White by Law: The Legal Construction of Race* (New York: New York University Press, 1996). Professor Lopez discusses the Naturalization Act of 1790 vis-à-vis the prerequisites cases of the twentieth century.

44. David Roediger, *The Wages of Whiteness: Race and the Making of the American Working Class* (New York: Verso, 1991); see also Noel Ignatiev, *How the Irish Became White* (New York: Routledge, 1995).

45. Edgar McManus, *Black Bondage in the North* (Syracuse, Syracuse University Press, 1973), 166–167. See John Adams' quote in Leon Litwack, *North of Slavery: The Negro in the Free States, 1790–1860* (Chicago, The University of Chicago Press, 1961), 6.

46. Litwack, "Black Laws," or anti-immigration laws restricting Blacks from migration to North—Ohio, Illinois, Indiana, Oregon, 70–72.

47. Arthur Zilversmith, *The First Emancipation: The Abolition of Slavery in the North* (Chicago: The University of Chicago Press, 1967), 180.

48. Zilversmith, 113–115; see also Malik Simba, *"Commonwealth v. Jennison, 1783,"* in *The Historical Encyclopedia of World Slavery,* ed. Junius P. Rodriquez (Santa Barbara: ABC–CLIO, 1997).

49. J. D. Cushing, "The Cushing Court and the Abolition of Slavery in Massachusetts: More Notes on the Quock Walker Case," *American Journal of Legal History* 5 (1961).

50. Malik Simba, *"Commonwealth v. Jennison,"* 118–119. See also Arthur Zilversmith, "Quock Walker, Mumbet, and the Abolition of Slavery in Massachusetts," *William and Mary Quarterly*, 3, XXV (October, 1968).

51. Zilversmith, 114.

52. McManus, *Blacks in Bondage*, note Massachusetts, 164–167; Connecticut, 169–170; Rhode Island, 168; Vermont, 160; New Hampshire, 168; Pennsylvania, 161; New Jersey, 178; New York, 171.

53. Donald G. Nieman, *Promises to Keep: African Americans and the Constitutional Order, 1776 to Present* (New York: Oxford University Press, 1991), 8.

54. Zilversmirh, 221–222.

55. David Waldstreicher, 81.

56. Senator William Smith, March 6, 1818, *Abridgements of the Debates of Congress: From 1789–1856* (New York: D. Appleton and Company, 1858), 36.

57. Duncan MacLeod, *Slavery, Race, and the American Revolution* (New York: Cambridge University Press, 1974). Excellent treatment of the South's response to the era of liberty and freedom during the post-Revolutionary period.

58. MacLeod, 109. Excellent treatment of these cases.

59. McManus, 60. Solid treatment of the term. However, McLeod is definitive, 111.

60. Higginbotham, see section entitled "White Male Domination and Interracial Sexual Relations," 40–47.

61. MacLeod, 116–118.

62. MacLeod, 112–113

63. MacLeod, 118–119.

64. MacLeod, 117–118.

65. Douglas Hay, "Property, Authority, and Criminal Law," in *Albion's Fatal Tree: Crime and Society in Eighteenth-Century England,* eds. Douglas Hay, Peter Linebaugh, John G, Rule, and Cal Winslow (New York: Random House/Pantheon, 1976); sexual domination was an appendage to class and racial domination. The autonomy of sexual ideology was not formally addressed until 1967 in the case of *Loving v. Virginia*, wherein the U.S. Supreme Court declared statutes that forbade interracial marriages unconstitutional. Virginia's lower court, in upholding the statute in question, referred to God's vision of geographic and sexual separation of races that should have precluded interracial sexual contact. See Higginbottom, 43–44.

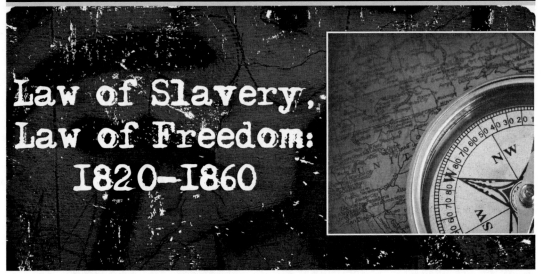

Law of Slavery, Law of Freedom: 1820–1860

The sum total of these relations of production constitutes the economic structure of society, the real foundation, on what rise a legal and political superstructure and which Corresponds {to} definite forms of social consciousness.

—KARL MARX, *A CONTRIBUTION TO THE CRITIQUE OF POLITICAL ECONOMY*[1]

Marx's observation on the dialectics between relations of production (e.g., master versus slave), which produces commodities for the market, the real foundation, and the corresponding ideology of race, expressed itself through the institution of the law of slavery. The critique of slave law originated during the 1830s abolition movement[2] and has been resurrected today. This chapter analyzes the contemporary historiography on American slave law and uses Marxist legal theory to critique how historians today attempted a clarification of the law. For the most part, slave law was used as "an instrument" against slaves and to "make them stand in fear."[3] Planters hoped that this instrumentalist legal coercion would correspond to better production, profit, and cultural/societal stability.[4] The four decades leading up to the Civil War have been characterized by noted legal historian Morton Horwitz as a period of judge-made law aimed at creating the conditions that would fuel commerce and economic interests.[5]

PART I: POLITICAL ECONOMY AND THE CONFLICT OF LAWS

Between the 1820s and the outbreak of the American Civil War, ideological and material developments confirmed much of our theoretical understanding of social and legal relations in a contradictory trajectory of conflict and consensus. On one level, we see a reciprocal relationship between two different economies under one capitalist political economy and "State" structure that at the same time produced modes of legal and cultural consciousness of the world that were, at times, Constitutionally consensual or diametrically opposed and conflicted. Supreme Court decisions alleviated Constitutional contestation at the federal and state levels. What is obvious is that the ideological conflicts, even when they appeared in radical form, either by Northern abolitionists or Southern apologists, were epiphenomenal to substantive material development concerning national political economy and territorial expansion. The "Market Revolution" pushed the Northern economy deeper into industrial capitalism, whereas the South, reinvigorated by Eli Whitney's cotton gin, evolved an economy dominated by "King Cotton." Plantations and planter-controlled slavocracy were based on the exploitation and control of African labor. The acquisition of new lands as a result of the war victory over Mexico led to the further solidification of different regional "class" interests.[6] The capitalist class came into conflict with itself, with one section located in the emerging industrial North and the other in the plantation South. The regional differences created opposing views regarding how the newly acquired lands would be developed and under what type of political economy. The views melted down to such propagandist ideas as "Free Soil/Federal Power of Antislavery" versus "State Sovereignty/Extraterritoriality for Slavery," with both proponents having a Constitutional perspective on why their positions were correct.[7]

The contradictions between the ideas of freedom and slavery, of slave labor versus free labor production, of capitalist class versus planter class, of federalism versus states' rights, was ultimately resolved in the throes of bloody antagonism on the battlefields of Bull Run, Antietam, Shiloh, Gettysburg, and ultimately Appomattox.

The various political and legal events in the decades leading up to the war revolved around the widening material developments in the North and South. The dominating class of both regions developed world views, value systems, and cultural assumptions explicitly and implicitly consistent with the revolution in the national market structure and the appearance of new and complex transportation and communication systems, such as steam-powered industrial technology. These national changes mirrored others in the finance and banking structures, the commercialization of the legal profession at all levels, immigration from abroad, and the further "domestication" of a large, third-generation African slave force in society.[8] In the North, commerce and business interests dominated and contoured these developments within a legal parameter that, according to Morton Horwitz, "entailed the transformation of the American common law from a fundamentally anti-commercial, anti-developmental body of doctrine that was protective, paternalistic, and expressive of the moral sense of the community, into an essentially amoral system of rules that promoted economic growth at all costs, subsidized large enterprises at the expense of small, and destroyed old forms of wealth and property in favor of newer ones."[9]

The deepening Northern commercial development was helped by this transformation in the common law, whereas the Southern agrarian–plantation economy developed an ambivalent law of slavery that at times was paternalistic, instrumentalist, horrific, formalistic, and commercial in its orientation. This ambivalence was based on the planter class's economic and political interests and their adherence to both the liberal legal tradition of formalism, individualism, equality, and freedom and another that relied on legal rigidity, authoritarian instrumentalism, and slavery.

The transformation of American law between the ratification of the Constitution and the infamous Dred Scott case of 1857 witnessed the development of the influence of the law on America's racial democracy and its legitimization of the privatization of property in the hands of self-willed and competing individuals as the sacred base for the rise of American capitalism. The United States Supreme Court, under the direction of its foremost Chief Justice, John Marshall, would use law as an instrument to ensure that aspiring capitalists used private property to enhance national economic growth rather than solely their narrow acquisitive interests.[10] Marshall and his fellow justices, especially his able Associate Justice, Joseph Storey, legislated law through their interpretive decisions to balance the relationship among slavery, rights of private property, and the new entrepreneurial spirit of the young Republic.[11] This balancing act of the conflict of laws and rights revolved, in part, around the insistence of Southerners that private property in slaves had paramount Constitutional protection, whereas their Northern capitalist adversaries, after first accepting this premise for the sake of creating the new Republic, grew tired and then antagonistic to the idea that slavery and capitalism could peacefully co-exist and prosper together.[12]

The first breach in the political rapprochement of 1787 was precipitated by Missouri's application to the Republic as a slave state in 1818. Growing concerns over the possible spread of slavery westward led Northern political leaders to oppose this admission by using the Constitutional provision that permitted "Congress . . . to dispose of and make all needful Rules and Regulations respecting the Territory or other Property belonging to the United States."[13] For these Northerners, "needful Rules" included slavery's prohibition. Southern planters responded, in part, by citing the Constitutional provision of the Fifth Amendment that "no person shall be deprived of property without due process of law; nor shall private property be taken for public use without just compensation."[14] Slavery or non-slavery became the line of division between two regional dominating classes as they vied over how Missouri, as well other states in the future, would be carved out of the Louisiana Purchase. This crisis was alleviated in 1820 by each ruling sectional class agreeing to a compromise that permitted Missouri's entry into the Union as a slave state and Maine's admission as a non-slave state, thus maintaining the same number and ratio of slave to non-slave states. The Missouri Compromise of 1820 also prohibited slavery in all parts of the Louisiana Purchase north of 36/30 north latitude.[15]

This compromise resolution eased sectional tensions because the Northern politicians were not ready to commit fully to antislavery as a political platform because of slavery's strong national economic underpinnings, as observed by many Northern capitalists who recognized that what enriches a part, enriches the whole.[16] In addition, most White Northerners viewed the African slave in the same light as Southerners—as human brutes doomed to slavery by their inferior nature. Furthermore, each side understood that slavery was also helping forge a "market revolution" within the nation.[17]

By the late 1820s and early 1830s, the Democratic Party solidified around the Southern figure of Andrew Jackson, who had strong popular Northern support that lessened the already decreasing power of the Old Whig politicians. However, the 1830 Webster–Hayne oratorical debates in the U.S. Senate epitomize the growing sectional tensions. Federalism (North) as opposed to states' rights (South) reflected the ideological differences between regional ruling classes, whose semantics and actions were dictated by divergent economic interests. However, individual rhetorical combatants aside, it was the emerging Democratic Party that dominated Congressional and presidential politics for most of the years preceding the firing on Fort Sumter. The Democratic political bureaucracy at the federal level became known by its detractors as the *slaveocracy* because the Democrats controlled all three branches of government. This ensured that the national policy agenda toward that "peculiar type of private property" would have federal protection.[18]

Racial federalism developed during this period because the ideology of race had become hegemonic throughout American life and institutions. In the North as well as the slave South, racialism pervaded all cultural aspects of society. The strange peculiarity of racialism after the first emancipation in the North was described by Litwack in his seminal work, *North of Slavery*:

> in virtually every phrase of existence, Negroes found themselves systematically separated from Whites. They were excluded from railway cars, omnibuses . . . they sat in secluded and remote corners of theaters and lecture halls; they could not enter most hotels, restaurants, and resorts, except as servants; they prayed in "Negro pews" in the White churches, and if partaking in the sacrament of the Lord's Supper, they waited until the Whites had been served the bread and wine. Moreover, they were often educated in segregated schools, punished in segregated prisons, nursed in segregated hospitals and buried in segregated cemeteries.[19]

Litwack recognized what the famous mid-18th century French traveler and astute essayist, Alexis de Tocqueville, observed: "It seemed that race prejudice appeared stronger in the areas of the country that no longer has slavery than where it exists at present."[20] What de Tocqueville saw was, in a sense, a confirmation of the Marxist theory that ideologies can take on a life of their own from the changing necessities of economy. This theoretical validation of the relative autonomy of the idea of race is probably more recognizable during the period after the destruction of American slavery in the North when that economy no longer needed it. Slavery was extinguished, but the ideology that was born of slavery continued culturally and legally. The rise of the ideological domination of race set the stage for conflicts over "second-class freedoms and citizenship" of quasi-free Blacks in non-slave areas.[21] De facto discrimination became as powerful as an oppressive system as slavery was with *de jure imprimatur*. Two examples demonstrate how ideologies take on a life of their own and confirm de Tocqueville's observation. In spite of the fact that the Quock Walker case of 1784 had abolished slavery, the Massachusetts Supreme Court, in *Roberts v. City of Boston*,[22] 1849, decided that Boston's school board could maintain separate schools for White and Black children and not violate the state's constitution that "all men are free and equal." And in Connecticut, which abolished slavery in 1784, Prudence Crandall[23] was fined by the state of Connecticut for violating a state law that prohibited the teaching of Blacks who were non-residents.[24] This *de jure* punishment mattered little because the White citizens of Canterbury had already demolished the school using the *de facto* customary ideology of White over Black. The first emancipation in the North created a Black proletariat that was quasi-free. The paradox of the states north of slavery was that it was here that birthed the anti-slavery movement. This anti-slavery impulse was revealed when various Northern states passed personal liberty laws[25] that gave fugitive slaves due process of law, Massachusetts passed a state constitution abolishing school segregation, small segments within White communities protected fugitive slaves within the Underground Railroad, a number of state courts ruled in favor of freedom in cases of slaves in transit, a number of abolitionists were elected to state office, and various colleges accepted Blacks as matriculants.[26] A stifling culture of racialism had explicit contradictions within it, and these contradictions, over time, institutionalized themselves and helped create the conditions for civil war. In spite of racism in the North, the North fought to maintain the Union, and in doing so, destroyed slavery.

However, the hegemonic ideology of race not only solidified race relations within states but made possible a racialist federalism supported by the apparatus of the national State as well. Southerners recognized the utility of such a hegemony and advocated the continued existence of the Union under the hegemonic racial guarantees of 1787. It was not until the perceived apogee of the Republican Party with Lincoln's election that the South turned to secession as an alternative to a racialized federal constitutionalism. As Arthur Bestor asserted in his exceptional work on state sovereignty and slavery, "Secession was the alternative to, not the purposed outcome of, the constitutional program that proslavery forces advocated . . . defenders of slavery wished the constitutional machinery to function in such a way as to give maximum protection to slavery."[27] An expanded and strengthened federal structure that protected slavery since 1787 was what the South cried for, and it was not until Lincoln's meteoric rise to political prominence that they changed their tune to anti-federalism and took on a pro-states' rights position.

Public policy that considered social consequences such as the maintenance of slavery was an acceptable fact in America's life and institution. Many American politicians abhorred this instrumentalist use of the law, for they still believed in "natural law" or the "Formal Style" of law making.[28] The formal style assumed that law has universal rules above and beyond the litigants, and that these rules can be applied objectively by jurists to remedies that are fair, impartial, and equitable. In approaching the issue of slavery the United States Supreme Court, under the firm Federalist hand of John Marshall, opted for what Karl Llewellyn called the "Grand Style," in which Marshall used his power as Chief Justice to form high court consensus around issues of public policy. In achieving this consensus, Marshall created law through decisions that recognized their social consequences. Law became an instrument by which the Marshall Court steered clear of the slavery controversy while solidifying the independency and autonomy of the Court in the federal system so that national economic growth could be Constitutionally sanctioned. Marshall's implemented vision helped make the high court the final arbiter of political disagreements and questions concerning the economic power between the varied social interests in the infant Republic.

Under a type of judicial restraint vis-a-vis slavery that ignored the social consequences of slavery, Marshall reminded his fellow jurists, in the infamous *Antelope* case, that "This court must not yield to feelings which might seduce it from the path of duty, and must obey the mandate of the law."[29] This 1825 case concerned the issue of whether Africans apprehended off the coast of

Florida, in violation of the 1808 Congressional prohibition against the international slave trade, should be freed or remanded to the foreign nations requesting them. Not wanting the Court to become involved in the murky and muddy waters of the slavery controversy, Marshall maneuvered the Court around the central issues of liberty versus property or freedom versus slavery. Marshall decided that as a conflict in law existed between the American prohibition and the permitted activity under international law and thus the laws of other nations, he would devise a formula by which some of the Africans were permitted to be claimed by the U.S. government and by two foreign nations, Portugal and Spain, involved in the case.[30] The path of duty for Marshall was to ensure that the Court did not become involved in this contentious, emotive issue, but in doing so, Marshall and his brethren revealed their inability to prioritize humanity before interest, thus verifying the substantive priority of economic interests in determining what was American law.

The ability of Marshall to control feelings and to uphold the mandate of law revealed that his emotive goals revolved around his insistence that the legal form should be contoured by those social classes who enslaved African humanity. As analyzed in Chapter 2, in the 1813 case of *Mima Queen v. Hepburn,* Marshall refused to permit hearsay evidence to be admitted into courts of law to aid slave plaintiffs who claimed that they had been told or that it was rumored that someone on their maternal side was of free ancestry. If this hearsay evidence could be admitted, then these plaintiffs would be able to continue to gain their freedom under the old colonial "law of the womb" statutes, stating that the legal status of children should follow the status of the mother—*partus sequitur ventrem.*[31] These statutes obviously overturned the English common law tradition in which children followed the status of the father. The change in this tradition recognized the constant duress of rape of African women by White colonial planters. The twist, however, was that many White lower-class women opted to cohabitate or marry men of African ancestry, thus creating the legal basis for the *Mima Queen* case of 1813. Even though hearsay evidence, which led to the freedom of such slaves, had been accepted in the state courts of Maryland, Virginia, and North Carolina for years, Marshall noted that admissibility of hearsay could only be in "cases of pedigree, of prescription, of custom, and in some cases, of boundary,"[32] but, inferentially, not in cases that might elevate the liberty of Africans over the property interests of planters.

On the question of slavery, neither the Marshall Court nor the Taney Court, which succeeded the Marshall Court, diverged greatly in the legitimization of the peculiar institution with Constitutional protection. However, Taney and his Court, unlike Marshall's, used *obiter dictum* and law to preach the triumphant nature of property in humans and the Constitutional rights of the states and the individual to exploit this property in their own economic interests. Previously, Marshall Court decisions reflected the settling propositions of industrial capitalism that property was identified with liberty. Material progress became the measure of individual merit and national greatness. And the corollary principle—that government should serve both individual and national progress by aiding capitalism—triumphed as well.[33]

In response, the Taney Court attempted to cautiously put the brakes on Marshall's entrepreneurial jurisprudence by appreciating the democratic nature of state legislatures and inviting them to regulate the new economic forces in the interest of the public and for the benefit of the common man.[34]

For Roger B. Taney, the *common man* meant men of European descent and absolutely not those of African descent. The Court, under Taney's watchful and guiding hand, restricted liberty for quasi-free Blacks as well as slaves themselves; neither one because of their color alone could be the common man.

The idea of the common man became embodied in the presidency in 1828, when Andrew Jackson was elected. The democratic impulse that ushered Jackson into the White House revolved around agrarian republicanism, states' rights, and proslavery sentiment. By 1837, six of the nine sitting justices had been nominated by Jackson.[35]

The racism of Jacksonian Democracy for White men could be recognized on three levels. The first is the treatment of the Native American Indian. Under Jackson's leadership, Congress passed the Indian Removal Act of 1832. Jackson epitomized the fruits of what the democratic impulse did for White men. Jackson not only fought, killed, and directed the removal of the Five Civilized Tribes (Cherokees, Choctaws, Chickasaws, Seminoles, and Creek), but he also prepared their vacated lands for cotton and land speculators like himself for tremendous profit. Jackson was the classic self-willed Indian killer, land speculator, and slave owner that characterized American manhood during the mid-nineteenth century.[36]

On the second level, institutional race domination was exhibited by the Jacksonian Congress, which passed the gag rule[37] prohibiting any discussion of slavery's abolition on the floor. The gag rule was Congress's response to the flood of antislavery petitions mailed to the federal government. With its passage, Congress effectively gagged the First Amendment rights of a segment of its citizens. This rule remained in effect between 1836 and 1844 and was eventually overturned as a result of the strenuous and tireless efforts of John Quincy Adams. This antislavery victory did not prevent Jackson's Postmaster General from prohibiting abolitionist literature from being conveyed by the U.S. mail, thus denying a Constitutional right to even White Americans who held antislavery opinions.

The third level consisted of the popular and paranoiac response of anti-abolitionist mobs that attacked, beat, tarred and feathered, and sometimes killed Americans of antislavery persuasion who exercised their Constitutional right of free speech.[38]

These events, coinciding with those of the other two levels, led many Northerners, for the first time, to question the *quid pro quo* agreement of 1787. They saw that the liberty and the property of dissenters could be destroyed by a racialist slavocracy determined to use the very fabric of ideals embodied in the rhetoric of the Declaration of Independence and the American Revolution in their race and class interests. It appeared and was recognized by many that the slaveocracy conception of freedom was restricted to those who believed that racial slavery was consistent with American liberty. In response, abolitionist ranks grew steadily throughout the 1830s and 1840s. Many White Americans were drawn to the standard of antislavery because of what they perceived as a threat to the "traditional" revolutionary rhetoric of higher law, the transcendental idea of the humanity of individuals, and how a republican form of government should treat its citizens. Abolitionism came to symbolize, for a growing number of Black and White Americans, a resurrection of what they perceived as the original social values of revolutionary Americanism. In trying to achieve this resurrection, more Americans began to see the validity of Garrison's words that the 1787 agreement was truly a "covenant with death, and an agreement with Hell."[39] Abolitionism clashed with American law and its cohort anti-abolitionism on both the state and federal levels.

The breakdown in interstate comity and thus the reciprocity of 1787 came through the efforts of the Boston Female Antislavery Society in 1836. These feminists came to the aid of a six-year-old slave girl name Med who was sojourning with her mistress in Boston. The Society's lawyer, Ellis Gray Loring, contended that morality, or *in favorem liberatis,* should take precedence over comity. Chief Justice Shaw, with unanimous support from his fellow justices, freed Med with dicta concerning slavery's immorality but rested his decision on the legal fact that human property is the exception to the rule of comity because this peculiar property is not recognized as such by all nations per se.[40] Southern courts countered even earlier and continued after *Aves* by refusing to recognize Northern court decisions that freed slaves in the North. Antislavery Constitutionalism continued to clash with Southern materialism with the breakdown in comity and federal efforts on behalf of owners of human property.[41]

Antislavery but pro-capitalist Supreme Court justices and others who presided over various Northern state appellate courts attempted to counteract the full weight of the racialist Jacksonian impulses and the personal predilections of Marshall and Taney. Using a utopian view of the law of nature as contravening the law of nations that positively legitimized slavery, Justice Story, the leading antislavery Supreme Court justice, handed down several bold decisions condemning the slave trade and slavery itself. In the 1822 case of *United States v. La Jeune Eugenie,* Story firmly stated that the slave trade was "repugnant to the great principles of Christian duty . . . the eternal maxims of social justice . . . And . . . is repugnant to the general principles of justice and humanity."[42] In the most famous 1842 *Amistad* case, Story ruled that Africans kidnapped as free men in Africa and transported on a slaver could commit "political" murder to achieve their freedom. This *cause célèbre* case gave Story an opportunity to vent his antislavery feelings.[43]

Other antislavery sentiments were echoed by Associate Justice McLean in a fugitive slave case when he asserted that "slavery had its origin in usurpation and injustice," whereas Judge Bissell of Connecticut, in a dissenting opinion, declared that "as a citizen and as a man, I may admit the injustices and immorality of slavery. . . . But as a jurist, I must look at . . . which the law proscribes."[44]

In Justice Bissell's dissent, one can readily perceive the moral dilemma confronting antislavery jurists within a society that promulgated proslavery law. It would be difficult being an antislavery justice within the world the slaveholders made.[45] As progressive segments in American society moved to confront the slavery issue at mid-century, cases concerning fugitive slaves illuminated the moral dilemma. The antislavery bar was composed of such legal minds as Salmon P. Chase (future Chief Justice of the Supreme Court); Samuel Sewall; Henry Dana, Jr.; Thaddeus Stevens; Charles Sumner; and William Seward. These future radical Republicans kept this dilemma in the forefront of the legal process by representing fugitive slaves and emphasizing in their defense the antithetical values between what the idealism of the Declaration of Independence declared and the material class interests protected by the Constitution.

The fugitive slave and the slave trade cases represented the legal response to the growing tide of sectional antagonism, both verbal and otherwise. The 1831 clarion of Garrison's *Liberator* newspaper called for the immediate abolition of slavery. Nat Turner's revolt earlier in the year set the tone for this clarion, while the torrential fear in the aftermath of Denmark Vesey's 1822 revolt had led, in part, to the sectional confrontation over South Carolina's Negro Seamen's Act.[46] South

Carolina became concerned that Northern-born, free Black merchant marine sailors, and particularly British free Black merchant marine sailors, were an obvious visual eyesore for slaveholding Whites and an inspiration for their slaves. South Carolina passed the Act, which required the incarceration of these "eye sores" in the local hoosegow while their ships were in ports of call and forced the captains of these ships to pay for the "room and board" for his men.[47] Following South Carolina's lead, other Southern states passed similar statutes. Federal power over interstate trade, foreign commerce, and foreign treaty as opposed to the Southern states' fears that lax controls over their ports might lead to slave insurrections became the sectional point of contention in this volatile situation. Federal treaties with foreign nations assured that these nations' sailors would have access to the port facilities. South Carolina's authorities knew that copies of the Black nationalist clarion *David Walker's Appeal*[48] were disseminated in 1829 by Black seamen from the North. In 1823, the Black seamen statutes were ruled unconstitutional by the United States Supreme Court in the case *Elkinson v. Deliesseline.*[49] Justice William Johnson noted the supremacy of federal law over interstate commerce and foreign policy, and argued that these acts interfered with that exclusive domain.

This case concerning Black seamen did not put to rest the issue of whether the federal or state governments had exclusive power to regulate interstate commerce. Like the South Carolina case, the 1841 Mississippi case of *Groves v. Slaughter*[50] revealed how divisive slavery could be vis-a-vis a non-slavery issue such as the commerce clause. Because Congress had the Constitutional right to "regulate commerce . . . among the several states," most abolitionists thought the Supreme Court could ban the nefarious interstate trade in commoditized human form, that is, slaves. Pro-slavery advocates argued that slaves were a special kind of property, meaning they were human, and thus not covered by the commercial term *articles of commerce.* These pro-slavery adherents argued in the negative when Mississippi decided that they could ban slave importation into the state by a state constitutional provision in 1822 that would go into effect in 1833. The 1841 case fostered four decisions by the Supreme Court justices, with Smith Thompson's decision holding for the Court. Thompson's opinion succinctly stated that the ban was invalid because the state constitutional clause needed additional actuating legislation that had not occurred. Several Justices issued their own *obiter dictums* either advocating for or against federal or state exclusivity over commerce. Abolitionist Justice McLean argued for federal control and the human qualities of Africans even as slaves, whereas pro-slavery Justice Taney retorted by restating his views that Congress did not have the power to control interstate commerce in slaves.[51]

The moral dilemma forced on American law by slavery was brought home in no uncertain terms in the case of the slave Margaret Morgan. Her case revealed the benign versus the malignant dilemma of master–slave relationships. Morgan's owner had permitted her parents as well as Margaret to live in a state of common-law freedom. This was not the usual case, for many anti-slavery slave owners, Quakers especially, purchased slaves with the aim of permitting them to live "free." What is different in Morgan's case is that she moved from Maryland, the state that recognized her slave status, to Pennsylvania, which did not. To further compound this conflict of laws, Margaret married a free Black man and had children who under the law of the womb—*partus sequitur ventrem*—took on the status of their mother. Maryland recognized this law and Pennsylvania did not. Except for the tensions caused by the occasional meandering slave catcher, Margaret and her family lived a relatively normal life.[52]

This benign master–slave relationship gave way to a malignant one when Margaret's owner died and his niece and heir, Margaret Ashmore, asserted her claim and sent the slave catcher, Edward Prigg, north to recapture her "human property," which included Morgan's children. After having been refused a recaptation writ by a local justice of the peace, Prigg took the Morgans back to Maryland and then returned to contest or "test" his conviction for violating Pennsylvania's personal liberty law.[53] Nominal freedom could have been the result of an intimate relationship with her master because Morgan's first child was born in Maryland and another child in Pennsylvania.[54]

Personal liberty laws were passed by various Northern states to protect their state citizens, White or Black but especially their quasi-free Black citizens, from forcible seizure and recaptation to a slave state. These laws also made it difficult to prosecute citizens who interfered with proslavery federal recaptation laws.[55] Personal liberty laws provided a wide range of due process guarantees that restricted the powers of professional slave catchers. *Prigg* and other professionals had broad powers of apprehension of fugitive slaves under the Fugitive Slave Act of 1793 and its earlier Constitutional provision. Personal liberty laws were aimed, therefore, at interposing state law over proslavery federal law or nullifying federal law entirely. Freedom as a national idea was the driving force behind the passage of these laws and thus created one more intersectional crisis within a nonconsensual generation.

Justice Story wrote the majority opinion in the *Prigg* case and remembering Bissell's dilemma, placed aside his repugnancy concerning slavery and did what the law prescribed. Story overturned the Pennsylvania law by upholding the Fugitive Slave Act of 1793 and the power of the Constitutional clause that gave slave law "extraterritoriality" outside of state boundaries.

This extraterritoriality permitted slave owners to recapture their slaves throughout the nation's free areas. This point was a direct refutation of the old 1772 King's Bench case of *Somerset v. Steward,* in which Lord Mansfield declared that slavery could only exist by positive law. Again, Pennsylvania had no positive legislation permitting slavery. Interestingly enough, Story began his decision by facetiously referring to the "courteous and friendly spirit"[56] of the states toward resolving this issue. Even at that, Story was in a no-win situation, because each state felt absolutely right on the issue. Story provided Pennsylvania with a face-saving antislavery loophole by seriously questioning whether state officials should have any responsibility in carrying out the administration of federal law. This legal interpretation validated the actions of the initial justice of the peace who refused to sign the order remanding Margaret Morgan back to her state of servitude. Absent of any administrative machinery and given the growing antislavery sentiment of Northerners, remanding slaves would be difficult indeed. Sadly, in the wake, of *Prigg,* a deeply troubled Story wrote to a friend in an attempt to assuage his guilt, "you know full well that I have ever been opposed to slavery. But I take my standard of duty as a judge from the Constitution."[57] It appeared that Justice Story not only could justify and deliver his decisions but could rationalize them to himself as well. Of the eight remaining justices, seven concurred in separate opinions, while the eighth, Justice McLean, dissented. He insisted that the states had broad police powers to regulate procedural guarantees within Congressional enactments. This argument, if agreed on by the brethren, would have retained the substance of personal liberty laws without disrupting federal sovereignty.

Issues of freedom and slavery involved a wide variety of incidences between the North and South. Black abolitionists and their communities fought to maintain their formal legal rights, but also fought against slavery when proslavery comity permitted its head to appear in their Northern communities. Frederick Douglass asserted that his community should fight the proslavery administration of the Constitution that warped its noble design.[58] Douglass argued the noble language of the document and the Declaration of Independence could be defined by a social activism which would elevate "all the people of this county, without regard to color, class, or clime."[59] Heeding Douglass's view, Black Bostonians and their White abolitionist allies fought for six-year-old Med in 1836, fought for six-year-old Sarah Roberts's right to integrate Boston's schools in 1849, and with the passage of the Fugitive Slave Act of 1850, fought successfully to prevent the remanding of the escaped slave, Shadrach, in February 1851, while failing to do likewise with another escapee, Thomas Sims, two months later.[60] However, the Sims case reveals the limits of Douglass's Constitutional analysis. In the Shadrach case, Black Bostonians used physical force to liberate the slave from Boston's hoosegow, but when Sims was incarcerated, the authorities took the necessary precautions based on their Shadrach experience. This experience led to the jail being protected by three military companies of Boston guards, 250 federal troops, and two artillery pieces.[61] Unarmed community activists could not match the combined state and federal armed coercion. Legal and Constitutional coercion rested on Massachusetts's Chief Justice Lemuel Shaw's decision to uphold the remanding of Sims in a summary manner. What Douglass did not grasp was that it was the administration of the 1850 Act that actually defined the noble language as ignoble. The noble language of freedom and equality was juxtaposed beside ignoble language such as, "In no trial or hearing under this Act [1850] shall the testimony of such alleged Fugitive be admitted as evidence."[62]

The inability of Shaw or his lower-court brethren to become antislavery justices did not inhibit others garbed in the Black robes of justice to walk another path. The autonomy of the ideas of freedom and equality led Justices McLean and Curtiss to dissent in the historic *Dred Scott v. Sanford* case of March 6, 1857.[63] The backdrop or early antecedents to the *Dred Scott* case centered on the issue of whether slavery should be permitted in the territories and thus future states that would be carved out from the lands acquired from the United States' military victory over Mexico in 1846. David Wilmot's infamous "Proviso" to a military appropriation bill sounded the clarion of how a segment of Americans tied racism to antislavery. Wilmot's Proviso declared, "neither slavery nor involuntary servitude shall exist in any part of said territory" acquired from Mexico once the victory was assured. The racial motivation behind such a prohibition was cried by Wilmot, "I plead the cause and rights for White freemen. I would preserve to free White labor a fair country, a rich inheritance, where the sons of toil, of my own race and own color, can live without the disgrace which association with negro slavery brings upon free labor."[64] However, the Proviso also suggested that Congress had exclusive power over the territories and their future per Article IV, Section 3, of the Constitution: "The Congress shall have power to dispose of and make all needful Rules and Regulations respecting the Territory or other Property belonging to the United States." The Compromise of 1820 in a sense had validated this Congressional power and its imprint on slavery because Congress limited slavery north of 36/30—the imaginary line extending westward and bordering the Southernmost boundary of Missouri.

Of course, Wilmot's Proviso was anathema to the proslavery Democrats. Those who tried to alleviate sectional conflict between sectional absolutes, such as Lewis Cass and Stephen A. Douglas, put forth the idea of *popular sovereignty*.[65] These compromisers argued that it should be left up to the individual citizens of each forming territory to determine their institutional social relationships before admittance into the Union. This was the most democratic solution they argued. The Compromise of 1850 would ultimately be agreed on based on the popular sovereignty formula.

In the Compromise of 1850, Congressional sectionalists agreed that Utah and New Mexico territories would be able to use popular sovereignty as their governmental formulation, California's request to be admitted as a free state would be accepted, the domestic slave-trading companies and their activities would be prohibited from the District of Columbia, and the Story's loophole in *Prigg* would be closed with an explicit monetary incentive that would help planters and their slave catchers capture fugitive slaves. This new fugitive slave clause, according to noted legal historian Loren Miller,

> provided for federally appointed commissioners to exercise the powers granted judges in the 1793 act. These commissioners were given concurrent jurisdiction with United States judges to give certificates to claimants and order the removal of fugitives. United States marshals and deputies were required to execute writs under the act on penalty of $1,000 fine, and if a slave escaped from the marshal, "with or without his assent," that official became liable for the value of the slave. . . . Commissioners were to be paid ten dollars for each fugitive ordered returned but only five dollars when the claim was refused! . . . Persons who aided or abetted in the rescue of a fugitive were liable to heavy fines and imprisonment.[66]

The political validation of popular sovereignty in the Compromise of 1850 set the stage for its ultimate legitimization in the Kansas–Nebraska Act of 1854, which, because both Kansas and Nebraska were above 36/30, repealed that relevant section of the Missouri Compromise of 1820. Slavery became a national institution supported by all three branches of government and the rule of law. Northerners perceived of these latest legislative *quid pro quos* as a defeat for their antislavery interests. These interests merged into the new Republican Party, rabidly sectional, ideological, and determined to reverse the trend toward the nationalization of slavery.[67]

The victory of the slaveocracy at the Congressional level set the stage for McLean and Curtiss's dissent at the juridical level in the infamous decision concerning a suit for freedom by Dred Scott. Taking the legislative lead and at the not-so-subtle behest of the executive branch,[68] the U.S. Supreme Court took the opportunity in the *Dred Scott* decision to complete the circle that would make slavery and slave owners' right paramount over the freedom of African slaves, the liberty of quasi-free Blacks, and the legal rights of progressive White abolitionist supporters. Dred Scott's suit for his freedom permitted the Supreme Court to put the final nail in the proverbial coffin by denying his lawsuit.

Dred Scott sued for his freedom based on the old *Somerset* case,[69] which established the dictum "free for a day, free forever." Scott claimed that because he had spent more than four years in the free state of Illinois and the free territory of Minnesota with his master, Dr. John Emerson, he was by default free. Scott submitted that he worked as a free waged laborer, had remarried, had a child, and in 1838 had voluntarily returned to the slave state of Missouri with Dr. Emerson. With the wages that he earned, Scott initially and unsuccessfully tried to purchase his and his family's freedom from Dr. Emerson's widow, Irene Emerson. Scott surely thought he was a free man in fact if not in law. As law would have it, Scott won his case at the state level using the principle of *Somerset* and the antislavery prohibition in the Missouri Compromise of 1820. However, in 1852, Ms. Emerson appealed her deceased husband's property "victory" to the Missouri Supreme Court, which overturned Scott's brief lower-court victory. The Missouri Supreme Court stated that Missouri need not give "comity" to another state's law of freedom. The determined Scott appealed to the U.S. Supreme Court. Interestingly, Irene Emerson had remarried to the anti-slavery Massachusetts Congressman Calvin G. Chaffee, who promptly conveyed his new wife's slave property to her brother, Dr. John Sanford of New York. Thus is the case of *Dred Scott v. Sanford*.[70]

This appeal placed Scott's legal fate in the hands of five justices, including the Chief Justice, who were Southerners and two who were, although Northerners, proslavery. On March 6, 1857, speaking for the majority of seven with McLean and Curtiss dissenting, Chief Justice Roger B. Taney stated clearly that Scott could not be a citizen because he was "a Negro and a slave."[71] Comity gave Missouri's slave law exterritoriality[72] throughout the nation. This proslavery comity over free state comity was based on Taney's reading of history. The Constitutional framers "regarded [Negroes] as beings of inferior order, and altogether unfit to associate with the White race, either in social or political relations, and so far inferior that they had no rights which the White man was bound to respect."[73] Taney went further and ruled the Missouri Compromise unconstitutional based both on his proslavery comity argument and his view that Congress can only legislate to affirm slave property rights. Any legislation that proscribed a master's property rights "could hardly be dignified by the name of due process of law."[74] In keeping with *stare decisis,* Scott's sojourn in free land had already been addressed and rejected in the 1850 case of *Strader v. Graham.*[75] One dissenter, Justice Curtiss, stated that Taney's history was pure propaganda, because in at least five of the original thirteen colonies and subsequent states, Blacks were citizens and used the franchise. As such, they were members of the original "contractual community."[76] Justice McLean expressed his moral outrage by strongly dissenting and stating that "a slave is not mere chattel. He bears the impress of his capital maker and is amenable to the laws of God."[77] Taney's views of how to resolve the sectional controversy via his instrumental use of law were completed in *Abelman v Booth.*[78] Sherman Booth, a Wisconsin abolitionist, was convicted in federal court for assisting fugitive slaves. On appeal to the Wisconsin Supreme Court, he won when that court issued a writ of *habeas corpus* and declaring the Fugitive Slave Law of 1850 unconstitutional. Federal Marshall Abelman appealed, and Taney and his proslavery brethren let Booth's original conviction stand.[79]

The Supreme Court, in *Prigg, Scott,* and *Booth,* was the "firebell in the night" pushing the two national sections to their "irrepressible conflict." The political discourse between Lincoln and Douglass further clarified the coming sectional cataclysm. Conflicting economies and interests even with a consensual ideology of race created Constitutional dilemmas. These dilemmas were addressed by the Supreme Court in a variety of conflict of laws cases. However, in the American South, the law of slavery had its own internal conflicts that were dilemmas created by the slave's humanity versus the planter's interests to make a profit from producing cotton for the international market.

PART II: LAW OF SLAVERY AND THE USE OF LAW AS AN INSTRUMENT OF CLASS DOMINATION

The law of American slavery embodied a fundamental contradiction that was that such a legal system existed even though the master's will over the slave was complete. The master was the law unto himself.[80] Slave law, as expounded by courts and legislatures, had to constantly place the master's complete domination of his slave within an inherited legal tradition of rule of law.[81] Unlike the blatantly harsh and unequivocal colonial law of slavery of the seventeenth and eighteenth centuries, the nineteenth-century law of slavery was restrained by capitalist market forces and a solidified antebellum legal and social culture of bourgeois origins. The rise of industrial capitalism in the Northeast with peripheral markets in the West had its counterpart, agriculturally, in the South. Cotton became "King" and was produced for the international market, and the demands of market capitalism placed comparable demands on the social and legal relationship between master and slave.

The mid-nineteenth-century market revolution ushered in new technologies of production and transportation that invaded the South. Industrial accidents and injuries to slaves, sometimes caused by slaves and sometimes by White free labor, led to bourgeois legal litigation. The use of slaves in mining, railroads, steamboats, and industrial factory production forced the law of slavery to mediate fault and blame by modifying bourgeois legal theory to the realities of slave buying, slave hiring, and slave dying.[82] As the law of slavery responded to the material economic changes of incipient industrialism, it rejected major trends of Northern courts and law that were confronting the major impetus of American industrialization. Southern courts did not accept the Massachusetts Supreme Court ruling in the *Farwell* decision that adopted the fellow servant rule.[83] Chief Justice Shaw's pro-business and anti-labor *Farwell* decision placed the assumption of risk on the worker in hazardous working conditions, and also limited the worker's right to sue his employer for negligence regarding an on-the-job injury.[84]

Southern courts refused to apply Shaw's logic vis-a-vis slaves because slaves who were hired out did not have the right to quit, give notice concerning how hazardous the work was, or receive extra compensation for such dangerous work.[85] Most important, slave hires could not decide the competency of the poor White worker who was to be his "fellow servant." In the famous case of *State v. Mann*,[86] which concerned the resistance of a female slave hire who was shot by her "temporary master," Judge Ruffin of South Carolina declared that the slave had no free will and the master's will over the slave was complete. Judge Lumpkin of Georgia in *Scudder v. Woodbridge*[87] agreed that Black slave and free White labor are so polar in their differences that "it would be strange and extraordinary indeed if the same principle should apply to both."[88]

Southern judges became instruments of the master class in consciously recognizing the different legal rules required of an economy based on free labor versus one based on slave labor. Southern tort and contract law concerning slaves had limited autonomy to develop in symmetry to Northern tort and contract law. Race relations and class relations were different social structures, and law reflected that reality. The protection of the master's interest in that peculiar type of human labor was first and foremost in the juridical mind of Southern judges and legislatures. *Caveat emptor* became a cardinal legal doctrine in bourgeois relationship in the North, but in the

South, the more traditional implied warranty and the sound price rule were retained to ensure that in return for the master's investment, he received from the seller a physically healthy and productive economic unit.[89]

Similar to how the law of slavery had to modify or reject bourgeois legal theory concerning tort and contract, slave law also had to do the same to protect the slave-owning class's economic interests in slaves accused of criminal acts or the acts of Whites who criminally harmed property of the master class. The questions for Southern judges were who shall be extended the protection of due process of law, and was this salient rule applicable in like manner from bourgeois theory to slavery's realities.[90]

Due process of law has been referred to as the miracle of Western criminal law. This idea refers to the procedural guarantees that emerged in Western legal tradition that provided rights to defendants in criminal proceedings. These rights became, in a strange sort of way, the basis of what many jurists and legal scholars believed to be *justice.* For these true believers, *justice* was achieved when a defendant was extended his or her Bill of Rights guarantees. Trial verdict, outcome, or result cannot and should not be the salient determinant of justice; rather, procedural guarantees should be the paramount basis for justice. This blind allegiance to due process has become the historical point of contention when historians, of late, have debated the merits of "a more equitable past" concerning the procedural justice meted out to slaves caught up in the vortex of the criminal law of slavery.[91] Due process, fairness, and formal adjudication can be seem in statutory requirement and in *obiter dictum* in a few cases, but given the absolutely small number of cases that reach the proverbial "law within the box or the appellate level, historians must be very careful in assessing who or what law actually 'protected.'" Formal judicial protection or non-protection of slaves must be assessed or balanced by the overwhelming number of cases of slave infraction settled by planter's authoritarian whim or Harriet Beecher Stowe's reference to this whim as the "absolute despotism of the most unmitigated form."[92] This personal and intimate despotism on the insular plantation was revealed quite clearly by James Dunwoody Brownson DeBow, who stated, "On our estates . . . we dispense with the whole machinery of public police and public courts of justice. Thus we try, decide, and execute the sentences in thousands of cases, which in other countries would go into the courts."[93]

Planter J.D.B. DeBow was obviously referring to the ability and the permissibility of a cultural hegemony of planter control over African labor that was the primary basis for the exploitation of this labor force for the production of cotton for the international market. This cultural hegemony was not only personal and intimate but legal—legal in the sense that the first bulwark to Black resistance was the planter who was a law unto himself, and on rare occasions, herself. The planter had the legal authority to lay on the lash without humanity because of his material interest in either profit and social control or both.

The South attempted to fashion a legal order grounded in the planter's absolute will with formal legal institutions standing guard on the periphery. This informal and formal juridicalism interacted dialectically to ensure social control and economic production. What glued the legal system together was the ideology of race that superseded liberal legal jurisprudence except in periodic *obiter dictums* when judges vented their concern at the depths to which such an inhumane legal and social order had descended. *Obitum dictum* represented the autonomy of the law, but had little effect on case decision itself and therefore the harsh social existence of slaves.

Chapter 3 ■ *Law of Slavery, Law of Freedom: 1820–1860*   **57**

Formal legal authority that recognized the absolutism of the planter's will over the repressed will of the slave was codified in a variety of state statutes and supported by case law. In the 1829 North Carolina case of *State v. Mann*, Chief Justice Thomas Ruffin noted that "the power of the master must be absolute to render the submission of the slave perfect."[94]

The facts of the case bring to light some critical dimensions of the workings of formal legal authority and how they were constrained by race, class, and political economy. The case involved the economic relations of White over Black in that various skilled slaves were often hired out to other interim masters to help them toward attaining a pecuniary/monetary goal via exploiting the hired slaves' labor. In this particular case, the hirer, Mann, had hired a slave woman by the name of Lydia who subsequently resisted Mann's imposed will by running off. In this attempt at resistance, Lydia was shot and wounded by Mann. Mann was indicted and convicted for assault and battery by a lower court. The Ruffin court overturned the lower-court efforts and created an innovative racist common law dictum by holding that "The established habits and uniform practice of the country in this respect is [are] the best evidence of the portion of power deemed by the whole community requisite to the preservation of the master's dominion."[95] Ruffin further emphasized that the entire purpose of slavery was for the "profit of the master, his security and the public safety."[96]

If we assume that Mann was a master without slaves or without a slave, then we can deduce several important factors. One, the lower court was only concerned with the class interests of the large planter whose property was damaged by a master of low economic status, whereas the Ruffin court understood the broader and deeper dimensions of race within the case. By this, I mean that Ruffin and his brethren understood the paramount need of Southern society to socially control the slave and quasi-free "Negroes," and they extended that authority over the slave to all "White" social classes within Southern society.

This attitude and the continuity of the attitude in the slave law among all Southern states were stipulated in statutes that permitted whipping and use of deadly force. The conjoining of social control, race, and slavery was reflected in the attitude of Justice John Belton O'Neal of the South Carolina Supreme Court, who noted that "I have always thought and while on the circuit ruled that words of impertinence and insolence addressed by a free negro to a White man, would justify an assault and battery."[97] In *Ex parte Boylston*, Judge D.L. Wardlaw of South Carolina noted that the state's slave statutes "contemplated throughout the subordination of the servile class to every free White person."[98] This absolute dominion of White over all Blacks would be tempered in any particular case by the pecuniary interests that a large planter might have in the slaves themselves. This factor looms greatly when one understands that the changing political economy in the South greatly affected poor Whites who were employed as slave patrollers, overseers, and free laborers who, at times, worked alongside slaves. Southern courts had to exercise a balancing act between class interests, racial domination, and the needs of a changing economy.

This convergence of race, class, and political economy can be seen in cases in which Southern courts had to use law as a direct instrument to resolve inherent contradictions in this convergence while using *obiter dictum* to assuage their liberal juridical heritage. Because of the weakness of the South's state power apparatus, courts took the lead in configuring the balance of interests between the slaveholders as a social class and any particular interests of an individual slaveholder. With few exceptions, most Southern courts dealt with Southern industrialization and the use of slaves therein outside of Northern legal sensibilities. The adaptation of common law resolutions to slave and free relationships became problematic. Market developments, industrial slavery,[99] and commerce led to litigation involving the violation and interpretation of contracts. Southern courts asserted jurisdiction over market-related problems while leaving the legal sentimentalism of the Dunwoody Debows to regulate their own relationships with their slaves within their insular plantations.

The rejection of Northern liberal, pro-capitalist legalism was revealed in how Southern courts dealt with Massachusetts's Chief Justice Lemuel Shaw's decision in *Farwell v. Boston* and the *Worcester Railroad* decision.[100] Most courts did not apply Shaw's new "fellow-servant rule" to industrial accidents, with Georgia and Florida rejecting the rule outright.[101] The pro-business rule rejected the "theory of respondeat superior. . . . 'The master is responsible for the acts of his servant, if done by his command, expressly or impliedly given.'"[102] Emphasizing the false equality of worker and capitalist, Shaw said that a worker's freedom of job choice, freedom to voice grievance, freedom to leave the place of employment, and every man's reasonable estimation of risks should take precedence over some inequitable and burdensome liability placed at the feet of the capitalist if a worker's injury should occur within the workplace owned and controlled by the capitalist.[103] Restricting the liability of employers certainly spurred entrepreneurial speculation and investments by eliminating fear of assuming the traditional risks of lawsuits based on the rejected theory of *respondeat superior.*

Except for North Carolina,[104] most Southern states followed Georgia's Chief Justice Lumpkin in *Scudder v. Woodridge* (1846), who argued successfully for limiting the fellow servant rule. Lumpkin noted in his decision that "The restriction of this rule is indispensable to the welfare of the slave," because in any industrial endeavor the slave will be paired with "po' Whites" who are "destitute of principle and bankrupt of fortune." Lumpkin feared that in risk-prone industries such as mining, bridge building, iron, timber, and railroads, hirers as interim owners would not take the necessary precautions to protect this human property, for they would not be liable if the fellow-servant rule was adopted. The divergence and the conflict of laws on this specific point, as represented by Shaw's and Lumpkin's decisions, illustrated how the two regions were responding to industrial growth, the concept of freedom, and the law's response to both. Protecting the slave and creating bourgeois freedoms for Northern workers reflected the trajectory of two cultures, two legal systems, and how the South's political economy required an entirely different juridical instrumentalism.

Lumpkin's reference to the social class that was morally bankrupt reveals a major problematic in Southern society. Because very few Whites owned slaves,[105] the rest of society had to become cultural strangers to the quality of life enjoyed by the planter elites, watching, hoping, and waiting for their chance to rise from the mudsill, more often than not in vain. In critiquing this intraracial conflict between White haves and have-nots, Hinton Rowan Helper wrote *The Impending Crisis and How to Meet It* in 1857. His analytical clarion to the White have-nots explained that "The lords of the lash are not only absolute masters of the Blacks, who are bought and sold, and driven about like so many cattle, but they are also the oracles and arbiters of all non-slaveholding Whites, whose freedom is merely nominal, and whose unparalleled illiteracy and degradation [are] purposely and fiendishly perpetuated."[106] This work attacked the peculiar institution as a process that destroyed the White workingman and called for a class war between the owners of slaves and the "noble, good White yeoman worker." Helper hoped that in the aftermath, the victorious White mudsill would colonize the slaves in a foreign land and truly make America a White man's country. Herein lies the dilemma of law and justice in the Old South according to Bertram Wyatt-Brown. This noted scholar of elite and "cracker" cultures in the Old South suggests that neither Marxian nor Gramscian theory can explain "how arrangements of law and class relations worked."[107] The predictability of such cracker expressions as Faulknerian "barn burnings," eye-gouging, ear-biting, or slave maiming or killing was treated as lower-class expectations by an elite hierarchy of local rulers who handed down retribution or mercy.[108] County criminal courts realized that unless lower-class violence got out of hand, their decisions should be about restoring proper class relationships and not about maintaining allegiance to formal legal rules that might undermine the social order.[109] Because most felonious and larcenous crimes were within the White poor social class itself, the exception could be handled by the planter class with grace and clemency. When this violence spilled over to the class of propertied humans, Justice Charles Colcock of South Carolina reminded masters that it was their responsibility to protect their slaves from wanton abuse by White lower-class slave patrollers. Masters must be aware that patrollers, "as unprincipled and unfeeling" crackers, would use their interim authority to abuse slaves.[110]

Southern law of slavery had to deal seriously with this antagonism directed at their more accessible property. Serving as low-wage employees in the industrial sector such as at Virginia's Tredegar Iron Works, poor Whites worked alongside slaves, supervised them as overseers on plantations, or controlled them as patrollers. These Whites were constantly faced with criminal charges for their abuse of someone else's property. In *Commonwealth v. Carver* (1827), the General Court of Virginia addressed this problem when it noted the following:

> It is for the benefit of the master, and consoling to his feelings, that a third person should be restrained under the pains and penalties of felony, from maiming and disabling his slave.[111]

Many cases penalized poor Whites who abused slaves even when they were carrying out their master's orders or when patrollers were overzealous in their use of force on slaves.[112] A case in point occurred in 1817, when a North Carolina judge rendered judgments and monetary damages against poor White patrollers who used excessive violence in subduing a slave who subsequently died. Judge James Louis Taylor's decision against these Whites, not of his class, probably revolved around the facts that the slave was on his master's plantation and had a pass from his master in hand.[113]

The constant contact between propertyless Whites and the human property, in an inverse manner in many circumstances, led to an intimacy in how stolen goods were exchanged, how resistance was carried out, and how sexual contact occurred. This sexual contact, as a customary taboo, was prohibited by law, even though planters violated this taboo quite often and poor Whites had their opportunities. In *State v. Hale* (1823), the North Carolina Supreme Court implied sexual intimacy between poor Whites and propertied humans in its support of an indictment handed down against a poor White who assaulted a slave. The court noted,

> These offenses are usually committed by men of dissolute habits, hanging loose upon society, who . . . take refuge in the company of coloured persons and slaves, who they

deprave by their example, embolden by their familiarity, and then beat, under the expectation that a slave dare not resent a blow from a White man.[114]

To illustrate this "familiarity" in an intimate setting, one need examine the case in which a slave was acquitted of raping a poor White female. In overturning the slave conviction for rape in the Tennessee case of *Major v. State,* the court proclaimed that "the invaluable right of fair trial by an impartial jury should not be disregarded . . . [this right] . . . was not placed in our Bill of Rights without motive, and can not be disregarded by the courts."[115] At first instance, this appears to be one of those cases that Professor Nash has referred to as upholding "procedural rights" for slave defendants; however, the court merely recognized the "depravity" and the "dissolute habits" of "po' White trash" who permitted the slave Major to sleep in the same room and become "familiar" with the girl as she grew into womanhood.[116] This case is obviously a case of judicial preachment or *obiter dictum* to this lower social class about not looking for judicial relief when they have violated a sacrosanct ideal of Southern elite culture.

Elite planters, with the support of their brethren planters in the judiciary, understood that their right to kill a rebellious slave was just about unlimited, only constrained by their collective social-class perception of what it took to "maintain slave discipline and property values . . . and the extent of White criminal liability . . . [would] vary according to the class identity of the White defendant."[117] One particular case confirms and illustrates this perception. In the 1834 case of *State v. Will,* the North Carolina Supreme Court overturned a murder conviction of the slave, Will, who killed his overseer on claim of self-defense. His conviction was "mitigated from murder to manslaughter."[118] The slave Will's life was certainly valued more than the poor White overseer whom he killed. In an ironic twist of fate, Will met his death by state execution in Mississippi when he murdered another slave.[119]

The planter class had to consider and balance its interests in slaves as a class versus poor White defendants, in this case, as victim. An interesting point concerning such cases of Black slaves defending themselves is that states varied in the amount of proceduralism handed out to slaves who defended themselves against poor Whites. Georgia and Alabama said there could be no mitigating circumstances that would permit a murder charge to be reduced to manslaughter when slaves killed their overseers.[120]

To understand the execution of Will in such ironic circumstances, one does not require a leap of faith to characterize a sense of Southern legal dualism as a conflict between humanity and interests as several noted researchers have done.[121] To argue this is to have failed to understand that Southerners came to think of their slaves as "propertied people." Kenneth Stammp reflected that Africans were "bartered, deeded, devised, pledged, seized, and auctioned. They were awarded as prizes in lotteries and raffles; they were wagered at gaming tables and horse races. They were, in short, property in fact, as well as law."[122] If a duality or dilemma existed, it existed at times in the autonomous legal consciousness of certain appellate justices who verbalized slave humanity while retaining a deep and abiding faith in slavery as a system of justice for the planter class.

A classic example of this racialist legal consciousness was exemplified by Keir Nash's most noted "fair and formalistic" judge, John Belton O'Neal of South Carolina, who reflected: "I have always thought [this] and while on the circuit ruled that words of impertinence and insolence addressed by a free negro to a White man, would justify an assault and battery."[123] Keep in mind that O'Neal is the judge that Nash argued had a severe conflict between perceiving slaves as property or as human beings. Certainly, insolence or impertinence for a slave according to a North Carolina judge could be "a look, the pointing of a finger, a refusal or neglect to step out of the way when a White person is seen to approach. . . . [S]uch acts violate the rules of propriety, and, if tolerated, would destroy that subordination, upon which our social system rests."[124]

The reality was that Southern judges as discrete human beings, as legalists trained, semi-trained, or not trained in the finer aspects of the law and legal reasoning, had no problem in sifting through the dialectics of humanity and interests because of their class position within the plantocracy and who rationalized judicial views via hegemonic function of race. As racialists, all judges—as with all Southerners—looked on propertied people in a dualistic manner and considered one aspect, or the other aspect, or both at the same time depending on circumstance, peculiarity, or familiarity. The ease judges had, without seemingly any personal tension at all, with dealing with the dualistic nature of human property was revealed in *State v. Jim* (1856). In this case, the North Carolina Supreme Court noted, "The slave is put on trial as a human being; entitled to have his guilt or innocence passed on by a jury. Is it not inconsistent, in the progress of the trial to treat him as property, like a chattel—a horse."[125]

The class question concerning interests, not humanity, was attended to by South Carolina as early as 1818, when a propertyless White was heavily fined for shooting and killing a runaway slave of a propertied White. The court firmly noted that "It can never be considered politic to subject a valuable species of property to the disposal of any unprincipled, unfeeling man in society; nor is it less impolitic with regard to the slaves themselves."[126] This case, for some historians, could be one that considered the humanity of the slave in reaching a decision, as indicated by the second clause in the quote. However, the concern is most likely a semantic one in dictum that balances proportionately one phrase to the other—e.g., politic versus impolitic. One should not seriously think that the court was trying to speak to the slaves' humanity via dictum to convince the slaves that the law is evenhanded, fair, and protective of them. Alabama and North Carolina addressed the issue of class interests by requiring juries to be made up of slave owners in criminal procedures involving slaves in order to "surround the life of the slave with additional safeguards, and more effectually to protect the property of the owner"[127] from dissolute White trash and to maintain a racial stratification that took into consideration property rights of elites in a social hierarchy bounded in terms of White intraclass power and powerlessness, planter domination, and a racialized and subjugated labor force.

If one was truly to search for the law's recognition of the slave's humanity before the Civil War, one must look toward the North and how Northern judges sped the nation toward its inevitable conflagration by rejecting interstate comity and asserting in case law as well as dictum, choices of law that confirmed the humanity of Africans who just happened to be slaves. The historically revered Lemuel Shaw, Chief Justice of Massachusetts's Supreme Court, led the legal assault on the infamous compromise of 1787. Shaw, conservative and an adherent to legal formalism, created the precedent in *Commonwealth v. Aves* (1836) for the refutation of racialist comity. The facts of the case revolved around the visit of a Southern "belle" to Massachusetts with her six-year-old slave girl, Med. In the tradition of true sisterhood, the Boston Female Antislavery Society filed suit in

Med's behalf, contending that the state's constitution freed all men and women except fugitive slaves. Using Mansfield's *Somerset* interpretation of comity, Shaw said that slavery was repugnant to natural law and owes its existence to local law; ergo, Massachusetts's prohibition took precedence over slave law. Shaw also, in a liberal fashion, stated that human property was not universally accepted among the laws of nations, and therefore comity could not apply to such property. *Aves* became the legal battleground over which slaveholders sojourning in Northern areas would have to contend. Most Southern judges had to follow, amend, or reject this decision, whereas most Northern judges eventually supported it. Massachusetts reaffirmed Shaw's decision in 1841, and other states followed *Aves* with Connecticut in 1837, Iowa in 1839, Illinois in 1852, Ohio in 1856, and New York in 1860.[128]

The force of abolitionism pressured Northern state courts to reverse their earlier allegiance to comity and compromise. In an earlier case in Illinois, *Willard v. State* (1843), the state court upheld *extraterritoriality*, which permitted slaveholders' own state law concerning human property to journey with them as they sojourned in the North. However, the state Supreme Court overturned and outlawed any extraterritoriality in 1857 in the case of *Rodney v. Illinois Central Railroad*.[129] The South responded with its own volley aimed at destroying this new antislavery comity. In Kentucky, within a one-year period, the state appeals court first affirmed a slave's freedom because of his sojourn, for two years, in a free state and then abruptly in *Collins v. America* (1849) affirmed the continued slave status of a plaintiff who had spent a considerable amount of time in a free state with his master's consent. The court declared that "[i]f the laws and Courts of Ohio may determine the condition of the slave while in that State, they cannot, by their own force or power, determine what shall be his condition when he has gone beyond their territorial jurisdiction."[130]

In this legal battle over comity, Southern judges appeared to have less ambivalence over their purpose whereas Northern judges had to deal with the reality that they were in fact switching horses in midstream. Sometimes they took the natural law approach to attack comity, while at other times they refused to stretch and fell back on the safety of formalism and their faith that federalism should be the steam valve that, it was hoped, would stave off the inevitable. Even Lemuel Shaw was caught in this dilemma. In assessing the status of a captured fugitive slave, Shaw fell back on formalism and federalism to maintain legal collegiality with the South by upholding the Fugitive Slave Act of 1850. Shaw noted sheepishly, like Taney in *Scott,* that the founding fathers had bargained with the devil and agreed that human property could coexist in the new Republic.[131] Being an antislavery justice within a proslavery legal system became a bed of thorns. The masks of formalism and a faith in the greatness of the ages could not and did not blunt its pricks. Robert Cover's *Justice Accused* brilliantly outlines these bleeding pricks in case after case. Antislavery judges were forced to choose between morality and law, law and their personal beliefs, or find the legal space between these opposites that would help them maintain their sanity and their jobs.[132] As indicated earlier, the tacit compromise between North and South placated bourgeois versus planter interests until William Lloyd Garrison's 1831 abolitionist clarion. In time, Northern judges responded favorably to Garrison's charge that comity and compromise defined the U.S. Constitution as "a covenant with death and an agreement with Hell." The abolitionist movement, located in the growing industrialized and capitalistic North, forced the slave-based plantocracy to defend its legal rights and cultural life.

This slavery's defense was summed up by one proslavery advocate with these words, "We must satisfy the conscience—we must allay the fears of our own people. We must satisfy them that slavery is of itself right—that it is not a sin against God."[133] However, the argument that slavery was now a positive and capitalism a negative fell on fewer receptive ears as abolitionism slowly gained strength in the Northern liberal populace and among professionals in the juridical field.[134]

Ultimately, the devolution of the political structure into state violence and a bloody civil war relieved these juridical individuals of this ongoing dilemma. The unambiguous process of the American Civil War forced judges, lawyers, and justices to reflect on their inability to stop the inevitable with appeals to divine law, natural law, positive law, comity, federalism, or other juridical compromises that in the last instance, became reflexive of deeper antagonism and divergent trajectories in the political economies of both North and South.

ENDNOTES

1. Karl Marx, quoted in Alan Haworth, *Understanding the Political Philosophers: From Ancient to Modern Times* (New York: Routledge, 2004), 222. See also Jose J. Nedumpara, *Political Economy and Class Contradictions: A Study* (New Delhi: Anmol Publicaitons, PVT.LTD, 2004), 9.
2. See John Codman Hurd, *The Law of Freedom and Bondage in the United States* (New York,1858–1862); Thomas R. R. Cobb, *An Inquiry into the Law of Negro Slavery* (New York, 1853); William Goodell, *The American Slave Code* (1967).
3. See Kenneth Stamp, *The Peculiar Institution: Slavery in the Ante-Bellum South* (New York: Vintage Books, 1956); see Chapter IV: "To Make Them Stand in Fear."
4. Many planters assumed that using coercion would discipline slave labor, which would in turn increase productivity.
5. Charles J. McClain, Jr. "Legal Change and Class Interests: A Review Essay on Morton Horwitz's 'The Transformation of American Law,'" *California Law Review,* 68 (1980), 383.
6. See Chaplain Morrison, *Democratic Politics and Sectionalism: The Wilmot Proviso Controversy* (Chapel Hill: University of North Carolina Press, 1967).
7. See Arthur Bestor, "State Sovereignty and Slavery: A Reinterpretation of Proslavery Constitutional Doctrine, 1846–1861," *Journal of the Illinois State Historical Society* 54 (1961, 119). See also Eric Foner, *Free Soil, Free Labor, Free Men: The Ideology of the Republican Party before the Civil War* (New York: Oxford University Press, 1970).
8. See R. Kent Newmyer, *The Supreme Court under Marshall and Taney* (New York: Thomas Cromwell, 1968).
9. McClain on Horwitz, 383.
10. Morton Horowitz, *The Transformation of American Law* (Boston: President and Fellows of Harvard College, 1977), 252–253.
11. See Donald Roper, "In Quest of Judicial Objectivity: The Marshall Court and the Legitimation of Slavery," *Stanford Law Review,* 21 (1969).
12. Note, "American Slavery and the Conflict of Laws," *Columbia Law Review,* 71, 1 (January 1971), 96–97.
13. United States Constitution, Article IV.
14. Fifth Amendment to the United States Constitution.
15. See Glover Moore, *The Missouri Controversy, 1819–1821* (Lexington: University of Kentucky Press, 1953); Richard H. Brown, "The Missouri Crisis, Slavery, and the Politics of Jacksonianism," *South Atlantic Quarterly,* 65 (1966).
16. See Paul Finkleman, "Slavery and the Founders," also quoted in video lecture at the Detroit African American Historical Museum (no date). See also Anne Farrow, Joel Lang, and Jenifer Frank, *Complicity: How the North Promoted, Prolonged, and Profited from Slavery* (New York: Ballantine Books, 2005); Governor Morris as quoted in Federalist #54.
17. See John B. Hutchens' review of George R. Taylor, *The Transportation Revolution, 1815–1860* (New York, 1962) in *The American Economic Review,* 42 (1952) 622–623; see also Harry N. Scheiber, "Federalism and the American

Economic Order, 1789–1910," *Law and Society* Fall (1975), 57–116. See Underground Railroad case of *Abelman v. Booth*, 76.

18. See Donald Roper on John Marshall and protection of property in people; Harry N. Scheiber, "Instrumentalism and Property Rights: A Reconsideration of American 'Style of Judicial Reasoning' in the 19th Century," *Wisconsin Law Review* (1975); Morton Horowitz, "The Rise of Legal Formalism," *American Journal of Legal History*, 19 (1975).

19. Leon Litwack, *North of Slavery : The Negro in the Free States, 1790–1860* (Chicago, University of Chicago Press, 1961), 97.

20. Litwack, 65; see an excellent analysis of Alexis de Tocqueville in Ronald Takaki, *Iron Cages: Race and Culture in 19th Century America* (New York: Oxford University Press, 1990), 110–111.

21. Litwack, 143. The negro-abolitionist attack on segregated schools achieved its greatest success in Boston.

22. Litwack, 143.

23. Litwack, 126–131.

24. Leonard Richards, *Gentlemen of Property and Standing: Anti-Abolition Mobs in Jacksonian America* (New York: Oxford University Press, 1970) 38–40. S. Strane, *Prudence Crandall and the Education of Black Folk* (New York: W.W. Norton, 1990).

25. See Thomas D. Morris, *Free Men All: The Personal Liberty Laws of the North, 1780–1861* (Union: New Jersey, The Lawbook Exchange, LTD. 2001).

26. Paul Finkleman, "Prelude to the 14th Amendment: Black Legal Rights in the Antebellum North," *Rutgers Law Review,* 17 (1986), 415.

27. Arthur Bestor, "State Sovereignty and Slavery," 119.

28. See Donald Roper, 539; see also William E. Nelson, "The Impact of the Antislavery Movement Upon Styles of Judicial Reasoning in Nineteenth America," 87 *Harvard Law Review* 3 (January 1974).

29. *The Antelope*, 23 U.S. 10 Wheat. 66 (1825); Donald Roper using Marshall's dictum; see also John T. Noonan, Jr., *The Antelope: The Ordeal of the Recaptured Africans in the Administration of James Monroe and John Quincy Adams* (Berkeley: University of California, 1977).

30. Roper, 539. See Noonan for excellent full treatment of this case.

31. Loren Miller, *The Petitioners: The Story of the Supreme Court of the United States and the Negro* (New York: Pantheon Books, 1966), 31.

32. Miller, 31–35.

33. Scheiber, "Instrumentalism and Property Rights"; R. Kent Newmyer, *The Supreme Court under Marshall and Taney*. Newmyer does an excellent analysis on the Taney approach to helping the common man, 38.

34. Kermit Hall, *Magic Mirror: Law in American History* (New York: Oxford University Press, 1989), 118. Vested rights and eminent domain issues took on a different vision with Taney.

35. Loren Miller, 43; Roper, 533. Jackson's influence on the Court to shift to a dualistic approach to federal–states' rights legalism. See Newmyer.

36. See Ronald Takaki, *Iron Cage: Race and Culture in 19th Century America* (New York: Oxford University Press, 1990); see Chapter V "Jackson: Metaphysician of Indian-Hating."

37. See Leonard Richards's study on Anti-Abolitionists mobs, 3. Cited in footnote 24. See also Lewis H. Lapham, *Gag Rule: On the Suppression of Dissent and the Stifling of Democracy* (New York: Penguin, 2004).

38. See Russell B. Nye, *Fettered Freedom* (East Lansing: Michigan State University Press, 1949); Harold M. Hyman and William M. Wiecek, *Equal Justice under Law: Constitutional Development, 1835–1875* (New York: Harper and Row 1982).

39. Paul S. Paludan, *Covenant with Death: The Constitution, Law, and Equality in the Civil War Era* (Urbana: University of Illinois Press, 1975).

40. See Paul Finkleman, *An Imperfect Union: Slavery, Federalism and Comity* (Union, New Jersey: The Lawbook Exchange, LTD 2000).

41. See Finkleman, *An Imperfect Union*.

42. Roper, 535; William R. Leslie, "The Influence of Joseph Story's Theory of the Conflict of Laws on Constitutional Nationalism," *Mississippi Valley Historical Review*, 35 (1948); Robert Cover, *Justice Accused: Antislavery and the Judicial Process* (New Haven: Yale University Press, 1975), 101–104. *U.S. v. La Jeune Eugenie* 23 U.S. 66 (1828).

43. Roper, 535.

44. Roper, 537.

45. This is Cover's thesis and analysis in his book.

46. Russel B. Nye, *Fettered Freedom: Civil Liberties and the Slavery Controversy, 1830–1860* (East Lansing: Michigan State College Press, 1972), 260.

47. Nye. The fear of slave insurrection led South Carolina to pass the Negro Seaman's Act.

48. See David L. Lighner, *Slavery and the Commerce Power: How the Struggle Against the Interstate Slave Trade Led to the Civil War* (Chelsea, Michigan: Sheridan Books, 2006), 66. Act was passed in the wake of the Denmark Vesey Slave conspiracy. It appeared Northern or British Black sailors had placed copies of the militant clarion *David Walkers' Appeal* in the hands of South Carolina slaves. See Nye, 153.

49. *Elkinson v. Deliesseline*, Federal Cases, No. 4366 (1823).

50. *Groves v. Slaughter,* 15 Peters 449 (1841).

51. Loren Miller, 45–46.

52. Donald Neiman, *Promises to Keep: African Americans and the Constitutional Order, 1776 to the Present* (New York: Oxford University Press, 1991), 18. Stanley W. Campbell, *The Slave Catchers: Enforcement of the Fugitive Slave Law, 1850–1860* (New York: W.W. Norton and Company, 1968).

53. Kermit Hall, *Magic Mirror,* 139. One can argue a test case because Edward Prigg knowingly returned to Pennsylvania after knowingly violating the state's personal liberty law. For a detailed analysis, see Joseph C. Burke, "What Did the *Prigg* Decision Really Decide?" *Pennsylvania Magazine of History and Biography*, 93 (1969). Detailed and excellent analysis of this case.

54. Donald Neiman, 18. See also issue of paternity in Loren Miller, *The Petitioners*, 48.

55. See Morris, *Free Men All: Personal Liberty Laws of the North, 1780–1861.*

56. Loren Miller, *The Petitioners,* 49.

57. Cover, 119.

58. Benjamin Quarles, *Frederick Douglass* (1966), 184; see also Philip S. Foner, *Frederick Douglass.*

59. Paul Finkleman, *An Imperfect Union: Slavery, Federalism, Comity* (Union, New Jersey: The Lawbook Exchange, LTD, 2000), 103–115. Philip S. Foner, *Frederick Douglass: Selected Speeches, Writings,* 350.

60. Cover discusses both the Shadrach and Sims cases extensively. 176–177, 218, 250. *Commonwealth v. Aves,* 18 Pick. (Mass.) 193 (1836). Better known as the case of Med, the slave girl.

61. Med's, Shadrach's, and Thomas Sims's cases are discussed at length in Paul Finkleman, *An Imperfect Union: Slavery, Federalism, and Comity*, 103–115. See also Paul Finkleman, *Slavery in the Courtroom: An Annotated Bibliography of American Cases* (Union, New Jersey: The Lawbook Exchange, LTD, 1998), 88.

62. Fugitive Slave Act, 1858.

63. *Dred Scott v. Sanford*, 19 Howard 393 (1857).

64. David Wilmot quoted in Ronald Takaki, *Iron Cages: Race and Culture in 19th Century America* (New York: Oxford University Press, 2000), 112.

65. See Bestor; see also Robert R. Russel, "Constitutional Doctrines with Regard to Slavery in Territories," *Journal of Southern History*, 32, 1 (November, 19660, 466–486). Chaplin Morrison, *Democratic Politics and Sectionalism: Wilmot Proviso Controversy* (1967); Eric Foner, "The Wilmot Proviso Revisited," *Journal of American History*, 56 d, 2 (September 1969), 262–279.

66. Loren Miller, *The Petitioners*, 51. See also Paul Finkleman, *Dred Scott v. Sandford* (Boston: Bedford Books, 1997), 29.

67. See Eric Foner, *Free Soil, Free Labor, Free Men: The Ideology of the Republican Party Before the Civil War* (New York: Oxford University Press, 1970).

68. President James K. Polk suggested "submit . . . [Missouri question] . . . to . . . the decision of the judicial tribunals"; see Loren Miller, *The Petitioners,* p. 55.

69. See A. Leon Higginbotham, Jr., *In the Matter of Color*, Chapter 9, "The Case of James Sommersett, a Negro."

70. See excellent brief overview of litigants in Paul Finkleman, *Dred Scott v. Sanford: A Brief History with Documents* (Boston: Bedford Books, 1997).

71. *Dred Scott v. Sandford*, 19 Howard 393 (1857). See also Neiman, 45.

72. See Paul Finkleman on his analysis of Taney's dictum on this point, 62.

73. Quoted in Loren Miller, *The Petitioners*, 72. See also Donald Neiman, *Promises to Keep*, 46.

74. Paul Finkleman, *Dred Scott v. Sanford*, 74.

75. *Strader v. Graham*, 10 Howard 82 (1850); see Finkleman's analysis on pp. 31–32.

76. See Steve Ferguson, "Social Contract as Bourgeois Ideology," *Cultural Logic*, ISSN 1097-3087, 2007.

77. Loren Miller, 77.

78. *Abelman v. Booth,* 21 Howard 506 (1859).

79. Donald E. Fehrenbacher, *The Dred Scott Case: Its Significance in American Law and Politics* (New York: Oxford University Press, 1978), 453.

80. Daniel J. Flanigan, "Criminal Procedure in Slave Trials in the Antebellum South," *The Journal of Southern History*, XL, 4 (November 1974), 539. Note planter DeBow's statement.

81. *State v. Mann* as analysis in Andrew Fede, "Legitimized Violent Slave Abuse in the American South, 1619–1865: A Case Study of Law and Social Change in Six Southern States," *The American Journal of Legal History*, XXIX (1985), 139.

82. See Paul Finkleman, "Slaves as Fellow Servants, Ideology, Law, and Industrialization," *American Journal of Legal History,* 31 (October 1987), 269–301. See also Andrew Fede, "Legal Protection for Slave Buyers in the U.S. South: A Caveat Concerning Caveat Emptor," *The American Journal of Legal History*, XXLXI (1987).

83. See Robert J. Cottrol, "Liberalism and Paternalism: Ideology, Economic Interest, and the Business Law of Slavery," *The American Journal of History,* XXXI (1987), 360–361; see also Paul Finkleman, "Slaves as Fellow Servants: Ideology, Law, and Industrialization," *The American Journal of Legal History*, XXXI (1987).

84. Cottrol, 360–361. Cottrol also cites Finkleman, 361.

85. Cottrol, 361. Cottrol states that *Farwell* in Shaw's dictum was "simple instrumentalism."

86. *State v. Mann*, 13 N.C. (1829); see book length analysis in Mark V. Tushnet, *Slave Law in the American South: State v. Mann in History and Literature* (Lawrence: University Press of Kansas, 2003).

87. *Scudder v. Woodridge*, 1 GA 195 (1846); see Cottroll, 368.

88. Cottrol, at footnote 41

89. See Fede's essay on *caveat emptor;* Fede argues that the great Karl Llewellyn ignored Southern law and missed an opportunity to be definitive on common law, 322.

90. For an interesting conservative look at this question, see A. E. Keir Nash, "A More Equitable Past? Southern Supreme Courts and the Protection of the Antebellum Negro," *North Carolina Law Review* 43 (1970); A. E. Keir Nash, "The Texas Supreme Court and Trial Rights of Blacks, 1845–1860," *The Journal of American History* 53, no. 3 (December 1971).

91. Nash, but also see Michael S. Hindus, "Black Justice Under Law: Criminal Prosecutions of Blacks in Antebellum South Carolina," *The Journal of American History* 63, no. 3 (December 1976), 575–599.

92. Quoted in Andrew Fede, "Toward a Solution of the Slave Law Dilemma: A Critique of Tushnet's 'The American Law of Slavery,'" *Law and History Review*, 2 (1989), 312.

93. Flaigan, 539.

94. *State v. Mann*; see full quote in Eugene Genovese, "The Hegemonic Function of the Law," 35. See Mark Tushnet's full-length monograph for a personal social history of Judge Thomas Ruffin, 90–91.

95. *State v. Mann,* 13 N. C. (1829); see exact quote in Mark Tushnet, 22.

96. Tushnet, 23.

97. Donald Neiman, *Promises to Keep: African Americans and the Constitutional Order, 1776 to the Present* (New York: Oxford University Press, 1991), 27.

98. Michael Hindus, "Black Justice Under White Law," 579.

99. Robert Starobin, *Industrial Slavery in the Old South* (New York: Oxford University Press, 1970).

100. Finkelman, 271–274.

101. Finklelman, 298.

102. Finklelman, 270.

103. Finkelman, 272: "and leave the service, if the common employer will not take such precautions."

104. Cottrol, 368, at footnote 41. Judge Lumpkin argued that the rule could only apply to free White servants.

105. "In 1860 only 383,673 White southerners (4.7 percent) out of a total White southern population of 8,9097,463 owned slaves." This statistic can be located in *African-American Odyssey*, Darlene Clark Hine, William C. Hine, and Stanley Harrold (Upper Sadder River, New Jersey: Pearson Prentice Hall, 2008), 143.

106. Ronald Takaki, *Iron Cages: Race and Culture in 19th Century America* (New York: Oxford University Press, 1979) 124.

107. Bertram Wyatt-Brown, "Community, Class, and Snopesian Crime: Local Justice in the Old South," 174–175. See quote in *Class, Conflict and Consensus: Antebellum Southern Community Studies*, eds., Orville Vernon Burton and Robert C. McMath, Jr. (Westport: Greenwood Press, 1982).

108. Bertram Wyatt-Brown, 174–175.

109. Andrew Fede, "Legitimized Violent Slave Abuse in the American South, 1619–1865: A Case Study of Law and Social Change in Six Southern States," *The Journal of American Legal History,* 29 (1985). Excellent study on racist common law and its mediation of strangers who abuse slaves.

110. Fede, 113, case of *Arthur v. Wells.* See also Fede, 106–107. Excellent description of poor White vagabonds. Note: "poor White trash."

111. Fede, "Legitimized Violent Slave Abuse in the American South," 128.

112. Fede, 129.

113. Flanigan, 551.

114. *State v. Hale* 9 N.C. (2 Hawks) 582 (1823) ; see also Fede, 130.

115. Flanigan, 552.

116. Flanigan, "Criminal Procedure in Slave Trials in the Antebellum South," p. 552

117. Fede on Tushnet, 316. Many slaveholders and judges created a "good ol' boy" network. See Fede, "Slave Abuse in the American South," 109.

118. Eugene Genovese, *Roll, Jordan, Roll: The World the Slaves Made* (New York: Vintage Books, 1976), 36

119. Genovese, 36.

120. Fede, "Legitimized Violent Slave Abuse in the American South," 126; see footnote 184: "killing cannot be mitigated to manslaughter when slave killed overseer." (Ala.); voluntary manslaughter conviction upheld (Ga.).

121. See A. E. Keir Nash, Michael Hindus, Daniel J. Flanigan, Andrew Fede, Mark Tushnet, and Paul Finkelman.

122. Stamp, 201.

123. Neiman, *Promises to Keep: African Americans and the Constitutional Order, 1776 to the Present* (New York: Oxford University Press, 1991), 27.

124. Neiman, 25.

125. Flanigan, 538.

126. Fede, "Slave Abuse in the American South," 113.

127. Flanigan, 551.

128. Kermit Hall, 140.

129. *Rodney v. Illinois Central Railroad* (1857) as cited in "Notes: American Slavery and the Conflict of Laws," 71 *Columbia Law Review,* no. 1 (1971), 96.

130. *Collins v. America* (1849), as cited in "Notes: American Slavery and the Conflict of Laws," 71 *Columbia Law Review,* no. 1 (1971), 97.

131. Robert Cover, *Justice Accused,* 250, 265, 266, 267. Cover discusses Shaw's moral–formal dilemma in a number of fugitive slave cases and uses theory of cognitive dissonance to explain Shaw's mindset.

132. See Cover. Again, note that Cover explains the moral dilemma on antislavery justices, holding true their oath to uphold constitutional slavery.

133. Ronald Takaki, *Iron Cages: Race and Culture in Nineteenth Century America* (New York: Oxford University Press, 1990), 120.

134. See William E. Nelson, "The Impact of the Antislavery Movement Upon Styles of Judicial Reasoning in Nineteenth Century America," 87 *Harvard Law Review,* no. 3 (January 1974).

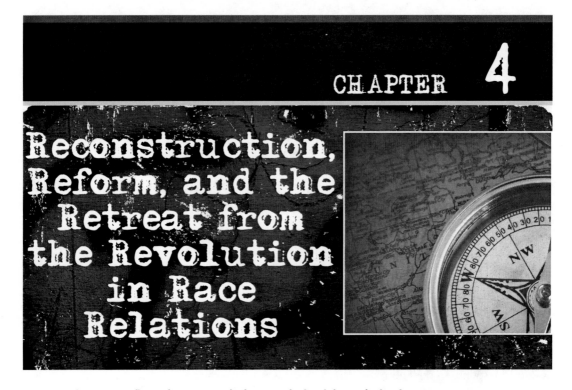

CHAPTER 4

Reconstruction, Reform, and the Retreat from the Revolution in Race Relations

It is disputes, conflicts of interests, which create the legal form, the legal superstructure.

—PASKUSKANIS[1]

The sectional dispute and the North and South conflicts of interest led to a Civil War and to Constitutional superstructure changes as manifested in the Thirteenth, Fourteenth, and Fifteenth Amendments. In a Marxist concept, these laws were products of a massive struggle between Northern merchant capital and the Southern planter class. These amendments reflected the exact movement of the Civil War from the Lincoln war to maintain the union, to an abolitionist war for freedom, and to a Radical Republican Reconstruction for equality and their party's domination over national affairs.[2] This chapter explains how law, used as an instrument of class power and racialism, as an institutionalized social force, led to a deferred commitment in reference to the war goal of equality.[3] However, this significant Constitutional change in the legal form was contoured by a conservative federalism and by events within the social relations of political economy with the rise of the New South.

PART I: CONSTITUTIONALISM AND THE FREEDPEOPLE

The Civil War ended one period of Constitutional conflict in which the great institutional issue of slavery was placed to rest. At the same time, another source of Constitutional conflict arose with the question, "What is to be done with the freedman and freedwoman and their families?" This "Black" social class totaled 7.75 million out of America's population of 35 million in 1865. Ninety percent of this oppressed social class lived in the Deep South. This question posed deeper juridical, ideological, and sociopolitical problems, and these problems were, simultaneously, contradictory, paradoxical, and enigmatic: contradictory in the sense that democracy was freed of this institutional antipode while its racial ideological hegemony was solidified; paradoxical in the sense that the freedpeople would still be the exploited laboring base by which "the South would attempt to rise again"; and enigmatic in the sense that these same freedpeople would cling to the possibility of attaining the American Dream of civic security and prosperity while daily experiencing its worst nightmare.

The possibility of achieving a dream of civil security and economic prosperity was based on the three Civil War Constitutional amendments and supportive enforcing legislation. Prior to the passage of these amendments, the Radical Republicans passed the Freedman Bureau Act in 1865, which was the first race-based federal assistance to aid the freedpeople's transition from slavery to freedom.[4] The Bureau would eventually oversee the establishment of Black schools and medical assistance and establish courts to protect Blacks, especially in labor relations with the planter class.[5] The Thirteenth Amendment, passed in 1867, abolished slavery and involuntary servitude and gave Congress power to enforce this amendment with appropriate legislation. As with the 1863 Emancipation Proclamation, which "freed slaves in those states in rebellion," the Thirteenth Amendment was a response to the "military conditions" on the ground war and the violent reaction by Southerners toward the freedpeople under Presidential Reconstruction.[6] Black codes, race riots, and exploitative labor contracts revealed the insurgent South's attempt to win the peace by creating a new South that mirrored the exact social relations of the old South.[7] The Radicals' response to the South's intransigence was to impeach their *de facto* supporter, President Andrew Johnson, and pass Reconstruction Acts that divided the Southern states into military districts under military occupation and martial law.[8]

Continuing on this "line of march," the Fourteenth and the Fifteenth Amendments were also Congressional responses to Southern resistance or insurgency. This insurgency, by the newly formed Ku Klux Klan, was aimed at placing the freedpeople into a new and certain kind of slavery.[9] As this resistance used law as an instrument to help create new social relations, the Radicals did the same.

The Fourteenth Amendment was predicated on the earlier Civil Rights Act of 1866 and the fear that the Act could be repealed by a later Congress. Congressional members such as Thaddeus Stevens (PA), John A. Bingham (OH), and Jacob M. Howard (PA), who sat on the Joint Committee of Fifteen on Reconstruction, wanted to give the freedpeople national civil rights protection. Both Bingham and Howard thought that incorporating the Bill of Rights into this amendment was a noble goal. Bingham said, "The proposition pending before the House is simply a proposition to arm the Congress . . . with the power to enforce the Bill of Rights."[10] Stevens was even more specific when he observed, "I can hardly believe that any person can be found who will not admit that every one of these provisions [in section 1] is just. They are all asserted . . . in our DECLARATION or organic law. But the Constitution limits only the actions of Congress, and is not a limitation on the States. This amendment supplies that effect."[11] The first section of the Fourteenth Amendment attempted to provide federal authorities with a legal form to attack the insurgency. This first section conferred citizenship on the freedman and stated that no State can deny any person the equal protection and the due process of the laws.

This section represented a clear recognition that insurgency was State orchestrated in many cases, and now Congress had the legal authority to break federalism and go into a state to prosecute insurgency. The Fourteenth Amendment was ratified in 1868 with five sections. Three sections addressed Southern resistance and another section gave Congress power to pass future supportive legislation for the amendment. **Section One,** the citizenship clause, read thusly: "All persons born or naturalized in the United States . . . are citizens of the United States and of the State wherein they reside. . . . [and] No State shall . . . abridge the privileges and immunities . . . of citizens . . . nor shall any person of life, liberty, or property, without due process of law. . . ." **Section Two** addressed voter discrimination and punishment: "But when the right to vote at any election is denied [federal] . . . to any of the male inhabitants of such State . . . the basis of representation therein shall be reduced. . . ." **Section Three** addressed Southern power and restrictions on it: "No person shall be a Senator or Representative . . . having previously taken an oath . . . as an officer of the United States . . . [having] engaged in insurrection or rebellion. . . ." **Section Four** removed Southern debt from the responsibility of the federal government: "Neither the United States nor any State shall assume or pay any debt or obligation incurred in aid of insurrection or rebellion . . . or any claim for the loss or emancipation of any slave. . . ." Finally, **Section Five** said, "The Congress shall have the power to enforce, by appropriate legislation, the provisions of this article."[12] To enhance this new Constitutional legal form, Congress passed, in 1870, the Fifteenth Amendment, which restricted Southern states from denying or abridging the right of "citizens of the United States to vote . . . on account of race, color, or previous condition of servitude."[13] This amendment also contained a section permitting Congress to pass enforcement legislation. It was a remarkable amendment in that Northern voters had "explicitly rejected black suffrage between 1865 and 1869."[14] Senator Jacob Howard was apprehensive of the Black vote when he stated that the American people are not "yet prepared to sanction so fundamental a change . . . the right of suffrage to the colored race."[15] This problem led the Radicals to create an amendment that was "not a positive extension of the franchise, but an injunction against the use of race in setting qualifications."[16] Political reality in the North against Black suffrage led to racial semantics within the Fifteenth Amendment that did not explicitly state who had the right to vote, but only permitted the states to regulate voting within limiting categories.[17]

However, the Fourteenth Amendment was different in that it was positive law and would be used as an instrument of class power to combat the insurgency of the Klan. In pursuant of the fifth section of the Fourteenth Amendment, Congress passed the Enforcement Act of 1870 and the Ku Klux Klan Act of 1871, which permitted federal authorities to arrest and prosecute members of the Southern insurgency, that is, the Ku Klux Klan.[18] Winning the peace by solidifying Republican Party control in the recalcitrant South was the driving force of the amendments and enforcing legislation. Constitutional law arose out of the political disputes and sectional controversy of Civil War and Reconstruction.[19] However, this change in legal superstructure would be limited by another autonomous ideology—race—and how this idea led both Northern capitalists and Southern planters to require the freedpeople to call "Their Old Master-Master."[20] Racism and the fatigue of combating the ongoing Southern insurgent resistance (Redeemers) led the Republicans to relinquish control of Southern states' internal political affairs to Redeemers and permit the Southern states to maintain, in the words of a Northern newspaper observation, "Status quo antebellum or things as they were before Lincoln, slavery excepted."[21] This retreat from enforcing the legal superstructural Constitutionalism was due to violent events on the ground and to a conservative Supreme Court within the age of enterprise.[22]

Constitutional change was blunted by a series of conservative and formalistic Supreme Court decisions. However, one can look at the change in the legal form and the conservative content of Court decisions as merely a reflection of real, concrete economic incentives. These incentives were characterized, according to one of the framers, Roscoe Conklin, by the use of the word "person" in Section One. Conklin claimed that persons and corporations were analogous, and, therefore, the Reconstruction plans of the Radicals would be "the method by which the 'Masters of Capital' . . . [would] exploit the resources of the Southern states" behind federal protection."[23] Both a person and a corporation would have the equal protection of the laws within the age of enterprise and amid the rising needs of corporations to be protected from populist state legislatures.[24] The material grounding of law and corporations as persons under the new amendments was bonded with a hegemonic racialism that was unquestioned, except by a number of Black leaders whose voices went unheard.[25] Given this context, the hegemony of White supremacy, overt in the South and covert in the North, would severely limit the aggressiveness of federal enforcement and the protection of the freedpeople within the New South's political economy of Black subservience and exploitation within the shadow of the plantation.[26]

The political dimensions of the question of what was to be done with the ex-slaves of African descent living in a White supremacist society was not resolved by Grant's victory at Appomattox; nor by the Supreme Court when it declared that "the Constitution, in all its provisions, looks to an indestructible Union, composed of indestructible States"; *Texas v. White* (1869),[27] nor by the passage of the Thirteenth, Fourteenth, and Fifteenth Amendments. The political dimension of this question was finally resolved in the aftermath of the bitterly contested and disputed presidential election of 1876. The Republican Party, wearied of its efforts to impose "Black rule" on the South, and the Democrats, determined to put an end to this GOP effort and establish "home-rule,"[28] agreed to the now infamous Compromise of 1877. If the Civil War was the "irrepressible conflict," then the Compromise of 1877 could rightly be termed the *inevitable reconciliation.*[29] The disparities and inherent contradictions between sectional political economies had brought about the Civil War. Now, in part, it was the American ideological belief in White supremacy that molded how Union restoration would proceed. Racial domination, as a hegemonic belie, was pervasive in both the North and the South before and after the Civil War.[30] This hegemony, as a dominant cultural institution, intertwined itself in every aspect of American religious, political, economic, and social life. Consequently, this racial ideology limited, in a hard and fast way, how Radicals viewed what they could do to change the state–federal relationships. By this, I mean that racialism made Constitutional conservatives of most members of Congress. It prevented them from going the Constitutional distance to implement revolutionary changes in federal–state relationships to enable the freedpeople to make substantive strives toward freedom. Radical Congressman George W. Julian summed up racialism as hegemony when he observed, "the real trouble is that we hate the negro,"[31] a view echoed by a Southerner who stated that the White Southerner "hates the negro as a force in politics, and he hates the party which has entitled him to be a force in politics."[32]

PART II: RACIAL FEDERALISM AND THE FREEDPEOPLE

Political compromise embodied in America's cultural life and institutions and based on the White supremacist majority view as well as the economic self-interests of the elite few had traditionally eased the sectional crisis and appeased the principles of "right" on the side of the North and "rights" on the side of the South.[33] The Civil War became the only dramatic departure from this political heritage of compromise based on White supremacy and economic self-interest—dramatic in the sense that it was and is the only time in which the American political culture of compromise stopped and devolved into civil war. White Americans from the states' rights section of the South and from the federal/centrist section of the North resorted to armed warfare to settle their differences. The North fought for federal supremacy and voiced those inspiring "rights of man" phonemes embodied in the Declaration of Independence, and the South fought for the slavery right[34] given to them in that most sacred document, the Constitution.[35] Both sections set aside compromise because of "rights of man" principles that both sides held so dear, yet in actuality were not too substantively different when it came to "the negro."[36]

The North, being victorious, tried to reestablish the pre-war federalism regarding what was understood to be the proper power relationship between federal and state political structures. The war, however, destroyed the old federalism only when it came to the race question. Congressional legal Reconstruction eradicated this old federalism and ensured that Americans of African ancestry would have formal Constitutional freedom, equality before the law and citizenship, and the right to protect these new freedoms with the right to vote, with the federal government maintaining the power to enforce these legal changes within the states themselves. The Southern states' new relationship with the federal government was established as each state was coerced into ratifying the Fourteenth and Fifteenth Amendments that had become the Republican party's litmus requirement for their readmission to the Union. These amendments' "pervading purpose," as the Court stated in *Slaughterhouse,* was to protect the federal rights of freedpeople against state actions that harmed them.[37] However, the majority of the freedpeople's social, economic, educational, and political rights were still under the purview of state authorities who had acquiesced reluctantly and under duress to accept the formal Constitutional changes ushered in by the Civil War. This traditional federalism was conservative, given the facts on the ground, which was Klan insurgency and terrorism. However, most Radicals believed that, in the words of Carl Schurz, "The political system of this Republic rests upon the right of the people to control their local concerns in their several states. . . . This system was not to be changed in the work of reconstruction."[38] Maintaining military occupation of the South and its exclusion from participating in the federal system would be contingent on Southern states ratifying the Fourteenth and Fifteenth Amendments.[39] Some Radicals realized the limited dimensions of this policy. Quickly returning rebellious states back into the Union who were just defeated but not really loyal was driven by an uncritical faith in the old federalism embodied in the Tenth Amendment.[40] According to one astute Northern critic of this conservative federalism, "the idea which underlay all this legislation was that if the freemen were clothed with the same powers as the Whites, had the same privileges and immunities, nothing more needed to be done, in their behalf."[41] This allegiance to basic formal rights limited legal protection within the proper federal–state relationship and, coupled with a racial ideological hegemony, was alluded to when, during his presidential campaign of 1868,

Grant clearly said, "Let us have peace."[42] The term *us* referred only to White Americans. Grant's comment was an explanation why he was so reluctant to use federal troops on behalf of the freed-people and their radical supporters when they were violently attacked by Redeemers.[43] Watchful waiting and wishful thinking in the face of racial violence were politically savvy, but morally corrupt.[44] Grant's Southern policy would, through his inaction, lead to the last massacre of the Civil War at Colfax, Louisiana, in 1874.[45] Racial violence as a political weapon became a hallmark of the activities of the insurgency between 1865 and the beginnings of the Mississippi Plan of 1890. In response, federal authorities indicted thousands of insurgents for civil rights infractions. In late 1871 and early 1872, they were successful in temporarily blunting insurgent violence. Winning convictions in 150 cases although dismissing 1,000 indictments, authorities disrupted the Klan.[46] Federal prosecutors indicted 1,200 persons in North Carolina, 750 persons in Mississippi, and 350 persons in Alabama.[47] These indictments described violence including murder, beatings, burnings, and rape.[48] This violence, setting aside federal authorities, was still effective in achieving its goals. Redeemers acquiesced to the federal requirement for readmission (i.e., agreeing to abide by the new amendments) and then used violence as their political instrument to control events on the ground. By 1868, reunion and reaction were predicated on acquiescent acceptance by all but three states of the old Confederacy of the coercive requirements for readmission to the Union.[49] The post-war federalism would be driven by the Union as it was defined by the Tenth Amendment and the Constitution as it has changed by the Reconstruction amendments.[50]

The coercive but conservative federalism of the victorious Republicans represented the "outer limits" of the party's willingness to expand the scope of federal power. Beyond giving the freed-people their federal rights, however, conservative elements of the party were particularly concerned with maintaining the autonomy of the states in regulating and proscribing the rights of their respective citizens. The idea of forcing liberal democracy government on the rebels with the support of Union bayonets quickly receded, not only because of conservative political theory embraced by Northern Republicans and Southern Democrats concerning the limits of federal power vis-à-vis states' rights, but also equally or more so because both political parties and their constituencies believed in the ideology of "race supremacy."[51] Both Southerners and their Northern adversaries hated "the negro," and this commonly held belief would facilitate reunion between two regional elites. The North hated slavery but also "hated the negro," and these two facts brought the nation to civil war but also to a failed policy on how to reconstruct the nation.[52]

The freedpeople were doomed by moderate Republicans and the Radicals, a true historical misnomer and false moniker, who were not radical enough and who could not move away from a conservative Constitutionalism. This conservative radicalism had, in part, a liberal tradition that involved the Radicals' antislavery heritage exhibited before the Civil War. This liberalism supported equality before the law for free Blacks in the North through the passage of personal liberty laws. Many Republicans, as state representatives and later as Congressmen, had sincerely fought to maintain Black rights in the free states. Noted Constitutional historian Paul Finkleman argued that this liberal tradition set the prelude for the Fourteenth Amendment. Finkleman recognized the degree of "negrophobia" in the North prior to Civil War, but he argued the picture was more complex. Northern White liberals not only passed personal liberty laws, but also spearheaded the Underground and Above Ground Railroad, supported the passage of the 1855 Massachusetts

Constitution banning school segregation, helped repeal various Black Laws, helped free slaves in transit, and supported various abolitionists to public office.[53] The idea of liberal legalism was clearly expressed by Abraham Lincoln during his Congressional debates with Stephen A. Douglas. Lincoln expressed support of an equality-before-the-law sentiment when he said, "I as well as Judge Douglas am in favor of the race to which I belong having the superior position . . . but I hold that . . . the negro is entitled to . . . the right of life, liberty and the pursuit of happiness."[54] Finkleman argued that these ideas were expressed in Northern law prior to the sectional conflict. Lincoln in this same debate said the "negro," even though he is not the equal of Whites in their intellectual, moral, and condition of color, still had "the right to eat the bread without leave of anybody else which his own hand earns."[55] The Radicals' approach to a conservative federalism and contractualism[56] laid the basis for how Northern capital would legalize labor contracts, via Freedman courts, between the planter class and Black sharecroppers. Coupling this contractualism and racialism, the Black share-cropper and those chained in peonage would be pushed down into a new kind of slavery that merely "substituted law for the lash."[57] Conservative federalism permitted Southerners to promulgate "Negro Law" and use law as an "instrument of their domination over Blacks."[58]

However, Eric Foner noted that Lincoln's views on legal equality and Northern legal formalism, applied either in the North or in Freedman court, were not consistent with the prevailing opinion of how most White Northerners believed in the idea of law and race.[59] Racial liberalism in the North was clothed in clear racial assumptions about Blacks. For many Northerners, slavery was evil, Blacks were inferior, and traditional federalism, in spite of civil war, should still remain the bedrock of American democracy.[60]

Hegemonic racialism was the prevailing belief of the Republican communities and constituencies who dragged their feet on the ratification of the civil rights amendments. John Hope Franklin noted, "few Northern states got around to considering the 14th Amendment until 1867 and in some states like Pennsylvania debate over ratification was bitter."[61] Carl Degler also observed that as pertaining to the Fifteenth Amendment, "as late as 1868, only four states outside of New England and New York granted the suffrage to Negroes–Nebraska, Iowa, Minnesota and Wisconsin. Colorado and Connecticut had rejected Negro suffrage in 1865; Ohio and Kansas did so in 1867, and Missouri and Michigan in 1868."[62]

Alexis de Tocqueville, while traveling in the North in the 1830s, noted that racial hegemony appeared to be stronger there than in the South.[63] This observation is supported by Leon Litwack's research, which indicated that

> In virtually every phase of existence, Negroes found themselves systematically separated from whites. They were either excluded from railway cars, omnibuses, . . . or assigned to special "Jim Crow" sections; they sat, when permitted, in secluded and remote corners of theaters and lecture halls; they could not enter hotels, restaurants, and resorts, except as servants; they prayed in "Negro pews" in the white churches; and if partaking of the sacrament of the Lord's Supper, they waited until the whites had been served the bread and wine. Moreover, they were often educated in segregated schools, punished in segregated prisons, nursed in segregated hospitals, and buried in segregated cemeteries.[64]

Many Northern Whites, prior to the Civil War, went along with their Southern counterparts in looking on people of African descent as an inferior race doomed to the lowest position in White civilized society. Many colonization schemes were aimed at maintaining America as a "White man's country." Lincoln's own Civil War colonization plan, which was implemented with taxpayer monies, was consistent with this goal.[65] Before the Civil War, many Northern states had statutes that prevented the quasi-free African's right to vote.[66] In essence, a system similar to Jim Crow was the norm for "North of Slavery" in the years preceding the Civil War.[67]

Racial supremacy as an essential cultural formation was clearly an intersectional or national phenomenon, and it certainly directed the sensibilities of the conservative, moderate, and radical factions within the Republican Party, thus inhibiting the party from securing social and political stability or economic security for the freedpeople.

This intersectional agreement on the idea of White over Black was the essential reason why political compromise over the question of the African's position in American society could be worked out with relative ease in the long period prior to the war between the states; thus, this is why the infamous 1876 compromise occurred so soon after the war. One Southern demagogue summed up this consensual attitude by explaining to his Northern brethren, "You do not love [nigras] any better than we do. You used to pretend that you did, but you no longer pretend it."[68]

Another contemporary wrote, "Thank God slavery is abolished, but the Negro is not, and never can be the equal of the White. His is of an inferior race and must always remain so."[69] Senator Lyman Trumbull of Illinois argued that his Republican party is "the White man's party. We are for free White men, and for making White labor respectable and honorable, which it can never be when negro slave labor is brought into competition with it."[70] Trumbull's Northern party colleagues had their own similar spin on White "democratic" nationalism and the Negro Question. Antislavery, Reconstruction, and federalism twisted in the wind of this racial hegemony on both the popular and institutional levels. Congressmen John Sherman of Ohio understood that Reconstruction was not about the "negro," but about securing opportunities of Northern capital.[71] In 1866, while commenting on the new civil rights legislation, George W. Julian admonished his colleagues with this observation: "the real trouble is that we hate the negro. It is not his ignorance that offends us, but his color."[72]

This belief in Black inferiority was the hegemony that pervaded Congress, the states, and the American people per se. To reconstruct the nation, to legislate new rights, and to enforce public policy in the interest of the freedpeople became an inevitable failure in the context of such a dominant cultural formation. This inevitability was stated clearly by Henry Wilson of Massachusetts when he told his colleagues in 1867, "There is not today a square mile in the United States where the advocacy of the equal rights and privileges of those colored men has not been in the past and is not now unpopular."[73] The war, of course, abolished slavery as a military necessity in spite of the victors' own racial views and systemic structures of race.[74] These views and the belief in American federalism would define and thus limit racial progress during Reconstruction.

Reconstruction's "progressive" Republicans, the Radicals, wanted the opportunity to harness the Southern elite's political power so that they could reconstruct the South in their own vision. This vision rested on giving the freedpeople the minimum protection of rule of law and enlarging the capitalist market economy in the South.[75] To accomplish this end, they had to impeach President Johnson to demonstrate that their Congressional power was supreme over the Executive in matters relating to Reconstruction. To assert this power, the Radicals had to persuade conservative and liberal Republicans to support their vision. A powerful persuasive tactic used by the Radicals was the tactic of "waving the bloody shirt,"[76] a term that referred to how some radical congressmen waved the bloody shirts of the many fathers, sons, and brothers who gave their lives for the "Blue" to maintain the Union. Vengeance with punishment was the essence of this tactic, which enabled the Radical Republicans to push their more moderate, liberal, and conservative congressmen to agree to include fundamental civil rights for the freed slaves within federal–state relationships to ensure that the South would not win the peace but also would be punished. However, once the passions of war had subsided and the readmission of the Old Confederate states completed, the ideology of race and federalism took center stage in determining the substance of what these new civil rights would be, not only for the ex-slaves, but also for the nation at large. By using the Constitution as an instrument in their interests while maintaining the validity and inviolability of federalism as a guiding principle, this approach restricted the extent to which the Radicals could go to secure the new rights of the freedpeople. This belief in the intrinsic worth of Constitutional federalism was deeply intertwined with the ideology of race. A good example of the adherence of race and federalism was President Johnson's willingness to benignly bring the "dead states" back into a federal–state structure because of his own racial affinity to his fellow Southerners and his and their antipathy toward the freedpeople. In some respects Johnson's plan was, in its implementation, a slight modification of Lincoln's 10 percent plan.[77]

Johnson's extensive conveying of pardons for ex-Confederate landowning elites led not only to their re-empowerment, but also to the passage of infamous Black Codes under his Presidential Reconstruction. Passed during the winter of 1865–1866, these laws were instruments of the defeated Confederates winning the peace. These codes were a hodgepodge of revised neo-like "slave codes" that forced freedpeople to continue to work on the plantations, restricted their physical mobility via vagrancy laws, used apprenticeship laws to force Black children into working for ex-masters, and used criminal law to ensure that a speedy but unfair trial would place Black defendants in a criminal justice system that hired them out to labor for planters.[78] Even though this reality, in part, caused his impeachment by the Radicals, both Johnson and his opponents believed in the intrinsic value of Constitutional structure that was clearly contoured by racial affinity and hierarchy. Black Codes were a natural result of the maintenance of a conservative, Constitutional federalism that permitted the Presidential Reconstruction states to quickly return to the pre-war social relationship of White over Black.

The retreat from or failure of Reconstruction was the result of how both conceptions of the political world, federalism and racism, created a death spiral for the freedpeople's interests. This spiral became a political dance, with racism leading its partner, conservative Constitutionalism, to the Rebel clarion tune, "Dixie," which sounded the death knell for Reconstruction. The romance of these intimate ideologies led to various reasons for the nation's retreat from Reconstruction. As Gillette noted, these causes were the "waning of popular support" due to conservatism, "the increasing desire for reconciliation on the part of Northerners despite the terrorism and repression" exhibited by redeemers in the South that was exacerbated by the "gradual reduction of federal troops in the South,"[79] and the restriction on federal action imposed by judicial decisions."[80] These judicial decisions reflected the internal coherence of racial legitimization.[81]

The retreat from Reconstruction was essentially a retreat from the Constitutional changes that could have permitted Northern control over national public policy while establishing Republican party leadership in the South based on the political coalition of freedpeople, carpetbaggers, and scalawags.[82] This coalition was not able to achieve its goals because Constitutional law, as an instrument of the conservative retreat, with its own autonomous, internal dynamics, molded the new amendments and enforcing legislation within a narrow federalism parameterized by the idea of race. The autonomous internal logic of the law interacting with racialism combined major ideologies that the U.S. Supreme Court embraced and that shaped how the Court determined the signification of new civil rights laws. These ideologies, bounded by the specific social and historical context of Reconstruction, led to legal decisions that created a certain type of freedom for the freedpeople while maintaining the *status quo* for White planter class within the New South.[83]

The Supreme Court, in 1869, set the tone for the post-war federalism when it affirmed that the Constitution imposes "an indestructible Union, composed of indestructible States."[84] This federal relationship, as a core value of governance, was extremely important because it permitted conservative Whites of both the North and South to mediate what the New South and the new freedoms for Blacks should be in terms of both a federalist and racialist hegemony. Both core beliefs prevailed to the detriment of the freedpeople's hopes and dreams. Jubilee's expectations were dashed on the rocks of this hegemonic adherence. This reciprocity between law and race gravely affected how the freedpeople fared within the Southern criminal justice system. As Hyman observes, this commitment to the traditional state-federal structure, quoting Wisconsin's ex-Senator Doolittle, meant that "the republic [was] restored to the normal condition, [and] the burdens of the federal government . . . will once more . . . rest as lightly upon our people . . . as they were before that terrible convulsion."[85] Law at the state and local level, controlled by Klansmen, White Leaguers, White Liners, and the like (many serving on all-White juries), became an instrument of terror with few restraints. Individual judges, holding to autonomous rules of law procedures, merely demonstrated the futile circumscription of the law and fair justice when faced with the class and racial warfare that exploded during Reconstruction. "White Terror"[86] consisted of numerous race riots with high Black mortality, a dramatic rise in the rape of Black women, murder by Klansmen and other similar White supremacist groups, and state governments' limiting Black educational opportunity by discriminating tax allocation policies, sharecropping, and *peonage* (exploitative laboring systems) that lengthened the shadow of slavery and the plantation.[87]

White Terror was not the only factor that prevented the Republicans from providing economic stability for the freed population. The strong beliefs in *laissez-faire* Constitutionalism and in the vested rights of private property also impaired the Republicans' vision of possible avenues in the creation of a truly equality before the law post-war America. These twin ideas had gained ascendancy in the post–Civil War age of enterprise.[88] The ideas of *laissez-faire* Constitutionalism and *laissez-faire* vested rights capitalism prevented any more interference into people's lives by the government than was absolutely necessary to maintain the legitimation of new social relations. Giving "forty acres and a mule" to newly freed slaves was certainly neither a necessity nor a requirement to maintain their existing allegiance to the party of Lincoln. Entrepreneurialism and the vested rights of property took precedence over the substantive needs of the freedpeople. The entrepreneurial values of maximization of profits with the minimization of losses helped, philosophically, the various dominant social classes to applaud reunion as a natural counterpart to Southern reaction.[89] Henry Grady's "New South" embraced and epitomized this line of thinking. Grady wanted the post–Civil War South to emulate the industrial and entrepreneurial North. He advocated the purchasing of machines and technology under a Jim Crow free-labor system borrowed, also, from the North.[90] Grady, however, was a moderate on the social question of race and strongly believed that *de facto* segregation, and not *de jure,* should be the basis of the New South. Black Anglo-Saxons, a la Booker T. Washington, should have a customary right to socialize with Whites in a discrete manner.[91]

PART III: LAW, CAPITAL, AND A CERTAIN KIND OF FREEDOM

The stability of the relationships between capital and labor at the point of production was the major concern of many Congressional legislators. The attitudes of both the Radicals and progressive White Southerners on the relationship between capital and labor were one and the same: that property-owning classes by their ownership of land and property have a natural authority to control their labor force and forces of production and the ability to exercise the function of state power in their respective interests. Recognizing that for Southerners, *labor* had meant *slave labor,* Henry Raymond, editor of *The New York Times,* called for "Southerners to learn the art of managing Negroes as paid laborers without the aid of the lash."[92] Managing the exploited class of the Black social caste involved economic and legal systems of peonage, convict labor, Jim Crow, and lynching, all of which the U.S. Supreme Court legitimized in high-profile cases and gave Constitutional protection to the New South's social relations of production.[93]

These hegemonic attitudes of capitalism presented formidable obstacles for a nation, just torn by civil war, to reconstruct itself on the novel principle of racial equality. An institution that was set up to moderate the hard edges of these obstacles was the Bureau of Refugees, Freedmen and Abandoned Lands, commonly known as the Freedmen's Bureau. Empowered by Congress on March 3, 1865, it was to supervise and manage all abandoned lands and to govern all matters relating to the new freedmen and freedwomen and their families. The Bureau became the first attempt by the federal government at mass social welfare aimed at uplifting a racial caste from slavery. A major Congressional charge for the Bureau was to "set apart for the loyal refugee or freedman, such tracts of land . . . as shall have been abandoned" in lots of "not more than forty acres."[94] The Radicals hoped that land redistribution would go a long way in constructing equitable social relationships in the new South, restrain the long shadow and legacy of slavery, and render the landowning and old political elites powerless. The protection of the law was the decisive variable that made Black land ownership a viable option.

General Oliver Otis Howard headed the Bureau and attempted to advertise the availability of land for the potential class of Black yeoman farmer. Ultimately, the actual land acquired by the ex-slaves was minimal because of Northern entrepreneurial speculation, Southern resistance, and Howard's lack of the political vision to understand the critical nature of the land question.

Another major factor that doomed land redistribution was President Andrew Johnson's Amnesty Proclamation in May 1865. It pardoned most ex-rebels and permitted those who owned property worth more than $20,000 to request pardons and thereby purchase their own abandoned lands.[95] Bureau head Howard quickly accepted Johnson's "live and let live" Reconstruction plans. Howard toured the South, advising White Southerners that the Freedmen's Bureau stood for stable labor systems and governmental control by capital. Howard told the freedpeople to sell their labor and that their ex-masters, at times their new employers, would be kind to them and would honor the labor law contracts signed with them. However, these contracts called for gang labor techniques reminiscent of slavery times. The contract system did not provide a set rate of payment scale for work completed, and some contracts set no wages at all but described the work to be performed "in the usual way."[96] Bourgeois concepts of contractual liberty doomed the freedpeople to lives of drudgery and extreme poverty.

These labor law contracts, monitored by Bureau agents, reflected only one of several types of labor systems that developed after the Civil War; sharecropping, tenant farming, convict lease, and debt peonage were others. Codes for Black labor, passed by Redeemer Southern governments, made it illegal to leave a job site within the duration of the contract, and violation of vagrancy laws forced many freedpeople onto chain gangs and into jailhouses where they were released to merchant–planters to labor in the traditional manner. Labor codes were a blatant attempt by planters to use law as an instrument to protect their class interests. Many freedpeople moved from one system to another several times in their lives. The shadow of slavery and plantation reflected the deep reluctance of Southerners to let loose of Black involuntary servitude, and planters' use of violence created a new South that was not very different from the old. The inability of the Bureau to ensure the obligation of contracts and civil rights protection for the freedpeople created "a certain kind of freedom"[97] devoid of freedom from fear, want, and, most important, the opportunity to acquire land. The relationship of land to freedom was poignantly stated by one ex-slave who asked, "What is the use of being free if you don't have land enough to be buried in? Might juss as well stay [a] slave all yo' days."[98] Land, this ex-slave understood, would give not only a burial plot but also an air of freedom from the watchful and coercive hand of his old master. A few chickens, corn, a cow, a small cabin, and the family on one's own land was the "milk and honey" the freedpeople understood as freedom.

An example of the complexities and failure of land reform was seen in the South Carolina Sea Islands. As early as February 1863, the "liberated contraband" (ex-slaves) at Port Royal had been permitted to purchase small lots of auctioned land totaling several thousand acres.[99] General Saxton and Governor Hunter supervised the sale of 50,000 acres to Black families around Savannah. General Sherman's field order no. 15 stipulated that the "entire coast from Charleston, SC, to St. James River in Florida and stretching 30 miles inland, [is] for the exclusive settlement of blacks . . . and divide the land . . . in farms not to exceed forty acres of arable land."[100]

However, much of the land auctioned off was bought by Edward Philbrick, representing a group of Boston speculators. Having attained more than 8,000 acres, Philbrick proposed to teach the ex-slaves individual self-reliance by thrusting them into free market work relationships under contract agreements. Philbrick, the lead man for Northern capitalism, would show the New South how to manage their ex-property without the lash but under a new type of slavery based on iron law of wages.[101] Wage slavery existed because many labor contracts were violated by those who hired the ex-slaves. Bureau professionals adjudicated these violations, succeeding at times in protecting Black rights and at other times failing. Federal legal protection was represented by these Bureau professionals, who adjudicated conflicts at law in such areas as contracts, criminal conflicts, and civil law. Crouch's study of these Bureau courts revealed that the freedpeople

> pressed their legal rights aggressively and with an awareness of what the law should do for them. The freedpeople brought cases to these government courts for numerous and varied reasons. . . . They realized they were part of the law and could not live outside it, nor did they desire to. Blacks simply wanted the legal system to remedy the injustice done them and to provide protection for their newly won rights and freedom.[102]

Crouch appears to argue in favor of some type of hegemony of law as freedpeople used the law in their own interests. However, the law could not extend to the freedpeople a reality that would dramatically help bring them up from slavery.[103]

In 1865, in Texas, while requiring that freedpeople continue to work under labor contracts with planters, Bureau officials insisted that now there would exist "an absolute equality of personal rights and rights of property between former masters and slaves, and the connection heretofore existing between them becomes that between employer and hired labor."[104] The Texas federal commissioner required all Bureau courts to give the freedpeople "impartial justice."[105] Even though the majority of the cases heard in the two years of the Bureau courts' existence concerned disputes about labor law contracts, these courts also heard cases concerning Black family disputes such as spousal abuse and adultery, but also cases concerning the forced apprenticeship of Black children to White planters. However, the limits of the law were again revealed in a conservative federalism that Bureau courts assumed restricted their interference in "intrastate equality of treatment . . . as intrinsic parts of each state's constitution, laws, and customs."[106] Within this dual system of law, Bureau courts and state and local courts handed down the law in similar and dissimilar ways. Of course, the freedpeople looked to the Bureau courts for legal remedies and relief, thus demonstrating their understanding that their new legal rights would be more likely "protected" by the federal government courts and would probably give them a degree of justice rather than state courts controlled by redeemers. Blacks, in reference to what equality of the law should mean, were quick learners about how law is used as an instrument of class and racial power.

In Mississippi, the early Presidential Reconstruction period reveals a similar sense that Blacks knew that they had new rights, and their assertion of these rights, even in state courts, reveals a determination, self-assertion, and moral verve in the face of adversity. State redeemers attempted to "substitute law for the lash"[107] by creating inferior courts and Black Codes legislation in response to Black self-assertion, a self-assertion that Whites believed would make Blacks unruly laborers because this labor would demand the equal protection of the law. Without the master's lash, the *Vicksburg Herald* said that the new freedom required the formal control of the law.[108] Redeemer vigilantism would take a back seat or co-exist with this new legal attempt at forcing the Blacks to live under the hegemony of Whites, although one journalist implied that vigilantism would be relied on if the "negro" does not abide by "civil laws of the State."[109] White Mississippians debated and differed on whether giving Blacks legal protection would control them better than violence. In the end, Black Codes as law were both ideological and co-ercive domination that co-existed and manifested themselves in both law courts and in lynch law. This co-existence was revealed by two Southerners, one of whom stated an extra-legalism that "nigger life's cheap now . . . when a white man feels aggrieved at anything a nigger's done, he just shoots him and puts an end to it;"[110] whereas another Southerner, Judge Warren Cowan of Vicksburg, strictly enforced legal formalism and rule of law in his county court that many times absolved Black defendants from the proverbial "noose" of planters' demand that law be used as an instrument in their interests. However, "negro law" developed in wide areas such as labor, vagrancy, family, and criminal law became almost common law in the hands of various Southern courts. Bureau courts and local courts handled cases involving prostitution, theft, as-sault, murder, and labor disputes. Even though all-White juries and judges predisposed fairness in their peculiar way, it did not prevent Blacks from using these county courts as well as Bureau courts to "take advantage of the smallest and most unimportant offense to come to the law."[111] Because most court officers attempted to follow the rules of procedure, Blacks became more and more aware of the autonomous nature of the law and the possibility, albeit limited, of using law as a weapon in their interests. Blacks used *habeas corpus* petitions to challenge false impris-onment as well as unreasonable bail. They learned the autonomous dimensions of the law from such individuals as Judge Cowan, who released Black defendants when the prosecutor's docu-ments were in technical error concerning, for example, the correct identification of the defen-dant in court documents.[112] The end of Presidential Reconstruction and the establishment of Radical Reconstruction led to the repeal of the Black Codes, but redemption in the South by the late 1870s assured that racist law and the lash would reappear again. However, Black dreams and hopes were not squashed by this ebb and flow, and freedpeople used all sorts of self-assertions, armed resistance, migration, and legal formalism to blunt the goals of the redeemer governments.[113]

The failure of land reform and the inability of Bureau and state officials to afford legal protection to the freedpeople were persistent realities during Reconstruction. The ideology of White su-premacy and the conservative political federalism of the radicals merged as a barrier to the ag-gressive enforcement of civil rights. The Congressional Constitutional amendments and support-ive legislation were, in part, passed to protect the political and civil rights of people of African descent who were implementing these newly acquired rights in that period so inaptly termed *Black Reconstruction*.[114] Reconstruction was short-lived and never Black controlled, and its end was anticlimactic. By 1868, all but three Southern states had been redeemed and home-rule estab-lished via White Terror violence and Northern acquiescence. The social and political events that led up to the Compromise of 1877 and the restoration of White supremacy saw federal equalitar-ian legislative efforts torn asunder under the weight of the expediency of a *quid pro quo*[115] recon-ciliation between the Democratic and Republican parties.

The events that led up to the Compromise were brought about by the determination of White Southerners to maintain their way of life. They resorted to a type of guerrilla warfare that in-cluded fraud, intimidation, and murder to reestablish their own control over the state govern-ments, which were then in the hands of Black Republicans, Northern carpetbaggers, and Southern scalawags. The implementation of "nigra" legislation, as seen by Southerners, by the federal government made the South even more determined to resist. The South saw the Civil

Rights amendments and subsequent Congressional enforcement legislation as the main threat to the Southern *status quo* of Black subservience and White supremacy. There was no place in Southern society for citizens of African ancestry protected by federal law. These laws, passed by an alien Congress, as the Southerners saw it, brought about the specter of Black formal equality that Southern Whites saw as the world turned upside down. The fear of Black political domination was probably exacerbated in states such as South Carolina, Mississippi, and Louisiana, where Africans outnumbered Whites, or in other counties where they were clearly a majority. The restoration of home-rule was led by White supremacist terrorist groups such as the Knights of the White Camellia in Louisiana, Knights of the Rising Sun in Texas, the White Line in Mississippi, and others with such names as the Pale Faces, the White Brotherhood, the Constitutional Union Guards, the Council of Safety, the White League, and other like organizations.[116] The '76 Association restored home-rule in Tennessee in 1869, whereas Virginia, North Carolina, and Georgia were reclaimed in 1870; Alabama, Arkansas, and Texas in 1874; and Mississippi in 1875. Only a strong coalition of freedpeople and White Unionists (scalawags and carpetbaggers) prevented redemption in South Carolina, Florida, and Louisiana.[117]

By the presidential election of 1876, the South had more or less regained its antebellum state political sovereignty and was ready and able to negotiate the removal of troops in the remaining Southern states. What prompted or initiated the negotiations and enabled the South to negotiate from a position of strength was the disputed Hayes–Tilden presidential election of 1876. The early election returns indicated that the Republican Rutherford B. Hayes, Civil War general and governor of Ohio, was the victor. However, the Democrat Samuel J. Tilden, respected reform governor of New York, had carried his home state, New Jersey, Connecticut, and Indiana, as well as all the Southern states. Tilden had accumulated 184 electoral votes and was convinced that he would pick up one more for victory. Hayes had 165 electoral votes and was convinced that he could secure all the disputed votes from the Republican-controlled and unredeemed states to bring victory home to his party.[118] Florida, South Carolina, and Louisiana were hotly contested and disputed.

Supporters of both candidates claimed victory and were determined to seat their man in the White House. This situation was exacerbated by a unipartisan electoral commission that, after examining the returns and refusing to investigate the biased Republican canvassing boards, gave the disputed electors to Hayes.[119] Tilden's supporters' reactions to the commission's decision were to attempt to interpose their will on the vote count so Hayes could not attain the White House.[120]

It was only through a series of quasi-secret meetings and discussions, known as the *Wormley Bargain* that certain Republican and Democratic leaders agreed on the decisions of the electoral commission and thus secured the White House for Hayes.[121] One noted historian, C. Vann Woodward, argued that the Wormley agreement had been exaggerated, although he does note that important promises that were to be a *quid pro quo* came out in these discussions and thereby sealed the victory for the GOP.[122]

The reciprocal promises were that the Republicans would concede a federal subsidy for the construction of the Texas and Pacific Railroad and other internal improvements to ease the South's economic plight. Hayes also promised to withdraw the remaining federal troops in the three unredeemed states and to appoint a Southerner as Postmaster General. In return, the South agreed with the electoral commission's decision and helped elect Republican James A. Garfield as Speaker of the House.[123]

On March 2, 1877, Hayes was formally announced the winner of the election. Within a short period, Hayes withdrew the federal troops that put an official end to Radical Reconstruction. He also appointed Senator David Key of Tennessee as Postmaster General. However, Southerners did not deliver enough votes to elect Garfield as Speaker, and the Republicans did not deliver enough votes to pass the Texas and Pacific Railroad bill. In the end, the North resigned political control of the South to the Democratic Party while retaining for itself control of national economic policies.

The Radicals failed to change federalism because they essentially embraced a racialist hierarchy that then led to a devolution of the effort to protect the freedpeople from Southern Whites bent on winning the peace after losing the war. The Radicals attempted to use law as an instrument of capital's domination was, according to most, a "soul-sickening spectacle . . . [by a] . . . vulgar, materialistic" government against the "intelligent" White people of the South. The Compromise symbolized the victorious peace effort and confirmed to most citizens in both regions that, according to the revered constitutionalist John W. Burgess, "It was a great wrong to civilization to put the White race of the South under the domination of the Negro race."[124]

The retreat from the Reconstruction goals of the radicals was, for those Whites and Black abolitionists who went South after the Civil War to help uplift the freedpeople from slavery to freedom, a disheartening turn of events. In his autobiography, one carpetbagger, Albion Winegar Tourgee, described his journey and those of others like him as a "Fool's Errand."[125] Tourgee recalled the effectiveness of White Terror because he believed that this terror broke the will of the freedpeople. Tourgee noted that before the widespread use of terror by the redeemers, "the negro manifested a most inveterate and invincible repugnance and disinclination towards allowing his former masters to define, regulate, and control his liberties."[126] That moment of defiance occurred when the Radicals took control of the process of Reconstruction. It was a brief moment. Redemption as a violent force took its toll. W.E.B. DuBois echoed Tourgee when he observed that what occurred after slavery's destruction was that "the slave when free; stood a brief moment in the sun; then moved back again toward slavery."[127] The inability of the Radicals to ensure land reform and civic protection doomed the freedpeople to worker status under the hegemony of redeemer racism that prompted a common refrain quoted earlier in this chapter—"What is the use of being free if you don't have land enough to be buried in?"[128] Despite the revolutionary if conservative legal changes wrought by Civil War and Reconstruction, the freedpeople were left lurching in the winds of hegemonic racialism that contoured American politics and labor relations in the last decades of the nineteenth century. African Americans' very lives, in all of their dimensions, were compromised because of this hegemony that contoured the infamous Compromise of 1877, which ended many Black dreams by establishing White justice under the Constitutional auspices of the United States Supreme Court. The high court's decisions not only supported legal developments in the Southern states, but also in some ways both set the tone and supported the realities on the ground. Supreme Court decisions interacting with state legislative law activities helped create the Black nightmare that became known as Jim Crow.

ENDNOTES

1. Ronnie Warrington, "Paskuskanis," in *Legality, Ideology, and the State*, ed. David Sugarman (London: Academic Press, 1983), 50.

2. Comer Vann Woodward, *Burden of Southern History* (Baton Rouge: Louisiana University Press, 1960); see Chapter 4, "Equality: The Deferred Commitment."

3. See Comer Vann Woodward, *The Strange Career of Jim Crow* (New York: Oxford University Press, 1964). Excellent analysis of how this commitment devolved during the period when the hopes of Reconstruction were dashed in the face of White terror.

4. See Eric Schnapper, "Affirmative Action and the Legislative History of the 14th Amendment," *Virginia Law Review,* 71 (1988).

5. Milton Cantor, ed., *Black Labor in America* (Westport: Negro University Press, 1969), 1–24; see Chapter 1 by Thomas Wagstaff, "Call Your Ol' Master-'Master': Southern Political Leaders and Negro Labor During Presidential Reconstruction."

6. John Hope Franklin, *Reconstruction: After the Civil War* (Chicago: The University of Chicago Press, 1961), 15–31, "Presidential Peacemaking"; Eric Foner, *Reconstruction: America's Unfinished Revolution, 1861–1870* (New York: Harper Collins, 1974).

7. Comer Vann Woodward, Origins of the *New South, 1877–1913* (Baton Rouge: Louisiana State University Press, 1961). Woodward, *Reunion and Reaction: The Compromise of 1877 and the End of Reconstruction* (New York: Doubleday, 1956).; Allen William Trelease, *White Terror: Ku Klux Klan Conspiracy and Southern Reconstruction* (Baton Rouge: Louisiana State University Press, 1972).

8. Enforcement Acts 1870 and 1871 (Ku Klux Klan Act). *Acts and Resolution*, 41st Cong. 2nd session, May 31, 1870; 41st Congress 1st session, S April 20, 1871.

9. Peter Daniel, "The Metamorphosis of Slavery, 1865–1900," *Journal of American History* 66, no. 1 (June 1979); see Trelease, *White Terror*; Leon Litwack, *Been in the Storm Too Long: The Aftermath of Slavery* (New York: Alfred A. Knopf, 1979).

10. Robert J. Kaczorowski, "Searching for the Intent of the Framers of Fourteenth Amendment," *Connecticut Law Review*, 5 (1972–3): 381–383.

11. Schapper, 787.

12. U.S. Constitution, Fourteenth Amendment (1868).

13. U.S. Constitution, Fifteenth Amendment (1870.).

14. D.G. Stephenson, Jr., "The Supreme Court, the Franchise, and the 15th Amendment: The First Sixty Years," *UMKC Law Review* 57, 1 (1988), 49.

15. Stephenson, 49.

16. Stephenson, 51.

17. Stephenson, 50.

18. See Marilyn R. Walter, "The Ku Klux Klan Act and the State Action Requirement of the Fourteenth Amendment," *Temple Law Quarterly,* 58 (1985).

19. Arthur Bestor, "State Sovereignty and Slavery: A Reinterpretation of Proslavery Constitutional Doctrine, 1846–1860," *Journal of Illinois State Historical Society,* 54 (1961), 117–180.

20. Thomas Wagstaff, "Call Your Old Master-'Master': Southern Political Leaders and Negro Labor During Presidential Reconstruction," in *Black Labor in America*, ed. Milton Cantor (Wesport: Negro University Press, 1969).

21. William Gillette, *Retreat from Reconstruction 1869–1879* (Baton Rouge: Louisiana State University Press, 1979) 379.

22. See Robert Green McCloskey, *American Conservatism in the Age of Enterprise, 1865–1910* (New York: Harper Row, 1951).

23. See Stanley Coben, "Northeastern Business and Radical Reconstruction: A Re-Examination," *The Mississippi Valley Historical Review,* 65 (1959).

24. See Andrew C. McLaughlin, "The Court, the Corporation, and Conkling," *American Historical Review,* 46 (1940); James F.S. Russell, "The Railroads and the 'Conspiracy Theory' of the Fourteenth Amendment," *Mississippi Valley Historical Review,* 41 (1955).

25. See James McPherson, *The Struggle for Equality: Abolitionists and the Negro in the Civil War and Reconstruction* (Princeton: Princeton University Press, 1964).

26. See Pete Daniel, *Shadow of Slavery: Peonage in the South, 1901–1960* (New York: Oxford University Press, 1973); see also Nicholas Lemann, *Redemption: The Last Battle of the Civil War* (New York: Farr, Straus and Giroux, 2006)

27. *Texas v. White*, 7 Wallace 700 (1869).

28. See Trelease, *White Terror* (Baton Rouge: Louisiana University Press, 1971)

29. See Woodward, *Reunion and Reaction: The Compromise of 1877 and the End of Reconstruction*

30. See Woodward, "White Racism and 'Black Emancipation,'" *The New York Review of Books* XII (February 27, 1964).

31. *Speeches on Political Questions by George W. Julian* (New York: Hurd and Houghton, 1872), 299.

32. Gillette, *Retreat From Reconstruction 1869–1879,* 377.

33. Rights and constitutionalism have been explored by various scholars. Northern abolitionists' "rights" embodied in the Declaration of Independence and Southern "rights" laid clear in the United States Constitution.

34. Arthur Bestor, in his essay on "State Sovereignty and Slavery," covers this ground quite well.

35. Read Bestor for a clear and precise trajectory of the changing rhetorical clarions by both sides.

36. Paul Finkleman has a different take on the racism north of slavery. "Prelude to the Fourteenth Amendment: Black Legal Rights in the Antebellum North," *Rutgers Law Journal* 17 (1986) 415.

37. "Justice Miller presented the Negro-rights theory of the purpose of the 14th Amendment." In Alfred H. Kelly, Winfred A. Harbison, and Herman Belz, *The Amerian Constitution: Its Origins and Development* (New York: W.W. Norton and Company, 1983), 400.

38. Michael Les Benedict, "Preserving the Constitution: The Conservative Basis of Radical Reconstruction," *The Journal of American History*, LXI (June 1974) 77.

39. Benedict, 83.

40. See Benedict and Earl Maltz, "Reconstruction Without Revolution: Republican Civil Rights Theory in the Era of the Fourteenth Amendment," *Houston Law Review*, 24, 2 (March 1987). See federalism structure in the Tenth Amendment that delegates limited power to the federal government while reserving important "rights" to the states.

41. See Albion Tourgee, quoted in Gillette, *Retreat from Reconstruction*, 365.

42. Gillette, 77; or see Benedict, 88.

43. Lemann, *Redemption: The Last Battle of the Civil War* (New York, Farrar, Straus, & Giroux, 2006).

44. See Lemann's interpretation of Grant's refusal to use federal troops to intervene at Colfax Massacre, 145.

45. LeeAnna Keith, *The Colfax Massacre: The Untold Story of Black Power, White Terror, and the Death of Reconstruction* (New York: Oxford University Press, 2008); Charles Lane, *The Day Freedom Died: The Colfax Massacre, The Supreme Court, and the Betrayal of Reconstruction* (New York: Henry Holt and Company, 2008).

46. Donald G. Nieman, *Promises to Keep: African-Americans and the Constitutional Order, 1776 to the Present* (New York: Oxford University Press, 1991), 84.

47. Neiman, 85.

48. Neiman, 85–86.

49. Woodward, *Reunion and Reaction.*

50. Mary Beth Norton, Carol Sheriff, David M. Katzman, David W. Blight, and Howard Chudacoff, *A People and A Nation: A History of the United States* (Boston: Houghton Mifflin, 2008), 444.

51. Paul Finkelman noted that Lincoln's racism asserted that he did not support civil and social equality "between the White and Black races." In "Prelude to the 14th Amendment: Black Legal Rights in the Antebellum North," *Rutgers Law Journal,* vol. 17 (1986) 3.

52. George W. Julian, "We Hate the Negro," see sources at footnote 31.

53. Finkelman, "Prelude to the 14th Amendment," 17.

54. Finkelman, 3.

55. Finkelman, 3.

56. See Steve Ferguson, "Social Contract as Bourgeois Ideology, *Cultural Logic, ISSN 1097-3087 (2007).*

57. See Christopher Waldrep, "Substitute Law for the Lash: Emancipation and Legal Formalism in a Mississippi County Court," *Journal of American History* 82, 4 (March 1996), 1425–1451.

58. Waldrep, 1425.

59. See Eric Foner's excellent study on this topic: *Free Soil, Free Men: The Ideology of the Republican Party Before the Civil War* (New York: Oxford University Press, 1995).

60. Michael Les Benedict, "Preserving the Constitution: The Conservative Basis of Radical Reconstruction," *The Journal of American History* LXI (June 1974).

61. John Hope Franklin, *Reconstruction: After the Civil War* (Chicago: The University of Chicago Press, 1961), 67–68.

62. Carl Degler, *Out of Our Past* (New York: Harper and Row: 1959), 216 at 5.

63. Alexis de Tocqueville quoted in Ronald Takaki, *Iron Cages: Race and Culture in 19th Century America* (New York: Oxford University Press, 1990), 110.

64. Leon Litwack, *North of Slavery: The Negro in the Free States, 1790–1860* (Chicago: The University of Chicago Press, 1961) 97.

65. See Gabor Boritt, ed. *The Lincoln Enigma* (New York: Oxford University Press, 2001); Lerone Bennett, *Forced into Glory: Abraham Lincoln's White Dream* (Chicago: Johnson Publishers, 2000).

66. See Richard Sewell, *Ballots for Freedom: Antislavery Politics in the United States, 1837–1860* (New York: Oxford University Press, 1976).

67. Litwack, *North of Slavery*, 99. Litwack demonstrates the clear racist attitudes of Northerners.

68. Quote by Senator Ben Tillman of South Carolina on the Senate Floor in Harold Underwood, *Politics, Reform, and Expansion, 1980–1900* (New York: Harper, 1959), 8.

69. Gillette, 191.

70. Eugene Berwanger, *The Frontier Against Slavery* (Urbana: University of Illinois Press, 1967) 133.

71. Degler, 193.

72. George W. Julian, *Speeches on Political Questions* (New York: Hurd and Houghton, 1872), 299.

73. Eugene C. Massie, *Proceedings of the Fifteenth Annual Meeting of the Virginia Bar Association* (Richmond, VA: Everett Waddey, 1903), 288–289.

74. Mary Berry, *Military and Civil Rights Policy: Black Citizenship and the Constitution, 1861–1868* (Port Washington: Kennikat, 1977).

75. See Senator Lyman Trumbull's thoughts on formal legal equality in Earl Maltz, "Reconstruction Without Revolution: Republican Civil Rights Theory in the Era of the Fourteenth Amendment," *Houston Law Review*, 24, no. 2 (March 1987).

76. Peter Camejo, *Racism, Revolution, and Reaction, 1861–1877* (New York: Monad Press, 1976), 82.

77. Norton, et al., *A People and a Nation* (New York: Houghton Mifflin Company, 2008) 437.

78. Christopher Waldrep, "Substituting Law for the Lash: Emancipation and Legal Formalism in a Mississippi County Court," *Journal of American History* (March 1996), 1425; see also Barry A. Crouch, "Black Dreams and White Justice," *Prolouge* (Winter 1974).

79. Gillette, *Retreat From Reconstruction*, xi.

80. *U.S. v. Cruikshank*, 25 Federal Case 707 (1874).

81. *Civil Rights Cases* 109 U.S. 3 (1883).

82. Camejo, 58, 93. See also Franklin's analysis of Union League, 120–123.

83. See economic basis on new slavery: Edward Magdol, *A Right to Land* (Westport: Greenwood Press, 1977); Roger L. Ranson and Richard Sutch, *One Kind of Freedom: The Economic Consequences of Emancipation* (New York: Cambridge University Press, 1977); Claued F. Oubre, *Forty Acres and a Mule: The Freemen's Bureau and Black Landownership* (Baton Rouge: Louisiana University Press, 1978).

84. *Texas v. White*, 7 Wallace 700 (1869).

85. Harold Hyman, *A More Perfect Union: The Impact of the Civil War and Reconstruction on the Constitution* (Boston: Houghton Mifflin, 1975), 547.

86. See Trelease, *White Terror*.

87. Peter Daniel, *The Shadow of Slavery*; and see John E. Fleming with John H. McClendon, *The Lengthening Shadow of Slavery: A Historical Justification for Affirmative Action for Blacks in Higher Education* (Washington: Howard University Press, 2008).

88. Michael Les Benedict, "Laissez-Faire and Liberty: A Re-Evaluation of the Meaning and Origins of Laissez-Faire Constitutionalism," *Law and History Review*, 3, 2 (Autumn 1985), 293–331.

89. For a Marxist analysis, see Camejo, especially Chapter 9, "The Republican Party's Betrayal."

90. See Ronald Takaki analysis in *Iron Cages*, 194–214.

91. See in Takaki on the social intimacy between George Washington Cable and Booker T. Washington, 210.

92. Thomas Wagstaff, "Call Your Old Master-'Master,'" quoting Raymond, 2.

93. See Michael Les Benedict, "Preserving Federalism: The Waite Court and Reconstruction," *Supreme Court Review* 1978 (1979).

94. See Donald Neiman, *To Set Law in Motion: The Freedman Bureau and the Legal Rights of Blacks, 1865–1868* (New York: KTO Press, 1976)

95. Norton, et al., 445.

96. William S. McFeely, "Unfinished Business: The Freedmen's Bureau and Federal Action in Race Relations," in Nathan I. Huggins, Martin Kilson, and Daniel M. Fox, *Key Issues in the Afro-American* Experience *II* (New York: Harcourt Brace Jovanovich, Inc. 1971), 14. See also Neiman, *To Set Law in Motion*; see also Barry A. Crouch, "Black Dreams and White Justice," *Prologue* (Winter 1974), 255–264, for an excellent analysis of Freedman's Bureau contract during this period.

97. Loren Schweninger, *Black Property Owners in the South, 1890–1915* (Urbana: University of Illinois Press, 1990), 144–145.

98. Heather Cox Richardson, *The Death of Reconstruction: Race, Labor and Politics in the Post–Civil Rights North, 1865–1901* (Cambridge: Harvard University Press, 2001), 33.

99. Willie Lee Rose, *Rehearsal for Reconstruction: The Port Royal Experiment* (Indianapolis: Bobbs Merrill, 1964), 272–296.

100. Louis S. Gerteis, *From Contraband to Freedman: Federal Policy Toward Southern Blacks, 1861–1865* (Wesport: Greenwood Press, 1973), 57.

101. Rose, 224–226; also see Gerties, 54–58.

102. Crouch, 265.

103. See Crouch and efforts of Freedman Bureau courts to hold to idea of equality.

104. Crouch, 256.

105. Crouch, 257.

106. Crouch, 264.

107. See Waldrep, "Substituting Law for the Lash: Emancipation and Legal Formalism in a Mississippi County Court, *The Journal of American History* (March 1996).

108. Waldrep, 1436.

109. Waldrep, 1436.

110. Waldrep, 1436.

111. Crouch, 265.

112. Waldrep, 1442–1445.

113. Joel Williamson, "Black Self-Assertion Before and After Emancipation," in Nathan I. Huggins, Martin Kilson, and Daniel M. Fox, *Key Issues in the Afro-American Experience* (New York: Harcourt Brace Jovanovich, Inc., 1971), 213–239.

114. See John Hope Franklin, *Reconstruction*.

115. See C. Vann Woodward, *Reunion and Reaction* (Boston: Little, Brown, and Company, 1951). See Chapter 3 "Quid Pro Quo," 55–72.

116. See Franklin, 155.

117. Franklin, 122–123. Franklin describes "Negro Militias and Union Leaguers."

118. Franklin, 214. Franklin is using Woodward's *Reunion and Reaction*.

119. Woodward, 179–200. See Chapter 7, "The Apostasy of the South."

120. Woodward, 161–178, "The Crisis Renewed."

121. Woodward, 1–23, "The Unknown Compromise." See also 201–220, "The End of the Crisis."

122. Franklin, 216.

123. Franklin, 216–217.

124. See John W. Burgess, *Reconstruction and the Constitution, 1860–1876* (New York: Charles Scribiner's and Sons, 1905), 215. The previous quote about the soul-sickening spectacle is also attributed to Burgess and can be found in Nicolas Lemann, *Redemption: The Last Battle of the Civil War* (New York: Farrar, Straus and Giroux, 2006), 191.

125. Albion Winegar Tourgee, *A Fool's Errand* (New York: Fords, Howard and Hulbert, 1880).

126. Tourgee, 295.

127. W.E.B. DuBois, *Black Reconstruction in America* (New York: Harcourt, Brace and Co., 1935), 30.

128. See Richardson, 33.

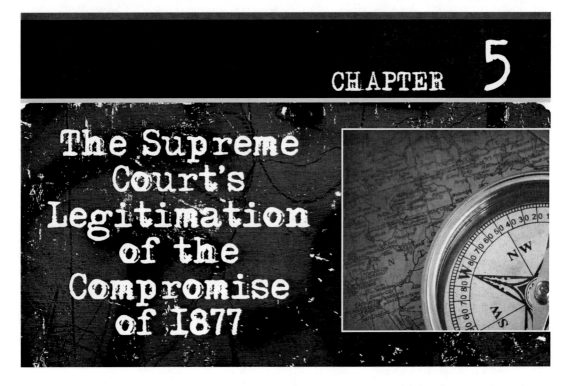

CHAPTER 5

The Supreme Court's Legitimation of the Compromise of 1877

> *As in the same way bourgeois demands for equality were accompanied by proletarian demands for equality . . . the proletarians took the bourgeois at its word: equality must not be merely apparent, . . . but also be real, must also be extended to the social, economic sphere.*[1]

—FREDERICK ENGELS, *ANTI-DUHRING*

PART I: RACIAL FORMALISM AND THE BETRAYAL OF THE NEGRO

The role of the Supreme Court was vital in creating the legal basis for a nationally recognized Jim Crow system. To do this, the Court had to legitimize the Compromise of 1877. The agreement to develop the South's economy with a railroad connection to the West was consistent with the Court's carte blanche to the emerging and increasingly powerful industrial capitalist corporate interests who were securing a stranglehold on the American economy.[2] The Court also carried into effect the Compromise as it related to state control of civil rights. The convergence of an economic and racial vision was implemented within the framework of the Fourteenth Amendment as interpreted by the Court. The Court formulated law with a broad interpretation of the Fourteenth Amendment in the interests of economic elites and a restrictive interpretation in the sphere of civil rights. It was virtually impossible for the high court to lead an equalitarian shift in the political position of the freedpeople as long as Black labor served as the basis of the South's political economy and race remained a hegemonic force throughout America's juridical, institutional, and philosophical life. Centered in this hegemony, the Supreme Court tried to use language and theory to legitimate racialist justice and bourgeois class interests.

Convinced that laissez-faire capitalism and hierarchical racialism should rule the nation, the Supreme Court justices, for the most part successful corporation lawyers and conservative in out-look,[3] set the judicial legitimation for the Compromise of 1877 when they reviewed and handed down a decision concerning environmental legislation in 1873. In this decision and others, the Court was determined to reestablish judicial supremacy, which had been eroded by Congress, presidential power, and the Civil War.[4] However, in achieving this goal, the Court also deliber-ately used legal formalism to create a new bourgeois legal definition of equality consistent with capital's demand for Black labor.[5] This was a certain type of equality made real within the con-text of the Compromise and the needs of Northern capital and Southern political economy.

Congress, in passing the Thirteenth, Fourteenth, and Fifteenth Amendments and subsequent acts (i.e., Civil Rights Act of 1866, Ku Klux Act of 1871, Enforcement Act of 1872, and Civil Rights Act of 1875), attempted to do what the *Dred Scott* case had failed to do, which was to settle the "Negro Question." Giving the freedpeople formal legal rights would be the answer to the ques-tion. Congress, in those pieces of "rights" legislation, said the following:

> Negroes were citizens of the United States and of the states in which they resided; they were part of the body politic; they enjoyed privileges and immunities conferred by the Constitution; they had the same rights as White men and White men were bound to respect those rights under the pains and penalties of punishment.[6]

These new formal legal rules would, in case law decisions, be contoured to meet the developing economic social relations of the "New South."[7] The Supreme Court would deliberate on the meaning of this new Civil Rights public policy with an understanding of Congressional intent within the context of the political, economic, and racial relations in the New South and the Court's own adherence to a federal structure.

Congressional intent as stated by Senator Roscoe Conkling of New York was to "give them [freed-people] liberty and rights as the South, and they will stay there and never come into a cold cli-mate [the North] to die."[8] Black rights would ensure not only Republican Party political control of the South, but would also make sure that Southern freedmen would not "swarm" northward in search of those rights denied by the ex-confederates in the South.[9] The fear that the ex-slaves would, in hordes, migrate northward to compete with free White labor was constantly debated as a possibility. For many Radicals, this possibility became a driving force that led them to sup-port justice for the freedpeople in the South as an expedient political choice to prevent a Black exodus northward. The Supreme Court justices interpreted the new Civil Rights legislation within the framework of these political concerns and their own juridical views on federalism. Federalism, as the basis of Constitutional Reconstruction, set limits on revolution in Constitutionalism ushered in by civil war. The case that initially outlined those limits occurred in 1873.

In the *Slaughterhouse* cases of 1873,[10] the Supreme Court began to limit and define what these new rights were in reference to federalism. The cases involved the right of White butchers to exercise their trade in New Orleans' slaughterhouse businesses. In 1869, the Louisiana legislature passed a law regulating slaughterhouses in Orleans, Jefferson, and St. Bernard parishes. The statute aimed at cleaning up the Mississippi River as an environmental hazard because of the excessive and unregulated dumping by butchers. The statute gave a single corporation a monopoly on the slaughterhouse trade. The excluded owners of other slaughterhouses who had been driven out of business by the statute charged that the law curtailed the right of a butcher to make a living, and the right to make a living was a property right in itself. The butchers contended that this right was one of those valuable privileges and immunities guaranteed by the recently adopted Fourteenth Amendment.

In the resulting cases brought before the United States Supreme Court, the Court's decision clarified to the nation what this new Fourteenth Amendment would mean to the social relations of race and class. It did this by reasserting[11] that there were two categories of citizens, "national and state and that the privileges and immunities did not protect rights flowing from state citizenship but only those arising out of national citizenship." National citizenship rights were restricted to such broad categories as right to international travel, right to transact business with the government, protection while residing in foreign lands, and the right to the use of navigable U.S. waters. The Court's decision permitted the regulation of the more fundamental rights (as embodied in the Bill of Rights) to the states, many of which had been redeemed by White supremacists. This decision undermined the intent of at least one of the framers of the amendment. Senator Jacob Howard of Michigan, one of the committee members who framed the amendment, said its aim was to

> forever disable everyone of them [the states] from passing laws trenching on those fundamental rights which pertain to citizens of the United States and to all persons who may happen to be within their jurisdiction. It establishes equality before the law, and it gives to the humblest, the poorest, the most despised of the race the same rights and the same protection before the law as it gives the most powerful, the most wealthy, or the most haughty.[12]

Turning a deaf ear to Howard's observation, Justice Samuel F. Miller, speaking for the majority, emphasized that the Fourteenth Amendment was not intended to change the federal system by bringing Civil Rights under the purview of national citizenship. This was a sort of judicial somersault, because Miller had, in this opinion, agreed that the purpose of the amendment was to protect the ex-slaves themselves. Certainly, redeemer governments would not use the amendment to protect its ex-slave population. It was obvious that Senator Howard's hopes could not be achieved if the federal system was dichotomized in a way that conveyed the protection of the more substantive civil rights to White supremacist state officials. It was also clear that those limited but enumerated national citizenship rights were of little use to a people just a few years removed from the yoke of slavery. It appears that the Court was more concerned with maintaining the balance between state and federal power than with securing the civil rights of its newly incorporated citizenry. The protection of the privilege and immunity clause, progressively interpreted, could have provided the basis for federal prosecution of freedman's civil rights; however, this would not be the case. One historian noted that *Slaughterhouse* severely weakened the clause, and "For all practical purposes the privileges and immunity clause passed into the realm of historical oddities."[13]

The Court kept in step with the Compromise in *U.S. vs. Cruikshank* (1875),[14] a case that demonstrated how formal legal rules would legitimize racial violence and murder. The justices examined the facts surrounding the violent disruption of a political meeting of Louisiana Blacks by William Cruikshank and other White supremacists. An ambivalent President Grant ordered federal troops not to interfere in the local disputes between radical Republicans and a coalition of Democrats and Liberal Republicans over a gubernatorial politics and 1872 outcome in the county seat at Grant Parish, Colfax, Louisiana.[15] When historians attempt to confront the continuity of White terror directed on Black people, they needed to look no further than the Massacre at Colfax.[16] After about 150 Blacks barricaded the county courthouse and it was surrounded by White Leaguers, the courthouse was torched. The leading historian of this incident describes what happened next: "[T]he Whites set fire to the courthouse. Some Blacks were burned alive; others were shot as they ran from the flaming building. The wounded were bayoneted. . . . The prisoners never even reached the jail, for their drunken guards opened fire on them during the nights. Their bodies were mutilated. Abdomens ripped open and brains blown out."[17] Cruikshank and several other companions were arrested and convicted under the Enforcement Act of May 30, 1870, in a federal circuit court in Louisiana.[18] On appeal to the U.S. Supreme Court, the men's convictions were overturned on the grounds that the Enforcement Act itself was not justifiable in that the states were responsible for the protection of their citizens. The justices said, "The Fourteenth Amendment prohibits a state from denying to any person within its jurisdiction the equal protection of its law," but did not prohibit actions of one citizen against another. Clearly, this was legal formalism gone berserk. It left a wide-open field for White power advocates to use violence to maintain their race and class position at the state level. The Court clearly sent a message to freedpeople that when White supremacists, as private citizens, attacked and killed them, they would have to seek protection or redress from the very state authorities who had not stopped the violators in the first place. The justices did not explain what would prompt Southern "Redeemers" and "Ku Klux" politicians to use state power at the behest and in the interests of Black people.

Redeemers in Colfax had addressed the voting and political activity of Blacks in a direct manner. Congress, in passing the Fifteenth Amendment, thought it could empower the freedpeople as potential voters to use the ballot to throw out of office redeemer politicians who revealed their Klan sympathies through state action or inaction when it came to protecting the civil rights of Blacks. The Court was clearly ambivalent about the length to which it would go to firmly protect the ballot for the freedpeople. In *U.S. vs. Reese* (1876),[19] the negative meaning of the Fifteenth Amendment, pointed out by the Supreme Court, was that the amendment did not "confer the right of suffrage upon anyone." The new law, the justices interpreted, only prohibited the states or federal government from denying the franchise to a person because of race, color, or previous condition of servitude. The control of the franchise that is who would get the vote and who would not remained within the power of state authorities. In *Reese*, the Court also declared sections three and four of the Enforcement Act of 1870 unconstitutional, because they gave Congress, in too broad of a fashion, the right to penalize anyone for attempting to deny or denying any person the use of the franchise. Chief Justice Waite said the Congress' right to legislate for state elections was restricted to areas concerning discrimination because of race, color, or previous condition of servitude. This decision revealed how the legal form can change and appear to be progressive whereas its Constitutional interpretation could be so formalistic that the content of the law solidified inequitable social relationships, "Southern style."[20] The formalism of the Fifteenth

Amendment, which prohibits "the United States or . . . any State" from abridging or denying the vote "on account of race, color, or previous condition of servitude,"[21] would be applied in a strict constructionist manner in various cases.

The Court supported federal power over the ballot in *Ex parte Yarbrough.* It upheld, in a formalistic manner, the power of Congress to protect the rights of Blacks voting in federal, but not state, elections. It then turned around and strengthened state "redeemer" power in *James vs. Bowman,*[22] when Justice David Brewer held, in a formalistic manner, that the Fifteenth Amendment did not give Congress the power to legislate against individuals who sought to interfere with voting rights of Blacks in state and local elections. Violence and intimidation in state and local levels would certainly send the message that freedpeople were also not welcome in federal elections. In *Bowman*, Justices William Day and Harlan dissented without opinion. A very formal reading of the Fifteenth Amendment and a strict application of its wording could and did lead to seemingly contradictory decisions. By the 1890s, the redeemed South, following Mississippi's lead, eventually used these and various other decisions to exclude Blacks from the franchise by creating such ingenious restrictive devices as the poll tax, the literacy test, the "grandfather clause," and ultimately the "White primary" law.[23]

The Supreme Court had another opportunity to support the national mood of reunion and reaction in the case of *U.S. v. Harris* (1883).[24] The ruling in this case was that an important provision in the Ku Klux Klan Act of 1871 was unconstitutional. This Act was the Radicals' attempt to use law as an instrument to close the "state action" loophole of the amendments and prohibit "two or more persons" from conspiring "by force, intimidation, or threat . . . to prevent any person from . . . holding any office . . . under the United States."[25] For the Court, that provision, which prohibited a conspiracy by two or more persons to deprive others of their civil rights, did not include the "twenty members of a Tennessee lynch mob" that "seized four Negro prisoners held by a state deputy sheriff and beat them severely, killing one."[26] The justices construed this provision to mean that the Fourteenth Amendment applied only to deprivations by the state, not by individuals or lynch mobs, and that "Congress has no power to enact any law making it a federal crime for private persons to lynch Negroes or otherwise deprive them of their civil rights."[27] Using a strict constructionist approach, the Court said, "The language of the 14th amendment does not leave this subject in doubt." Unless the State is proactive in abridging the life, liberty, or property rights of individuals, then there can be no Constitutional protection.[28] Justice John Marshall Harlan dissented without opinion. The *Harris* case, following the *Cruikshank* case in being so formalistic and ignoring the facts on the ground, left no federal protection for Blacks as they confronted reunion and reaction. The Court could have looked to the intent of the framers of these amendments, as it would do in a later case, and ruled that Congress did have the power to federally protect its United States citizens within the states in which they resided.[29]

In the same 1883 term, the high court ruled unconstitutional, in the *Civil Rights Cases*, several sections of the Civil Rights Act of 1875.[30] The 1875 Act clearly stated in section 1, "That all persons . . . shall be entitled to the full and equal enjoyment of the accommodations, advantages, facilities, and privileges of inns, public conveyance on land or water, theatres, and other places of public amusement." Section 2 of the act permitted federal enforcement of section 1. However, the Court's ruling rejected Congressional intent. The ruling involved five cases as they pertained to sections 1 and 2 of the Act of 1875. A number of persons were indicted under the Act for deny-ing hotel and theater accommodations, as well as equal accommodations in a railroad car, to Blacks because of their race. The hotel accommodation cases stemmed from the acts of discrimi-nation in the states of Kansas and Missouri, the theater denials from San Francisco and New York City, and the railroad denials from Tennessee. Racist hegemony as national culture was clearly demonstrated as only one of these cases had its origin below the "cotton curtain."[31]

The Civil Rights Act of 1875 was framed to protect freedpeople from the invasion of their newly acquired civil rights by acts of private individuals as well as by action of the states. The primary question in the cases was as follows: Could Congress legislate under the Fourteenth Amendment against citizens of respective states, thus contravening the police powers of the states? The Court answered this question by delivering an opinion that stated that Congress was powerless to estab-lish federal regulations controlling the acts of private citizens in the states in which they reside and that Congress could only enforce the amendments' prohibitions against "state action" or the racial actions of state officials. The Court also noted that racial discrimination does not stamp the badge of slavery on freedpeople in violation of the Thirteenth Amendment. In declaring these sec-tions unconstitutional, Justice Bradley's perspective was ahistorical, and thus extremely contra-dictory. On the one hand, he admitted that Congress did have the power, under the Thirteenth Amendment, to legislate against individuals within the states; however, the use of private prop-erty had higher sanctity and judicial protection than the alleged "badges of slavery" purported in this case. In fact, Bradley believed that "It would be running the slavery argument into the ground to make it apply to every act of discrimination which a person may see fit to make as to the guests he will entertain, or . . . take into his coach . . . or admit to his . . . theater."[32] Obviously, Bradley favored the private property rights of home, coach, theater, and so on over the rights of freedpeople. The right of Congress to "enact all necessary and proper laws for the oblit-eration and prevention of slavery with all its badges and incidents," in Bradley's own words, stopped at the doors of the White citizens' property rights. Moreover, Bradley's dictum in these cases revealed how quickly the nation had become tiresome of the divisiveness caused by the Negro Question. Bradley stated irksomely that

> When a man has emerged from slavery, and by the aid of beneficent legislation has
> shaken off the inseparable concomitant of that state, there must be some stage in the
> progress of his elevation when he takes the rank of a mere citizen, and ceases to be the
> special favorite of the laws, and when his rights as a citizen, or a man, are to be pro-
> tected in the ordinary modes by which other men's rights are protected.[33]

Bradley's decision can only be seem as instrumentalist law, clearly and directly supporting the Compromise of 1877 and the agreement to give the South "home rule" so that national peace and entrepreneurial growth would not be hindered by the Negro Question. When one examines Bradley's dissenting opinion in *Slaughterhouse* thirteen years before he heard the civil rights cases, one sees an entirely different type of formalistic thinking taking place. In this case, Bradley's dis-sent revealed a broad interpretation of the powers of Congress under the Fourteenth Amendment to reach discrimination within the States "to prevent the invasion of any clear and undoubted in-dividual rights of the citizen which are secured by the Constitution."[34] One should note that his broad reading of this amendment involved the rights of White butchers and not Black peons or sharecroppers. The politics of race was the fulcrum of Bradley's changed legal thinking between the two cases. This change, according to one legal historian, reflected Bradley's keeping in compliance with his decision, while serving on the special electoral commission of 1877, which gave Rutherford B. Hayes his ticket to the White House. Bradley was part and parcel of the *quid pro quo* that ended Reconstruction, and his legal thinking became a manifestation of his support and involvement. Granting home rule to the South and using law to support planter class domination formed the real basis of Bradley's tortured logic in the 1883 *Civil Rights Cases.*

The rhetoric used against the Act of 1875 reaffirmed that the Court would continue to legitimize reunion and reaction at the expense of the rights of freedpeople. The Court used the philosophical view of conservative federalism to determine that Congress had no power under the Fourteenth Amendment to initiate direct and affirmative legislation that would invade or destroy the police power of the redeemed states. Charles Warren, noted Constitutional historian, commented on the Civil Rights Cases and other redeeming judicial decisions:

> Viewed in historical perspective now [1922], however, there can be no question that the decisions in these cases were most fortunate. They largely eliminated from national politics the Negro question which had so long embittered Congressional debates; they relegated the burden and the duty of protecting the Negro to the States, to whom they properly belonged; and they served to restore confidence in the Southern states.[35]

Warren's view mirrored the hegemonic social consciousness of White dominating social classes and their concomitant intellectual elites of which Charles Warren was first and foremost. The historical writing of the Court during the segregationist era is analyzed today as the "Betrayal of the Negro."[36]

In departure from his social class, Justice John Marshall Harlan dissented in the Civil Rights Cases. Harlan pointed out that both the Fugitive Slave Law of 1793 and that of 1850 imposed penalties against private persons (i.e., persons who gave assistance to runaway slaves). Both laws had been held as Constitutional in *Prigg v. Pennsylvania* and in *Abelman v. Booth.* Harlan reasoned that if laws of Congress could be enacted to protect slave owners and their property against infringements by individual abolitionists, then why were similar laws that secured the civil rights of freedpeople against infringements by White supremacists unconstitutional. In addition, Harlan suggested that the Thirteenth Amendment not only prohibited slavery, but also gave Congress the power to enact laws forbidding the manifestations of slavery in such things as Black Codes and racial discrimination in public accommodations.

A degree of legal autonomy and formalistic reasoning did influence the Court to rule, in a limited fashion, to uphold the rights of Black people to serve on juries in *Strauder v. West Virginia* (1880)[37] and in *Ex parte Virginia* (1880).[38] This minor concession to Black liberty was negated for all practical purposes when the Court ruled in *Virginia v. Rives*[39] that the mere absence of Blacks from a jury did not necessarily mean a denial of the right of jury service. The decision in *Rives* emphasized that the Fourteenth Amendment is not violated if it cannot be proved that Blacks are excluded from jury service on the ground of race when the jury is all White. The burden of proof was placed on the excluded freedpeople even though the historical and contemporary context clearly demonstrated that this badge of slavery, jury exclusion, was maintained to control the freedpeople and prevent them from exerting an instrumental influence on the justice system in their own interests.

These redeeming judicial decisions against the use of federal power on behalf of the freedpeople gave the South the assurance to reassert the hegemony of race throughout its New South institutional state structures. Northern society was essentially tired of the effort to win the peace in the face of continual resistance and gave up on its goal of protecting the freedpeople by recreating the South in the image of the North. In essence, the North was too

> hard at work building railroads, spawning corporations, winning the West, creating great fortunes, welcoming hordes of immigrants from Europe to do the necessary labor—and quite willing to resign the Negro to the tender mercies of the South.[40]

This national entrepreneurial context and Supreme Court decisions coincided, moreover, with a series of Southern political and intellectual developments that accentuated and gave momentum to the restoration of White supremacy in the South. These events are very important to understand because much of the twentieth-century efforts by the NAACP to change racist law rested on how these political and intellectual events created a Jim Crow America. W.E.B. DuBois, a founder of the NAACP, referred to these events in one of his most famous observations, that "the problem of the twentieth century is the problem of the color line."[41]

PART II: POPULISM: RACE FIRST OR CLASS FIRST?

The origins of the color line lay in events that ripped across the South in the last two decades of the nineteenth century. In the 1880s, several Southern *redeemer* (also known as *Conservatives* or *Democrats*) governments were involved in financial scandals, a situation that was even more embarrassing because financial impropriety was one of the main grievances used by the redeemers against the unionist coalition governments of carpetbaggers, scalawags, and Blacks.[42]

Beginning in the 1870s, the agrarian unrest of Black and White farmers, sharecroppers, and tenants caused by widespread economic disparity between the haves and the have-nots frightened the Democratic White supremacist elites. These elites had regained control or "redeemed" their states in the 1870s. The coalition of agrarian populists and Black and White have-nots had its origins in the loss of economic stability for both groups due to a faltering Southern economy. The freedpeople joined the popular agrarian movement to maintained what little gains they had acquired since the ending of slavery or because they saw the coalition as a progressive step upwards from the condition of servitude. The downturn in Southern economy cut across race and class lines. In the post-bellum economy, the "[White] farmer, former masters, . . . along with former slaves and yeomen, had been reduced to a state of peonage to the town merchant."[43]

Peonage, based on the vicious cycle of the lien system not only bound the small farmer to high-price merchant's credit, but also bound the freedpeople who, because of their indebtedness, were in turn coercively bound to the farmers.[44] Debt was the basis for being incarcerated in the condition of peonage. Congress had abolished this condition in the Anti-Peonage Act of 1867, which was legislation passed on the basis of the enforcement powers of the Thirteenth Amendment.

However, law could not address the emotions of race within social class resting at the mudsill of society.[45]

The farmers and the freedpeople were divided by race but exploited by class by the same "financial despotism" of merchant credit. With cotton dropping from thirty-one cents a pound in 1866 to nine cents in 1886 and to six cents in 1893, the lien system assured the ascendancy of the "financial aristocracy" of the new conservative social class composed of merchants, bankers, and large landowners. This new social class came to be known in history as the *Bourbon Democrats*.[46] The Bourbons were more apt than regular Democrats to use the race card to aid in the redemption of their state governments from the Republican radicals. As Nathaniel B. Meade of Virginia clearly stated, "To save the state we must make the issue of White and Black race against race and the canvass red hot—the position must be made so odious that no decent White man can support the radical ticket and look a gentleman in the face."[47]

The political response to this aristocracy was the rise of the White agrarian Southern Alliance under the leadership of Georgia's Tom Watson and, in Texas, with Black labor leaders organizing under the banner of the Colored Farmers' National Alliance. The coalition between these groups was the grand attempt to place class first and therefore bury the divisive concept of race and unite along lines of common economic interests. Class consciousness versus race consciousness would make this social movement unique in the history of the South and nation at large.[48]

With over a million members[49] in the Colored Alliance alone, the cooperation with the Southern Alliance presented a formidable foe to the Bourbon Democrats. After several conventions in which a joint platform of common interests was mapped out, a third-party movement was initiated and was named the People's Party. At the Cincinnati meeting of 1891, the convention overwhelmingly defeated a proposal to segregate the Colored Alliance delegates. Organizations as diverse as the Knights of Labor and the Union Labor Party attended the convention, and Terence W. Powderly, head of the Knights, spoke to the delegates urging "justice and equal rights for negro and White."

This equalitarian, anti-racist rhetoric was reflected in the early speeches of the foremost leader of the agrarian revolt, Tom Watson. Watson, being the People Party's first Congressman-elect, sought to appeal to the class consciousness of both races for solidarity by downplaying the race card and explaining it as a tool of "Boss Rule and Monied Elites" that exploited both racial groups. Watson pleaded

> You are kept apart that you may be separately fleeced of your earnings. You are made to hate each other—you are deceived and blinded—race antagonism perpetuates a monetary system which [makes] beggars of [you] both.[50]

Black agrarians of all sorts responded with enthusiasm to this appeal for the solidarity of the exploited class. Uncountable numbers of Black Populists were murdered by conservative interests while attempting to organize for the Alliances throughout the South. Black blood and toil for the Populist cause rested on certain *quid pro quos* that Blacks hoped would be assured to them by the Southern Alliance, basically to reform the election laws, the convict lease system, and the schools.[51] Constitutional issues evolved out of all three areas of assurances. Unfortunately, it was these essential issues that eventually split the coalition along the lines of racism, a split supported by Constitutional case law.[52] Class solidarity battled racism during this period, but ultimately failed in the face of *de facto* traditionalism and *de jure* hegemonic Constitutionalism.[53]

The assurances that split the agrarian revolt were hotly contested. Blacks wanted the implementation of the Australian ballot (secret voting procedures), but this assurance was met with mixed emotions. It was a double-edge sword. It could help prevent the fraudulent electoral tactics of the Democrats, but Democrats still employed literacy requirements to seriously dilute the Alliances' voting strength. Some Populists rejected the Australian ballot and warned that this type of ballot played into the hands of "educated or bourgeois nigras" to the detriment of "po' Whites." Not being able to formulate specific election reforms that would have drawn the large Black vote to their cause, the White Populists played into the hands of the Democrats, who continually used literacy requirements and coercion to control Black voters, which led to the defeat of various White Populists who ran for state political office. In the wake of these defeats, racial bitterness and accusations of blame were heard within the Populists' fragile coalition.[54]

The convict lease system was a coercive legal system by which thousands of Black workers were given lengthy jail sentences for trivial offenses and then hired out to industrialists for their mining, lumbering, or railroad projects. The use of law as an instrument of class domination is clearly seen in the convict lease system, and the high court provided Constitutional permission for such laws.[55] Southern industrialists saved hundreds of thousands of dollars in wages by using this exploitive forced labor system. With the death rate in several Southern states' lease systems running at more than twenty percent,[56] one can readily understand why the Colored Alliances insisted on a change in Southern penal corrections. Southern Alliance platforms in general condemned this system of forced labor, but Tennessee (White) Populists opposed any changes at all and attacked the Conservatives for allocating money for a new state penitentiary.[57] The system of convict lease did not change, and it remained one of the major grievances of Black agrarians.

Concerning the education issue, Tom Watson supported equal funding for segregated schools. This was a major paradox within the Southern Alliance. White agrarians could bring themselves to use the Black ballot by enticing the freedman with the plum of legal equality but refuse to budge on the *status quo* of social inequality and the segregation of the races. The specter of social equality brought home to the White Populists that close cooperation with Black agrarians would have to be achieved at arm's length. This contradiction between economic interests versus racial etiquette would doom or negate the Alliance's opportunity to reach common goals based on common class interests.

The racist contradictions within the interracial agrarian alliance proved to be too substantive to overcome. White bitterness and their blaming of the Blacks for the repeated failures to attain the coalition's political goals resulted in and increased race-based murder, many via the method of lynching. Even in Populist-controlled areas, at the height of the agrarian revolt, one could witness such politically motivated violence. Between 1889 and 1894, more than 300 Blacks were lynched in five Southern states alone.[58] In Texas, the Populist nominee for governor refused to come out strongly for anti-lynching measures, whereas his White Democratic opponent did. Lynching in this coalition period would be a harbinger of and a prelude to the explosion of lynching that occurred during the last decade of the nineteenth century that continued, abated at times, throughout the first four decades of the twentieth century.[59]

The failure of Southern Populism attests to the retentive and hegemonic values of White racism. In the end, White racism forced both the Southern Alliance and Democrats to admit that because of their common genotype of color, they had more in common with each other than the genotype of the Blacks. Both the Bourbon Democrats and the Tom Watson–led Populists wanted the Black vote to serve their interests. However, the autonomy of racial ideology subsumed class divisions within the White South as a whole. As one historian correctly noted, for the Southern Alliance to "advo[cate] . . . social equality would have been political suicide; it was also contrary to beliefs the Populists held in common with other White Southerners."[60]

The convergence of White Populism and redeemer reaction rested not only on race, but class as well. C. Vann Woodward notes that the Populist ideology "was that of the landowners, and at that time the landowning farmers about equaled the landless farmers. On the other hand, the great majority of Negro farmers owned no land."[61] The interests of those who owned land were stronger than the ideology of interracialism. This class contradiction and subsequent antagonism appeared when the Colored Alliance proposed to call a general strike of cotton pickers in 1891. The Southern Alliance opposed it vehemently. They, the landed White farmers, refused to pay the higher wages asked by the potential strikers. Even though the strike happened, it clearly exposed the intense class divisions, contoured by race, within the agrarians' ranks. The second agrarian note of discord occurred when the Colored Alliance endorsed the Lodge Force Bill of 1890. This Congressional legislation sought to protect the registration of Black voters and secure better ed-ucational facilities for them. This force bill would be the Radicals' last attempt to use law as a weapon in the interests of the freedpeople.[62] The Southern Alliance declared its opposition to the Lodge Bill and one political observer stated, "The White men of Mississippi . . . must stand to-gether."[63]

This manipulative use of the Black ballot disrupted Southern politics for decades. In Mississippi the Populists failed to include a single Black on their ticket, nor did they advocate the franchise for them.[64] Virginia Populists instituted separate Black clubs and also failed to "include political equality for the Negro" in their platform.[65] In North Carolina, the Populists' platform of 1900 "affirmed the basic fact [that] the Populist party in North Carolina was a White man's party and proposed the elimination of Negro office-holding by amending the state constitution."[66]

After the Populists failed to win in the national and state elections in both 1892 and 1896, Tom Watson echoed the general sentiments of White agrarians: "Financially I was flat on my back. How near I came to loss of mind only God who made me knows. . . . If ever a poor devil had been . . . vilified . . . mobbed . . . and hooted . . ., I was he."[67] The Southern Alliance had gained very little in its battles against the Democrats. Not willing to divest themselves of their racialism and eager to use tactics of political fraud and anti-Black violence, which the Democrats knew artfully well, the White agrarians still lost election after election. Bitterly disappointed, White Populists looked for a scapegoat to blame and thus explain why they had failed. The freedpeople became that scapegoat.[68]

The coup de grace of race–class fusion politics came in 1906 when Hoke Smith, conservative Democrat, appealed to Tom Watson for political support. The ex-Populist and landed gentry (by then he had rebounded financially and was worth more than a quarter of a million dollars) agreed to support Smith's liberal platform. However, Smith's platform called for big business regulation and with a final ironic twist promised "the elimination of the Negro from Politics . . . By legal and Constitutional Methods . . . without Disfranchising a single White man."[69] The old Populist insistence on the Australian ballot was buried by the closed ranks of Bourbon liberalism and Southern racialism.

Engineering the threat of *Africanization* (i.e., Black political and cultural control of the South through their newly acquired civil rights) and giving the solution to the threat as one of Whites' closing their inter-class ranks. This new Democrats' credo was conveyed by numerous individuals such as James K. Vardaman, who became governor of Mississippi by screaming such epithets as, "We would be justified in slaughtering every Ethiop on Earth to preserve unsullied the honor of one Caucasian home."[70] On another occasion, he thundered

> I am opposed to Negro voting; . . . I am just as much opposed to Booker Washington as a voter, with all his Anglo-Saxon reinforcements, as I am to the cocoanut-headed, chocolate-colored typical little coon, Andy Dotson, who Blacks my shoes every morning. Neither is fit to perform the supreme function of citizenship.

South Carolina's Ben Tillman cried, "Governor as I am I'd lead a mob to lynch a man—Black man—who had ravished a White woman . . . I justify lynching for rape and before Almighty God, I'm not ashamed of it."[71] Tom Watson's support of Hoke Smith was verbally stated when he said that he

> was equally certain that the Negro had no comprehension of virtue, honesty, truth, gratitude and principle . . . and the South was forced to lynch him occasionally, and flog him, now and then, to keep him from blaspheming the Almighty by his conduct, on account of his smell and color.[72]

The Democrats and their philosophy of White supremacy and Negro-phobia had gained ascendancy not only in the South, but in the North as well in the final decade of the nineteenth century. Racism, as a dominant hegemonic expression of the social relationship of Black exploitation and White profits, maintained and solidified itself in the political economy of industrial capitalism.[73]

The Northern liberals, seeing the Black race as the symbol of sectional strife and not wanting to upset the "spirit of 1877," joined the parade of reaction with supportive help from such all-American newspapers and magazines as *The Nation, Chicago Tribune, North American, Harpers' Weekly,* the *North American Review,* and *Atlantic Monthly,* among many others. These publications carried the same racist stereotypes of White supremacy regarding Blacks. Both *Harpers'* and *Century,* highly respected Northern literary magazines, gave credence to Joel Chandler Harris' caricature of Blacks when they published rave reviews of his works. Harris' interpretation and characterizations of Blacks embodied in his infamous Uncle Remus tales verified the White supremacy credo when Harris placed words like these in Uncle Remus' mouth:

> Hit's [education is] de ruiashun er dis country . . . Put a spelling'-book in a nigger's hans en right den en dar' you loozes a plowhand . . . What's a nigger gwineter 'larn outen books? Ikin take a bar'l stave an' fling mo' sense inter a nigger in one Midgin...Wid ine bar'l stave I kin fa'rly lif' do vail or ignunce.[74]

Meanwhile the *Atlantic,* in March 1878, gave editorial approval of Hayes' troop withdrawals from the South and regretted that the troops had not been withdrawn sooner, while the *North American*

Review conducted a symposium in March 1879, the topic being, "Ought the Negro to be Disenfranchised? Ought He to Have Been Enfranchised?" The discussion wavered regarding both questions. When it came to publishing articles on the new pseudo-scientific theories regarding Black inferiority, such as Social Darwinism, the *North American Review* surpassed all others. In 1877, the *Review* published an article by Charles Gayarre, a well-known Louisiana writer, stating the following:

> If contrary to the teachings of history and science, the Negro should rise to an equality of intelligence and energy with the Caucasian, there would be a final struggle between the two races from which the Caucasian would emerge victorious.[75]

Pseudo-scientific theories also encompassed institutional racism when, in 1896, the American Economic Association published Frederick L. Hoffman's *Race Traits and Tendencies of the American Negro*. Hoffman attempted to correlate the supposedly high incidence of tuberculosis, syphilis, gonorrhea, and scrofula with his fallacious theory that these diseases and others among Blacks would lead to their extinction as a race. Rejecting the argument that better living conditions would improve the health of Blacks, Hoffman stated

> "the root of evil" was the "immense amount of immorality, which is a race trait." "It is not in *the condition of life*" that we should look for reasons for the poor health record of Negroes, but in the *race traits and tendencies* that we find the causes of excessive mortality. So long as these tendencies are persisted in, so long as immorality and vice are a habit of life of the vast majority of the colored population, the effect will be to increase the mortality by hereditary transmission of weak constitutions, and to lower still further the rate of natural increase, until the births fall below the deaths, and gradual extinction results.[76]

John Hope Franklin, the late historian, stated that these pseudo-scientific theories were important because they continued an earlier pre-Civil War racial consciousness. These late-nineteenth century views were reminiscent of the pro-slavery thoughts of the Old South apologists like Bledsoe, Cartwright, and Elliot.[77] Black economic subjugation and racial rationalization were the dominant themes that contoured the history of the South.

Going along with what he thought to be the inevitable restoration of White supremacy, Booker T. Washington, the leading Black spokesperson, bowed to these political and intellectual developments by accommodating philosophically and institutionally to these national and local trends. In 1895, Washington's position was conveyed in his infamous Atlanta Exposition speech. Hoping that he could allay the Negro-phobia of White folk concerning the right of Blacks to vote and have access to equal public facilities, Mr. Washington, "feeling like a man on his way to the gallows," said,

> the wisest among my race understand that agitation of questions of social equality is the extremist folly. . . . In all things that are purely social we can be as separate as the fingers, yet one as the hand in all things essential to mutual progress.[78]

Southern reaction and redemption and the African-American response to these developments coincided with the Supreme Court decisions curtailing Black civil rights at the close of the nineteenth century. Law reflected the reestablishment of the social and political conditions of Black labor's exploitation. The law adjusted the legal superstructure to maintain a consistent symmetry with the rise of industrial capitalism and Jim Crow America. The issues in the Populist coalition—criminal justice, equity in education, economic stability, and political power—were major Constitutional issues of the twentieth-century struggle for freedom for African Americans. The retreat from a reconstructed South based on a racial legal formalism to one based on blatant lynch law involved the submission to race first by Democrats, Populists, and federal authorities. The social relationships of America's Whiteness[79] involved the dialectics of race and class struggle between the freedpeople and opponents of their freedom struggle. Law became an instrument and an ideological tool used by authorities at the state and national level to legitimize the Compromise of 1877. One Supreme Court case in particular that embraced the instrumentalism of this period and became the high mark of this tragic history of Reconstruction and reaction within the South and the nation at large was the case known as *Plessy v. Ferguson*.

ENDNOTES

1. Maureen Cain and Alan Hunt, eds., *Marx and Engels on Law* (London: Academic Press, 1979), 122–123.
2. *Santa Clara County v. Southern Pacific Railroad Co.*, 118 U.S. (1886); *U.S. v. E.C. Knight Co.*, 156 U.S. 1 (1895); see Arnold Paul, *Conservative Crisis and the Rule of Law* (Ithaca, New York: Cornell University Press, 1960)
3. Fred Israel and Leon Friedman, eds., *The Justices*, vol. 2; Justice Field's dissent in *Munn v. Illinois* (1877) was soon accepted constitutional interpretation. Field's dissent stated, "I deny the power of any legislature under our government to fix the price one shall receive for his property of any kind." See quote in Robert G. McCloskey, *American Conservatism in the Age of Enterprise* (New York: Harper Row, 1951), 114.
4. See activities of Chase Court in Leonard Levy, ed., *American Constitutional History* (New York: Collier MacMillan, 1986); note essay by William Wiecek, "Chase Court, 1864–1873"
5. See David E. Bernstein, "Roots of the 'Underclass': The Decline of Laissez-Faire Jurisprudence and the Rise of Racist Labor Legislation," *American University Law Review*, 43 (Fall 1993); Harold Baron, *Demand for Black Labor: Historical Notes on the Political Economy of Racism, Radical America*, 5, No.2 (March–April 1971), 435–462; Clarence Munford, *Production Relations, Class and Black Liberation: A Marxist Perspective in Afro-American Studies* (Amsterdam: B.R. Gruner Publishing, 1978).
6. Loren Miller, *The Petitioners: The Story of the Supreme Court of the United States and the Negro* (New York: Pantheon Books, 1966) 101.
7. See C. Vann Woodward, *The Origins of the New South, 1877–1913* (Baton Rouge: Louisiana State University Press, 1951).
8. Roscoe Conklin, *The State of the Union–House of Representatives*, January 30, 1861. See also Conkling quoted in C. Vann Woodward, "Seeds of Failure in Radical Race Policy," *Proceedings of the American Philosophical Society*, 10, 1 (February 18, 1966), 1–9.
9. See V. Jacquie Voegeli, "A Rejected Alternative: Union Policy and the Relocation of Southern 'Contraband' at the Dawn of Emancipation," *Journal of Southern History,* 69 (2003). Professor Voegeli studies anti-Black Northern attitudes by examining a little known effort to relocate Virginia freedpeople to Massachusetts.
10. See Woodward's essay, "Seeds of Failure in Radical Race Policy."
11. *Slaughterhouse Cases*, 16 Wall 36 (1873)
12. Miller, 103–104.
13. Eugene Gressman, "Postwar Revolution in Civil Rights and Judicial Counter-Revolution," in Arnold Paul, ed., *Black Americans and the Supreme Court Since Emancipation: The Betrayal or Protection?* (New York: Holt, Rinehart & Winston, 1972), 17.
14. *United Sates v. Cruikshank*, 92 U.S. 542 (1876)

15. See excellent outline of these events in LeeAnna Keith, *The Colfax Massacre: The Untold Story of Black Power, White Terror, and the Death of Reconstruction* (New York: Oxford University Press, 2008).

16. See Charles Lane, *The Day Freedom Died: The Colfax Massacre, the Supreme Court, and the Betrayal of Reconstruction* (New York: Henry Holt and Company, 2008).

17. William Gillette, *Retreat from Reconstruction, 1869–1879* (Baton Rouge: Louisiana State University Press, 1979), 115.

18. Donald G. Nieman, *Promises to Keep: African-Americans and the Constitutional Order, 1776 to the Present* (New York: Oxford University Press, 1991) 95.

19. *United States v. Reese*, 92 U.S. 214 (1876).

20. For a humorous examination of "Southern style," see Bertram Wyatt-Brown's "Community, Class, and Snopesian Crime: Local Justice in the Old South" in Orville Vernon Burton and Robert C. McMath, *Class, Conflict, and Consensus: Antebellum Southern Community Studies* (Westport: Greenwood Press, 1982).

21. Fifteenth Amendment, *United States Constitution*.

22. *James v. Bowman*, 190 U.S. 127 (1903).

23. Albert Kirwan, *Revolt of the Rednecks: Mississippi Politics, 1876–1925* (New York: Harper and Sons, 1951), 68. Excellent examination of the Redeemers' efforts to use such devices to eliminate the Black vote.

24. *United States v. Harris*, 106 U.S. 692 (1883).

25. Richard Bardolph, ed., *The Civil Rights Record: Black Americans and the Law: 1849–1970* (New York: Thomas Y. Crowell Company, 1970), 52.

26. Bardolph, 67.

27. Bardolph, 67.

28. Bardolph, 67.

29. *Yick Wo v. Hopkins*, 118 U.S. 356 (1886). Case involved the city of San Francisco discriminating against its citizens of Chinese ancestry. Even though the discriminatory law was "fair on its face," the Court examined the intent by looking at how the law was applied in a discriminatory manner.

30. *Civil Rights Act of 1875*, U.S. Statute at Large, XVIII, March 1, 1875.

31. Loren Miller, *The Petitioners: The Story of the. Supreme Court and the Negro* (New York: Pantheon Books, 1966), 137.

32. *Civil Rights Cases*, 109 U.S. 3 (1883) at 25.

33. See citation 32 or see Derrick A. Bell, Jr., *Race, Racism, and American Law* (New York: Little, Brown and Company, 1973), 200.

34. Bell, 202.

35. Charles Warren, *The Supreme Court in United States History* (Boston: Little, Brown and Company, 1922), vol. 2, 608. See also Rayford W. Logan, *The Betrayal of the Negro: From Rutherford B. Hayes to Woodrow Wilson* (London: Collier-Macmillan, Ltd., 1954), 117.

36. Logan, Chapter 6, "The Supreme Court and the Negro."

37. *Strauder v. West Virginia*, 100 U.S. 303 (1880).

38. *Ex parte Virginia*, 100 U.S. 339 (188).

39. *Virginia v. Rives* 100 U.S. 545 (1880).

40. Miller, *The Petitioners*, 114.

41. W.E.B. DuBois, *The Souls of Black Folk* (Chicago: A.C. McClurg and Co., 1909) vii; see also John Hope Franklin, *The Color Line: Legacy for the 21st Century* (Columbia: University of Missouri Press, 1993).

42. John Hope Franklin, *Reconstruction: After the Civil War* (Chicago: The University of Chicago Press, 1961), 226.

43. C. Vann Woodward, *Tom Watson: Agrarian Rebel* (New York: Macmillan Company, 1938), 129.

44. Best study on peonage during this period is Pete Daniel, *The Shadow of Slavery: Peonage in the South, 1901–1969* (New York: Oxford University Press, 1973).

45. "Mudsills and the Bottom Rails," is Chapter 7 in C. Vann Woodward, *The Origins of the New South, 1877–1913* (Baton Rouge: Louisiana State University Press, 1951) .

46. Peter Camjo, *Racism, Revolution, Reaction, 1861–1877: The Rise and Fall of Radical Reconstruction* (New York: Monad Press, 1976), 188, 233, 241.

47. Nathaniel B. Meade quoted in Michael Perman, *The Road to Redemption: Southern Politics, 1869–1879* (Chapel Hill: University of North Carolina Press, 1984), 155.

48. Camejo, 66–67; see also Woodward, *Tom Watson*; see also endnote 49 by Jack Abramowitz.

49. See Jack Abramowitz, "The Negro in the Agrarian Revolt," *Agricultural History,*—24, No. 2 (April 1950), 89–95.; John Hicks, *The Populist Revolt* (Lincoln: University of Nebraska Press, 1961).

50. C. Vann Woodward, "Tom Watson and the Negro in Agrarian Politics," *The Journal of Southern History*, 4 (February 1938) 18.

51. Robert Saunders, "Southern Populists and the Negro: 1893–1895," *Journal of Negro History*, 54 (1969) 242.

52. See Logan, "The Supreme Court and the Negro," 105–124.

53. See J. Morgan Kousser, *The Shaping of Southern Politics: Suffrage Restriction and the Establishment of the One-Party South, 1880–1910.* (New Haven: Yale University Press, 1977).

54. Saunders, 246.

55. See Logan, "The Supreme Court and the Negro," 105–124.

56. Paul Worthman and James R. Green, "Black Workers in the New South, 1865–1915" in Nathan Huggins, Martin Kilson, and Daniel M. Fox, *Key Issues in the Afro-American Experience*, vol. II (New York: Harcourt Brace Jovanovich, Inc., 1971), 49.

57. Saunders, 243.

58. Fremise A. Logan, *The Negro in North Carolina, 1876–1894* (Chapel Hill: University of North Carolina Press, 1964) 186.

59. See Ida B. Well, *Red Record*, reproduced in *Southern Horrors and Other Writings: The Anti-Lynching Campaign of Ida B. Wells, 1892–1900* (Boston: Bedford Books, 1997).

60. Saunders, 246.

61. Woodward, "Tom Watson and the Negro in Agrarian Politics," 23.

62. Peter Camejo, *Racism, Revolution, Reaction, 1861–1877: The Rise and Fall of Radical Reconstruction* (New York: Monad Press, 1976), 186.

63. Albert D. Kirwan, *Revolt of the Rednecks: Mississippi Politics, 1876–1925* (Gloucester, Massachesetts: Peter Smith, 1964), 115.

64. Kirwan, 66–68.

65. Charles Wynes, *Race Relations in Virginia, 1870–1902* (Charlottesville: University of Virginia Press, 1951), 48.

66. Helen Edmunds, *The Negro in Fusion Politics in North Carolina, 1894–1901* (Chapel Hill: University of North Carolina Press, 1951), 199.

67. Woodward, 25.

68. Woodward, 25.

69. Woodward, 27.

70. Bardolph, 101.

71. Bardolph, 101.

72. Bardolph, 101.

73. See excellent study by Mel Leiman, *Political Economy of Racism* (London: Pluto Press, 1993).

74. Logan, *Betrayal of the Negro*, 168.

75. Rayford Logan, 269.

76. Thomas F. Gossett, *Race: The History of an Idea in America* (Dallas: Southern Methodist University Press, 1963), 281–282.

77. John Hope Franklin, "History of Racial Segregation in the United States," *Annals of American Academy*, 304 (March 1956),

78. Gossett, 276.

CHAPTER 6

Plessy v. Ferguson: Anatomy of Legal Hegemony

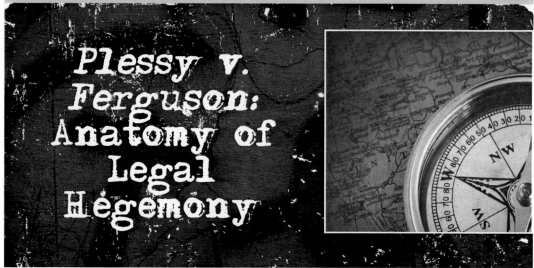

In a modern state, law must not only correspond to the general economic condition and be its expression, but must also be an internally coherent expression, which does not, owing to internal conflicts, contradict itself. . . . All the more so the rarely it happens that a code of law is the blunt, unmitigated, unadulterated expression of the domination of a class.[1]

—FREDERICK ENGELS, "LETTERS TO SCHMIDT," 1890

Understanding the triumphs of *laissez-faire* capitalism and racist ideologies within the Supreme Court and the nation at the close of the nineteenth century, one tends to view the Court's decisions validating these triumphs as reaching a high point in the case of *Plessy v. Ferguson* in 1896. In the *Plessy* decision, the Supreme Court adopted the now infamous "separate but equal" doctrine.[2] Looking at the Court's prior decisions, one can see how they, especially in the *Civil Rights Cases* of 1883, set up the Constitutional logic for the *Plessy* decision and how the outcome, that of Jim Crow, had a sense of inevitability.

In view of the highly politically and economically charged atmosphere that was the social context in which the Supreme Court handed down this decision, one can see that the justices had to develop a case logic that appeared to abide by the old, idealistic judicial concept of *judicial neutrality* based on the "static" Constitution or the idea of the "received law." Two noted Constitutional historians, Arthur S. Miller and Ronald F. Howell, refer to this antiquated concept as the *myth of judicial neutrality*.[3] The myth refers to the often violated idea that judges could reach decisions not in accordance with who the litigants were or the nature or consequences of the results that might come from the decision, but in accordance with known or ascertainable objective standards derived from the Constitution. These standards were neutral because they have an existence independent of the litigants. Miller and Howell suggest that the idea of judicial neutrality has never been a fact, because these standards are socially constructed along the lines of human-made self-interest. The possibility of any type of judicial neutrality was negated with the inclusion of racist pro-slavery clauses in the Constitution, and when the political forces of Civil War rejected these clauses, the Court used law as an instrument to breathe new life into a racially based post-Civil War Constitution.

The Constitutional standards of the Civil War amendments and enforcing legislation had been, prior to *Plessy*, defined in such a racial subjectivity that any litigants or issues involved in subsequent legal contestations could not be clothed in a protected judicial neutrality. The separate but equal doctrine was an attempt by the Court to create an ideological form that would mold mass consciousness and, in the process, legitimize the material interests of a dominant racial caste while obscuring the substantive inequality of the social relationships of Jim Crow.

In *Plessy v. Ferguson*, and other redeeming decisions, judicial biases are glaring, and any sense of neutrality or objectivity is nonexistent. The social and political values of capitalist interests and New South interests became the obvious momentum of judicial activism. Miller and Howell stated that "choices among values are unavoidable in that these choices are motivated by the entire biography and heredity of the individual making them."[4] The various Supreme Court decisions consistent with the Compromise of 1877 demonstrate that the capitalistic and racialist ideologies[5] embedded in the American cultural formation influenced the justices decisively. Living in such a hegemonic formation, the justices made static judicial principles mutable or congruent with the political economy of Jim Crow. These decisions made progressive legislation such as the Thirteenth, Fourteenth, and Fifteenth Amendments paper shields in face of the onslaught of Klan terror.

The lone dissenter on the Court in these decisions, beginning with *U.S. v. Harris* (1883),[6] was John Marshall Harlan. Harlan was a Kentucky-Unionist, an ex-slaveholder, a one-time Union Army officer, and an initial enemy of the Thirteenth Amendment. He was transformed into a Republican by 1868, the year in which he campaigned with the Republicans for the election of General Ulysses S. Grant.

The elements that gave rise to Harlan's transformation involved Harlan's war-time experiences in which he commanded first-generation southern European immigrants who helped him reject his "Know Nothing" suspicions of Catholics and immigrants. He was also repulsed by the wave of lynchings and other brutalities that Kentucky redeemers used against the ex-slaves.[7] Reviewing his racialism in the post-war era, Harlan withstood self-directed personal invectives and attempted the long and lonely process of embracing a more positive view of humankind. Harlan was unsuccessful in his bid for the governorship in 1871 on the Republican ticket and later threw in his political hat with Rutherford B. Hayes in 1876. When Justice Davis resigned from the Supreme Court in the spring of 1877, President Hayes decided to appoint a Southerner to the position, and Harlan was the natural choice.[8]

Harlan supported the rights of the freedpeople in all but two cases. In the first, *Pace v. Alabama* (1882),[9] Harlan joined a unanimous Court in holding that it was not a violation of equal protection for a state to punish adultery or fornication between Whites and Blacks more severely than the same crime committed between two Whites, so long as the more severe penalty applied equally to both the White and Black offender. In the second, *Cummings v. Board of Education* (1889),[10] Harlan, speaking for a unanimous Court, declared that a Georgia school board could close down, "for economic reasons," a public high school for Blacks while financially maintaining the White high school. Justice Harlan "admit[ed] that the benefits and burdens of public taxation must be shared by citizens without discrimination against any class on account of their race," unless there was a clear and unmistakable mismanagement of such schools in regards to racial discrimination.[11] For Harlan, if discrimination could be proved, then educational management of such facilities belonged under the purview of state police power. The question Harlan refused to face was whether the state of Georgia, when given a choice with a budget shortfall, would ever permit a Black school to stay open while closing a White school. In *Pace*, the sexual taboo of "Black on top of White" was obviously too deeply felt for Harlan to stretch into that forbidden area.

Even with these two exceptions, Harlan's other dissents represented the only consistent protestations against the legal devolution of the Constitutional rights recently passed by Congress in the interests of the freedpeople. However, even the supportive dissents cannot be viewed as completely color-blind in regard to the freedpeople. Alan Westin's research indicates that even Harlan's *Plessy* dissent, with its immortal statement that the Constitution is blind to color, also asserted that the White race was "the most dominant race in this country,"[12] and he thought it would continue to be so. Harlan expounded that assertion with pride, as being a natural product of heredity, legal tradition, and justice.

However, Harlan's dissent in *Plessy*, which concerned a Louisiana statute requiring racial segregation on railroadeet cars, rang with a high moral and equalitarian tone as compared to the majority verbiage. The response of the Black community in New Orleans, which had a well-established petit-bourgeois class and a high degree of literacy, set the philosophical tone for the twentieth-century fight against Jim Crow.

This highly educated Black community had fought against a segregated streetcar system in New Orleans in 1860 and achieved success with the aid of "reunion" in the late 1890s.[13] In 1890, another proposed Jim Crow railroad car bill appeared in the Louisiana legislature, and Blacks in New Orleans organized to defeat the bill. The franchise was still held by many Blacks in the city; consequently, there were sixteen Black senators and representatives in the Louisiana General Assembly. The pro-Jim Crow sponsors of the bill had wide local White support. For example, the New Orleans *Daily Picayune* noted, "an almost unanimous demand on the part of the White people of the state for the enactment of such a law."[14]

Opposition to the bill came from an interracial coalition who delivered a plea to the legislature entitled "Protest of the American Citizens." This letter of protest was sent to the legislature by the American Citizens' Equal Rights Association of Louisiana Against Class Legislation. Louis A. Martinet, a member and one of the founders of the Association, was probably the leading spirit of defiance against the Jim Crow bill. Martinet participated in the early 1880s in the Democratic Party, but was soon driven back to the Republican fold by the relentless racialism of the Bourbon Party, and in 1889 began editing the outspoken weekly newspaper the *New Orleans Crusader*.[15]

A coalition of the Black caucus and the railroad corporations formed to try to defeat the bill. The railroad corporations supported the Black caucus because they did not want to deal with the bother and cost of a system of enforced segregation. Adding hundreds of segregated coaches would be a costly operation. Their money interests superseded their race interests on this specific issue. With this coalition, the Jim Crow bill was temporarily defeated, but two days later it passed because of the naive tactics of the Black legislators who agreed to help override a gubernatorial veto of the state lottery bill in return for the assurance that the segregation statute would be defeated.[16] However, with the lottery bill passed, the majority Democrats reconsidered the Jim Crow statute and passed it.

Martinet and a close associate of his, R.I. Desdunes, who was also a member of the Equal Rights Association, both blamed the passage on the naïveté of the Black legislators. Martinet's *Crusader* newspaper rang with the words:

> The bill is now a law. The next thing is what are we going to do? The next thing . . . is to begin to gather funds to test the Constitutionality of this law. We'll make a case, a test case, and bring it before the Federal Courts.[17]

Martinet and Desdunes, along with sixteen other men, formed a "Citizens' Committee to Test the Constitutionality of the Separate Car Law" on September 1, 1891. By October 11, after collecting sufficient funds, the Citizens' Committee turned to Albion Winegar Tourgee, famed ex-carpetbagger, radical Republican judge of North Carolina, and now an ardent champion of civil rights for Black people, for legal aid. Tourgee accepted without remuneration the Committee test case. Tourgee also used "his weekly editorial column in the Chicago *Inter Ocean*" to "begin directing national attention and support to the project."[18]

Tourgee promptly announced that a "nearly White" person should be chosen for the defendant in the test case. After some doubts by Martinet on the difficulty of a too nearly White person being refused admission to a White car, Martinet pointed out that Blacks of fair complexion have a "large degree of immunity" from racism. However, Martinet was also concerned about "accusations from darker Negroes that those involved in the test project were all nearly White or wanted to pass for White."[19] Nevertheless, Tourgee's suggestion won the day, and on February 24, 1892, twenty-one year old, fair-complexioned Daniel F. Desdunes, son of Martinet's close associate R.I. Desdunes, purchased a ticket on the Louisville and Nashville Railroad for a destination outside the state. Young Desdunes seated himself in the White passenger coach and, on his refusal to comply with the conductor's order that he move into the appropriate Negro coach, was arrested by three policemen.

James C. Walker, a White Republican lawyer and Tourgee's associate, was retained to handle the local litigation. However, the Desdunes case came to an abrupt end when the State Supreme Court, in *State ex rel. Abbott v. Hicks*,[20] reversed the ruling of a lower court and upheld the Pullman Company's pleas that the Jim Crow law was unconstitutional insofar as it applied to interstate passengers. Martinet greeted the decision with high hopes in his *Crusader*: "The Jim Crow car is ditched and will remain in the ditch. Reactionists may foam at the mouth, and Bourbon organs may squirm, but Jim Crow is dead as a door nail."[21] However, Desdunes' attorneys, Tourgee and Walker, were well aware that the decision was limited and that a new test case must involve an intrastate decision on the Jim Crow law to make the victory complete.

Within two weeks, Homer Adolph Plessy, defined by the state's racialist law as seven-eighths Caucasian and one-eighth Negroid, boarded the East Louisiana Railroad bound for Covington, Louisiana, and took a seat in the White coach. Stating that he was indeed a Black man when asked by the conductor, Homer Plessy was promptly arrested by Detective Chris C. Cain for violating the Jim Crow law. It is quite possible that the conductor and Cain were tipped off by Tourgee and Walker to make sure that the light-skinned Plessy would be recognized correctly.

Tourgee and Walker then entered a plea before Judge John H. Ferguson of the Criminal Court of the Parish of New Orleans. They charged that the Jim Crow law that Homer Plessy was accused of violating was null and void because it established

> an insidious distinction and discrimination between citizens of the United States based on race which is obnoxious to the fundamental principles of National Citizenship, perpetuates involuntary servitude as regards Citizens of the Colored Race under the merest pretense of promoting the comfort of passengers on railway trains, and in further respects abridges the privileges and immunities of Citizens of the United States and the rights secured by the 13th and 14h Amendments to the Federal Constitution.[22]

Judge Ferguson promptly cited several legal precedents upholding the state statute and ruled against the two lawyers, his client, and their entire social and racial class. Ferguson's decision was greeted jubilantly by the *Times Democrat*, which hoped that the judge's words would

> have some effect on the silly Negroes who are trying to fight this law. The sooner they drop their so-called "crusade" against the "Jim Crow car," and stop wasting their money in combating too well-established a principle—the right to separate the races in cars elsewhere—the better for them.[23]

Plessy, through his attorneys, applied to the State Supreme Court for a writ of prohibition and certiorari and was given a hearing in November 1892. The case of *Plessy v. Ferguson* was thus born. Chief Justice Francis Tillou Nicholls, the 1877 Redeemer Governor of Louisiana and the 1890 Governor who had signed the Jim Crow Act, presided over the State Supreme Court. Justice Charles E. Fenner delivered the opinion asserting that enforced separation did not conflict with that equality bestowed upon Black people by the Fourteenth Amendment.

Two historically significant pre-Civil War Northern decisions referred to by Justice Fenner in his defense of Jim Crow were: (1) the Roberts' decision of 1849 upholding Bostonian school segregation against a legal attack led by Charles A. Sumner and the Black community; and (2) a Pennsylvania decision involving segregated transportation that stated that being separated is not to say that either race is inferior, but rather that, "following the Order of Divine Providence," equalitarian authority should not coerce these grossly separate races to "intermix."[24] This was the life-experience reasoning that sustained the basic justification for Jim Crow, whereby justice was denied not by any divine providence, but by a society predicated on racial hierarchy.

Justice Nicholls, probably remembering the time he was the "Redeeming" governor and the verbiage by which he had denounced extreme race bigotry and advocated concessions to the Black community, granted Plessy's petition for a writ of error, which allowed Plessy to seek redress before the United States Supreme Court.

Plessy's brief was submitted to the Supreme Court on his behalf and finally argued on April 13, 1896. The argument against the statute was presented by Tourgee and a young scalawag of a prominent North Carolina family, Samuel F. Phillips. Tourgee argued that Homer Plessy had been deprived of property without due process of law. Plessy's property was his "seven-eighths Caucasian and one-eighth African blood," which gave him the appearance of being White. Tourgee continued by saying that a White skin is "the most valuable sort of property being the master-key that unlocks the golden door of opportunity."[25] Plessy's reputation of being White was thereby endangered by such a law that any man suspected of having African blood would be excluded from avenues of wealth, prestige, and opportunity.

Tourgee concluded that "probably most White persons if given the choice would prefer death to life in the United States as colored persons."[26] Tourgee emphasized the incompatibility of segregation laws with the spirit and intent of the Thirteenth and Fourteenth Amendments by the framers. Segregation attempts to restamp the badge of servitude on Black people and thus is coincidental with the institution of slavery, contended Tourgee. Tourgee concluded: "the question is not as to the equality of privileges enjoyed, but the right of the State to label one citizen as White and another as colored in the common enjoyment of a public highway."[27] This last argument by Tourgee was pivotal, because the Supreme Court, in the *Civil Rights Cases*, had maintained, despite its weakening of the Fourteenth Amendment, that state governments could not unjustly discriminate against Blacks, that

> the law in the states shall be the same for the Blacks as for the Whites; that all persons, whether colored or White, shall stand equal before the laws of the States, and in regard to the colored race, for whose protection the Amendment was primarily designed, that no discrimination shall be made against them by law because of their color.[28]

On May 18, 1896, Justice Henry Billings Brown delivered, with the affirmation of six justices, the *Plessy* case decision. These seven justices who affirmed the separate but equal decision of the Louisiana lower courts were all Northern born and were politically either Republicans or pro-Union Democrats.[29] Brown, who delivered the decision, was born and raised in a middle-class Protestant community in Massachusetts. He was educated at Yale and Harvard. Brown spent his middle years in Detroit, Michigan, obtaining an appointment as Deputy United States Marshall. After one unsuccessful bid for a Court nomination, one that his ex-Yale classmate David Brewer attained, Brown attained his appointment to the high court on the death of Justice Samuel F. Miller in 1890.[30]

Brown's decision in the *Plessy* case reflected the attachment of his belief in the philosophy of Social Darwinism to the national hegemony of racialism. The Darwinian racialism was overt in Brown's decision. Brown's opinion reflected what he thought was beneficial to the fittest "Anglo-Saxon Race."[31] Brown believed that "a vast number of questions that should be settled in some way then they should be settled right."[32] Brown's argument in favor of separating social races confirms that this was one question in the context of a vast number of race-based problematics that would be settled and rationalized within a racially biased intellectual legal culture.

The Chief Justice presiding in the *Plessy* decision was Melville Fuller, born in Maine and educated in that Northern academic citadel, Harvard. Migrating to Illinois in 1856, Fuller supported popular sovereignty and admitted that slavery was morally evil but out of the legal reach of federal power. In the 1861 Illinois Constitutional Convention, Fuller supported a provision that excluded Blacks from the franchise and forbade them from immigrating into the state. Furthermore, as a state representative, Fuller introduced a bill to ratify the proposed national amendment that would prohibit federal interference with slavery. He also denounced the Emancipation Proclamation.[33]

Justice Stephen J. Field, born in Connecticut and educated in law at his brother's New York law office, believed that "law must be adapted by the judge to the circumstances he faces."[34] Field used this philosophical approach to help the Court become a "Supreme Censor" of state legislation threatening *laissez-faire* capitalism in the age of enterprise. The social circumstances of the New South and the spirit of 1877 permitted him to concur in the *Civil Rights Cases* and to join the majority in *Plessy*.

Another concurring justice, George Shiras, Jr., was born in Pennsylvania and also educated at Yale. Shiras became a wealthy lawyer defending Pittsburgh's great industrial corporations and the Baltimore and Ohio Railroads and was appointed to the Court in 1881. Sitting on the Court and prior to *Plessy*, Shiras joined the majority in various decisions that rolled back the substantive basis of the Civil War amendments and civil rights statutes.[35]

The fifth supporting justice, Horace Gray,[36] was also born in the Northern liberal city of Boston, Massachusetts. Educated at Harvard, Gray became imbued with White racialism with his involvement and support of the Free-Soil Party that he left to join the Republicans. Gray viewed Lincoln's Emancipation Proclamation as unconstitutional and leaning in the direction of authoritarian rule. Although Gray agreed with the majority in the *Civil Rights Cases*, he limited state power in *Logan v. U.S.*[37] when he held that citizens had a right to be protected from vigilante justice while in the custody of federal officers.

The last supporting Justice, Rufus Peckham, was born in Albany, New York, and became a proponent of the entrepreneurial jurisprudence by being "receptive to the new definition of individual liberty with their laissez-faire implications."[38] Peckham's judicial decisions were pro-business,[39] and he also concurred in the *Civil Rights Cases*. As one Constitutional historian noted, "Peckham's presence on the Court helped fashion its contemporary image as a safe, solid bulwark against social disorder and experimentation."[40]

Ironically, it was not these Northern-born and bred justices who attempted to protect the freedpeople's interests, but a Southern-born and bred justice, John Marshall Harlan, who did. National racial hegemony socialized the Northern-born and bred justices to agree to a standard of equality that barely hid its real substantive inequality.

Another ironic point in the *Plessy* case was that like the Louisiana court, the Supreme Court also used Massachusetts's Lemuel Shaw's dictum in the *Roberts* case that prejudice "is not created by law and probably cannot be changed by law"[41] to rationalize and validate the idea of separate but equal. Using the *Roberts* case and other decisions of lower courts, the Supreme Court, with Justice Brown delivering the decision, diverged from the norm because the high court is never required to and seldom follows the decisions of lower courts. The Court, in following Louisiana's lead, was looking for "authority that segregation of the races had been recognized as within the competency of the state legislature in the exercise of its police power."[42] The Court cited seven cases distinguishable in material facts from *Plessy*. Only six of those cases upheld this doctrine, and each considered school segregation.[43]

Because the high court had never considered whether racially segregated transportation—that is, railroads—was Constitutional, it appeared, by looking at the way the high court diverged from the norm by gathering precedents from inferior courts and by the case precedents themselves, that the Court was searching for authority in these cases to buttress a specific type of opinion that would answer the question, "Has a state the power to require that railroad trains within her limits shall have separate accommodations for the two races?"[44]

In approaching the *Plessy* decision, the Supreme Court further relied on recent decisions that curtailed freedpeople's rights.[45] Justice Brown argued that separate but equal was Constitutional because Louisiana police powers were exercised in a reasonable way according to the established usages. Brown noted that

> every exercise of the police power must be reasonable and extend only to such laws as are enacted in good faith for the promotion of the public good, and not for the annoyance or oppression of a particular class.[46]

The rationale in this case by the majority justices confirms that legal ideology and the institution of law reflect the interests of the dominating classes. Reunion of both the Northern and Southern dominating classes permitted the law to follow and legitimize this rapprochement. Reunion and reaction were materially grounded in the nation's political economy and solidified by the hegemonic function of the rule of law.

However, Justice Harlan in his dissent asserted that candor demanded recognition that "the statute in question had its origin in the purpose . . . to exclude colored people from the coaches" of White people. Harlan maintained that Jim Crow law was designed as an annoyance and an oppressive device that marked the freedpeople with a "brand of servitude and degradation."[47] He went on to say that the majority's legal semantics of rationalization were but a "thin disguise of equal accommodations for passengers . . . [that] will not mislead anyone nor atone for the wrong this day done."[48]

Justice Brown's decision wrote conservative social science into law. Brown argued that the standard of reasonableness for any statute is determined "with reference to the established usages, custom and traditions of the people."[49] However, if law is reasonable when it follows custom, then Brown and his colleagues misread Southern history. Noted Southern historian C. Vann Woodward says that segregation was not consistent with custom or tradition in the South, because the system of slavery would have been virtually inoperative had there been a separation of the races. His research clearly demonstrates that Jim Crow did not spontaneously arise after the war, but that Blacks rode "exactly as White people . . . and in the same cars" in Virginia.[50] Woodward states that "Up to 1900 the only law of this type adopted by the majority of Southern states applied to passengers aboard trains."[51] Separation of the races law came late with adaptation by North Carolina in 1899 and South Carolina and Virginia in 1900. Woodward's research clarifies that the Supreme Court had erred in its historical explanation that sought to give *Plessy* a standard of objectivity.

Popular condemnation of this decision was left up to a unanimous Black news press that denounced the decision. *The Weekly Blade*, of Parsons, Kansas, called the Court's decision a "damnable outrage." The editorial went on to declare

> the Supreme Court of the United States has wantonly disgraced . . . the highest tribunal of this the land that has proclaimed it the world over that "all men are created equal" by declaring the "Jim Crow" car laws of the South to [be] constitutional. When such an august body stoops so low, then it is time to put an end to the existence of

infernal, infamous bodies. . . . Justice Harlan was the only one on that bench with grit enough in him to utter a protest against this damnable outrage upon a race that for more than 275 years labored under the yoke of bondage.[52]

Another Black publication, the *A. M. E. Church Review*, after ridiculing Brown's legal arguments as "plausible sophistry," said this of Harlan's dissent:

Justice Harlan takes the ground that the intent and purpose of the constitution was to wipe out all official knowledge of race among citizens, by both state and nation, and that greater evils are in store by validating laws made in hate than can result from standing upon the broad grounds of right and humanity.[53]

The White press, for the most part, wavered between approval and disapproval of the decision. *The New Tribune* of Duluth, Minnesota, stated that

The necessity for such a law exists only in the south and the statute would never have been enacted but for conditions which made the separation of the races in railroad travel apparently unavoidable in order to secure the comfort of all concerned.[54]

The Dispatch of Richmond, Virginia, published an editorial entitled "Hardly Expected" that commented favorably on the decision because

Some colored people make themselves so disagreeable on the cars that their conduct leads white men to ponder the question whether such a law as that of Louisiana is not needed in all the Southern states.[55]

Some White newspapers, such as the *Republican* of Springfield, Massachusetts, responded by observing,

The South ought to be happy now that the United States Supreme Court has affirmed the constitutionality of the Louisiana law. . . . The law may now be expected to spread like the measles in those commonwealths where white supremacy is thought to be in peril. Did the southerners ever pause to indict the Almighty for allowing Negroes to be born on the same earth with white men?[56]

The most incisive disapproving commentary on *Plessy* and the analogous events was given in *Donohoe's Magazine*. The editorial suggested that the decision was inconsistent with the Constitutional amendments passed by Congress after the Civil War, but typical of what was occurring in America's life and institutions at that particular time. This editorial stated,

Events [are] shaping themselves strangely in this free land of late. With legislation against the negro backed up by the highest tribunal in the country (just as if the *Dred Scott* decision had not passed into lasting infamy, and as if there had been no Civil War); with Congress passing restrictive immigration laws directed . . . unfairly against special European nationalities; . . . the United States presents to the world a sad spectacle of inconsistency upon our boasted human freedom and brotherhood. Selfishness—individual, class, sectional and racial selfishness-is the great curse and danger of the American republic today.[57]

It is without doubt that the Supreme Court and Congress, in keeping in step with the Compromise of 1877, helped to shape the previously mentioned strange events, as well as those events not mentioned in the editorial: the final genocide of the red man, the violation of Mexican-American rights in the Southwest, and the Chinese exclusion and peonage on the West Coast of California. At the close of the nineteenth century, powerful capitalistic corporate interests were in control of the governmental structures, and White supremacy had become a hegemonic cultural formation within this political economy. The Supreme Court in the *Plessy* and other "redeeming" decisions returned to the White South home rule and gave full support to the entrepreneurial "Great Barbeque"[58] already in progress.

ENDNOTES

1. Frederick Engels, "Letters to Schmidt," in *Marx and Engels on Law* eds., Maureen Cain and Alan Hunt (London: Academic Press, 1979), 56–57.
2. *Plessy v. Ferguson*, 163 U.S. 537 (1896); See Frank J. Scaturro, *The Supreme Court's Retreat from Reconstruction: A Distortion of Constitutional and Jurisprudence* (Wesport: Greenwood Press, 2000).
3. Arthur S. Miller and Ronald F. Howell, "The Myth of Neutrality in Constitutional Adjudication" *University of Chicago Law Review* 27 (Summer 1960), 663–664.
4. See Miller and Howell, "The Myth of Neutrality in Constitutional Adjudication."
5. Mel Leiman, *The Political Economy of Racism* (Boulder: Pluto Press, 1993), 39–49.
6. *United States v. Harris,* 106 U.S. 629 (1883).
7. Alan Westin, "Harlan: Transformation of a Southerner," *Yale Law Journal*, 66 (1957).
8. See Westin, "Harlan: Transformation of a Southerner." See also C. Vann Woodward, "*Plessy v. Ferguson*," in *Historical Viewpoint: Notable Articles from American Heritage Magazine,* ed. John Garraty, vol. 2: Since 1865 (New York: Harper and Row, 1970), 65.
9. *Pace v. Alabama*, 106 U.S. 583 (1882).
10. *Cummings v. County Board of Education*, 175 U.S. 528 (1899).
11. See Cummings' case as cited in note 9; see also Garraty, 67.
12. *Plessy* case dissenting opinion, Justice John Marshall Harlan. Interestingly, Woodward does not mention this negative in his analysis of this case.
13. Jim Crow laws requiring railroads to carry Blacks in separate cars or behind partitions were adopted in the late 1880s by Florida, Mississippi, Texas, and in Louisiana, Arkansas, Georgia, Tennessee, and Kentucky in the 1890s. The Supreme Court, in an earlier decision in 1878, closed off this type of legislation in *Hall v. DeCuir*, 95 U.S. 485 (1878). The Court held constitutional a Louisiana statue forbidding discrimination on railroad cars on account of race because it places a direct burden on interstate commerce. By 1890, the Court, in place and time, approved state laws requiring racial separation on railroad cars in *Louisville, New Orleans and Texas Railroads v. Mississippi*.
14. Otto H. Olsen, *The Thin Disguise* (New York: Humanities Press, 1967), 9.
15. Olsen, 9. See also essay by C. Vann Woodward in *Quarrels That Have Shaped the Constitution,* Chapter X, "The Case of the Louisiana Traveler. . .," ed. John A. Garraty (New York: Harper and Row, 1987), 160.
16. Olsen, 10. Louis Ruchames notes that abolitionists who fought the original Jim Crow cars in 1841 Massachusetts argued that segregation was an expression of the ruling-class within state public policy. He argued that railroads, with their great wealth and power, "had enabled them to flout public opinion and to secure the sympathetic decisions of those court justices before whom suits had been brought" 71 in Louis Ruchammes, "Jim Crow Railroads in Massachusetts, *American* Quarterly, 8, No. 1(1956) 61–75.
17. Woodward, "The Case of the Louisiana Traveler," quoted in *Quarrels That Have Shaped the Constitution,* ed. John A. Garraty (New York: Harper and Row, 1987), 161.
18. Olsen, *The Thin Disguise*, 12. See also Woodward in *Quarrels*, 162. Albion Winegar Tourgee was described as "a Northerner who resembled a Southerner: in his insolence, his independence, and readiness to accept a challenge," 162. Tourgee established himself as the one of the leading advocates for equality between the races. See his autobiography of this period in his novel *A Fool's Errand* (New York: Fords, Howard and Hulbert, 1880).
19. Quoting Martinet to Tourgee, December 7, 1891, Tourgee Papers; See also *Quarrels*, 163.

20. *State ex rel. Abbott v. Hicks,* 44 La. Ann. 770. 11 S. 74 (1892).

21. Olsen, 13, as quoted in *Crusader* by Martinet; see also analysis by Brook Thomas, ed., *Plessy v. Ferguson: A Brief History with Documents* (Boston: Bedford/St. Martins, 1997), 5.

22. Olsen, 14.

23. Olsen, 14. It should be noted that Justice John Howard Ferguson was a carpetbagger from Massachusetts who had married into a prominent New Orleans family. Obviously, Ferguson "went native" in marriage and social sensibilities. See also Brook Thomas, 5. Woodward notes that Justice Henry Billings Brown was a resident of Michigan, but a native of Massachusetts.

24. Olsen, 15.

25. *Plessy v. Ferguson,* 163 U.S. 537 (1896). Brief submitted by Homer Plessy's lawyer, Albion W. Tourgee. See also Woodard in *Quarrels,* 167.

26. Woodward in Garraty's *Quarrels,* 167. Quoted from actual case text.

27. Brook Thomas, 30. Quoted from actual case text.

28. *Civil Rights Cases,* 109 U.S. 3 (1883); see also Olsen, *Thin Disguise,* 16.

29. Justice Edward Douglass White of Tennessee voted with the majority in the *Plessy* decision, whereas Justice David Brewer did not participate in the decision. See Fred Israel and Leon Friedman's book cited in note 30. See also Woodward in Garraty's "Historical Viewpoints."

30. Fred Israel and Leon Friedman, *The Justices of the United States Supreme Court, 1789–1969* (New York: Chelsea House Publications, 1969), 1–4.

31. Israel and Friedman, 2: "Henry Billings Brown" by Joel Goldfarb, 1555.

32. Israel and Friedman, "Henry Billings Brown" by Joel Goldfarb, 1558.

33. Israel and Friedman, "Melvin Fuller," by Irving Shiffman, 1474.

34. Israel and Friedman, "Stephen J. Fields," by Robert McCloskey, 1072.

35. Israel and Friedman, "George Shiras, Jr.," by Arnold Paul, 775–790. XXX.

36. Israel and Friedman, "Horace Gray," by Louis Filler, 1385.

37. *Logan v. United States,* 144 U.S. 263 (1892).

38. Israel and Friedman, "Rufus Peckham," by Richard Skolnick, 1692.

39. *People v. Budd,* 117 New York 1 (1889); *Lochner v. New York,* 198 U.S. 45 (1905).

40. Richard Skolnick, 1686.

41. *Roberts v. City of Boston* (1849); see case analysis by Bernstein in note 42.

42. Barton J. Bernstein, "Case Law in *Plessy v. Ferguson,*" *Journal of Negro History,* 47, 3 (July 1962), 190.

43. Bernstein, 190.

44. Bernstein, 193.

45. Bernstein, 194; note how the Court flipped from the *Hall* case to the *Louisville* railroad case concerning what "burdens" interstate commerce.

46. Barton J. Bernstein, "Conservative Sociological Jurisprudence," *Journal of Negro History* 48, 3 (July 1963), 198.

47. Harlan's dissent in *Plessy;* full text in *Plessy v. Ferguson: A Brief History with Documents,* ed. Brook Thomas (Boston: Bedford/St. Martins Press,1997), 5–59.

48. Harlan' dissent; Brook Thomas, 59.

49. Brown's majority comment; Brook Thomas, 50.

50. Bernstein, quoting Woodward's "strange career" citation on 200.

51. C. Vann Woodward, *The Strange Career of Jim Crow* (New York: Oxford University Press, 1974), 97.

52. Otto Olsen, *Thin Disguise:* "A Damnable Outrage," *Weekly Blade,* May 30, 1896.

53. Olsen, 125: "Plausible Sophistry," *A.M.E. Church Review* 13 (1896), 156–162.

54. Olsen, 126: *News Tribune* (Duluth, Minnesota), May 22, 1896.

55. Olsen, 126: "Hardly Expected," *Dispatch* (Richmond, Virginia), May 21, 1896).

56. Olsen, 127; "Like the Measles," *Republican* (Springfield, Massachusetts), May 20, 1895.

57. Olsen, 127: "A Sad Spectacle," *Donohoe's Magazine,* 36 (1896), 100–101.

58. *Great Barbeque* refers to the avaricious exploitation of America's natural environ that produced consumer commodities and great disparities in wealth. The Gilded Age is defined as a "great barbeque" of exploitation, consumerism, and the "aroma" of class antagonisms. See Mark Twain (Samuel Clemens) and Charles Dudley Warner, *The Gilded Age: A Tale of Today* (Hartford: American Publishing Company, 1874).

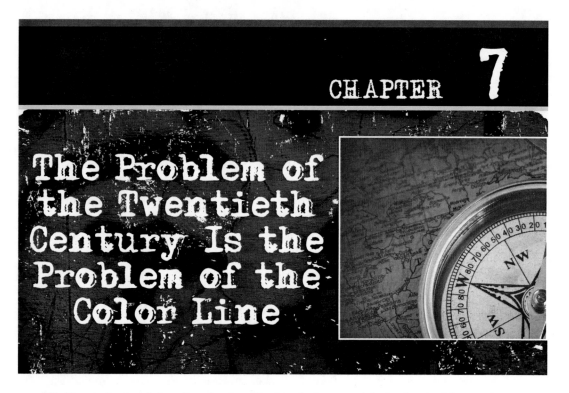

CHAPTER 7

The Problem of the Twentieth Century Is the Problem of the Color Line

The historical unity of the ruling class is realized in the State. . . . The fundamental historical unity, concretely results from the organic relations between State or political society and civil society.

—ANTONIO GRAMSCI, *NOTES ON ITALIAN HISTORY*[1]

CONSTITUTIONAL COLOR-BLINDNESS: AN IDEOLOGY OF STATE-SPONSORED INEQUALITY

Reunion unified the two regional sectional ruling classes into the industrial capitalist State under a new Constitutional order that followed the demarcations of the color line. The momentary disruption in this ruling class unity was created by the Civil War, but the U.S. Supreme Court was able to gently legitimize political rapprochement and thus prepare the country for the entrepreneurial age driven by science, technological Taylorism, and the consumer society.[2] In commenting on the impact of racist Constitutionalism, foremost Constitutional historians observed, "Yet even in the militantly racist atmosphere of the early twentieth-century reconstruction did not quite end."[3] These constitutionalists were referring to the post-*Plessy* solidification of legal, formal, and legitimized racial classification.[4] Another Constitutional historian also supported this understanding by noting that "As important as the *Plessy* decision is, it can be argued that it was possible only within the context of a complicated network of political considerations and beliefs about the role of race in society that are more important than the decision itself."[5]

The long shadow of Reconstruction was assured because the Court's redeeming decision permitted a separate but equal dictum to be Constitutional in the material manifestation of a complicated and contradictory structure of the Jim Crow political economy. The definition of color-specific America had to be worked out in case law. The law was used as an instrument to maintain Jim Crow, and the hegemonic function of law would be challenged early on by the newly organized National Association for the Advancement of Colored People (NAACP).[6] Formed in 1905, the NAACP's grand aim was to attack the denial of civil rights of African Americans by aggressively pursuing litigation that would overturn the racist redeeming case law precedents. In actively seeking to achieve this goal, the NAACP also felt it would blunt and reject the "accommodation" philosophy of Booker T. Washington.[7] The NAACP charged that Booker Washington had asked "Negroes" to give up three vital rights in hopes of surviving the onslaught of Klan violence: their interests in political power, civil rights, and higher education.[8] The struggle for the aggressive enforcement of the Civil War Amendments[9] was the driving force of NAACP litigation and what became known as the twentieth-century Civil Rights Movement.[10]

This incipient civil rights struggle clashed along the color line with conservative Constitutionalism in the second decade of the twentieth century. The NAACP, the Urban League, and other organizations challenged the high court to stop its solidification of Jim Crow into American law and institutions. There was very little of the law's relative autonomy as expressed in the rule of law. The Supreme Court accepted Southern states' regulation of Blacks' basic "rights," and Southerners used this Constitutional permission to confirm and reshape a racial hierarchy that was congruent with the stage of social organization called *monopoly capitalism*.[11] The Supreme Court utilized new legal theory to blunt the growing labor movement, and did the same to dilute and emasculate the newly won Civil War Amendments.[12] The Court implemented these new legal theories such that law became a constitutive element in the formation of race and class in the new industrial order.[13]

By the first decade of the twentieth century, the Supreme Court had established an impassable abyss between what the framers of the Civil War Amendments and subsequent civil rights legislation intended and the reality of an unequal and separate America. The framers sought to create a legal formalism that would permit the freedpeople to stand equal to Whites before the law. However, the hegemony of race, driven by the separate but equal doctrine, permitted the Court to interpretatively answer a part of Douglass's query: For whom and for what was the Constitution made?[14]

If the antebellum Court ensured that the Constitution would provide for the interests of White Americans and leave no respect for the interests of Americans of African ancestry, then the post–Civil War Court made sure that this dialectic would continue. The Court's interpretations in the *Slaughterhouse Cases,* the *Cruikshank Case, Civil Rights Cases, Reese* and other voting rights cases, *Virginia v. Rives* and other jury rights cases, and finally *Plessy,* reduced the social class of freedpeople

> to a despairing second-class citizenship: voteless in the South; helpless in the face of constant and brutal aggression; indicted by all-White grand juries and convicted by all-White trial juries; denied access to places of public accommodation; represented in public office by those whose very elections were dependent on their promises to White voters to double and redouble his disabilities; forced to scrounge and cadge for education; segregated in every phase of life; . . . with no place to turn for redress of his grievances except to

the Court that had approved the devices used to reduce him to his helpless and almost hopeless degradation.[15]

These cases truly proved Harlan's dissent in *Plessy* to be prophetic. In that dissent, Harlan argued that giving judicial legitimacy to the South's Jim Crow system would

> not only stimulate aggressions, more or less brutal and irritating, upon the admitted rights of colored citizens . . . what can more certainly arouse race hate, what can more certainly create and perpetuate a feeling of distrust between these races, than state enactments, which, in fact proceed on the ground that colored citizens are so inferior and degraded that they cannot be allowed to sit in public coaches occupied by White citizens.[16]

Harlan knew already that legal lynching, a la Colfax Massacre, had received a judicial free pass, and such violence had begun during Presidential Reconstruction. However, Harlan's prophecy would be readily seen in the wave of lynchings from 1889 through 1901, when 1,955 lynching were recorded, race riots exploded in both the North and South, and Jim Crow laws steadily proliferated. The freedpeople responded by establishing a variety of civil rights organizations, holding conferences on civil rights issues, and protesting by migrating from the source of the violence, litigating court cases against the onslaught of White supremacy, or using armed resistance in self defense.[17]

The Supreme Court, during this period, 1896–1936, rarely overruled its "redeeming decisions" and therefore confirmed Du Bois' observation that the problem of the twentieth century would be one of White over Black. The Court girded the caste relations[18] of color and convinced the South that even though it had lost the Civil War, it was victorious regarding Constitutional law.[19]

The South's effort at maintaining the caste order involved restricting the franchise. The specific plan for disfranchisement was implemented by Mississippi in 1890, when voting barriers were implemented in the state constitution based on property or literacy qualification, good character clauses, and reading and understanding the Constitution clauses. The plan also left loopholes for Whites to vote, such as the infamous grandfather clause, which permanently enfranchised descendants of those who voted before 1866.[20] Between 1890 and 1910, all the cotton states had developed various aspects of this initial plan of disfranchisement. Florida, Tennessee, Texas, and Arkansas had added a further device, the poll tax, which required an annual head tax to vote. This was essentially a piece of class legislation because the vast majority of freedpeople were involved in debt peonage and could not afford to pay the tax and thus vote. The effect of these devices on Black voting patterns was enormous. For example, Louisiana amended its constitution with many of the plan's devices in 1898, and its Black voter registration dropped from 130,334 in 1896 to 1,324 in 1904; ninety-nine out of every one hundred Black voters were denied the right to vote.[21]

Another disfranchisement device used was the primary system. Initially not set up to prevent Blacks from voting, it was soon recognized for this potential. Converting the primary system into a Whites-only exercise, most Southern states, between 1896 and 1915, adopted the state-wide "all White" Democratic primary system.[22] If Blacks could not vote in the primaries because they were excluded from party membership, then they had little hope of circumventing this structure in the following all-White general elections. The all-White primary essentially became the general election itself.

The Supreme Court reviewed some of these disfranchisement practices in the case of *Williams vs. Mississippi* (1897).[23] In this case, the Court upheld a state statute that required any voter to read and interpret any part of the U.S. Constitution and to be able to pay a poll tax as a requirement for voting. This left the fate of the Black ballot in the hands of Southern officials. Justice McKenna, speaking for the Court, held that the Mississippi Constitution and codes

> do not, on their face, discriminate between the White and Negro races, and do not amount to a denial of equal protection of the law, secured by the Fourteenth Amendment . . . and it has not been shown that their actual administration was evil but only that evil was possible under them.[24]

Alabama followed suit in 1901, and amended its constitution per Mississippi's. A deadline was set up for voter registration, and those who registered before that date would be permanently enfranchised. Those who registered after that date would be required to pass those difficult and interpretive reading and literacy tests. One question posed to a Black person attempting to register was to explain the "difference between Jeffersonian Democracy and the Calhoun principles as compared to the Monroe Doctrine."[25] The Court legitimized Alabama's devices in the 1903 case of *Giles vs. Harris,*[26] saying that a denial of the franchise is a political wrong, and those Black individuals suffering such a wrong must look to the legislative department of the federal government for redress. As long as legal formal law appeared "equal," then, according to Justice Harlan, the Court cannot assume a fact of unconstitutionality.[27] These evasive semantics could not hide the fact that the Court had asked Blacks to seek redress from the same body, Congress, that the Court had previously prevented from protecting the franchise by diluting the teeth of the Fifteenth Amendment in the *Reese* case.[28] In *Reese,* it had overruled sections three and four of the Enforcement Act of 1870, which was aimed at preventing the specific disfranchising schemes that William Giles faced in Alabama.[29] Alabama, with assistance from the law, had risen from the ashes of Reconstruction to the highest level of White supremacy by excluding Mr. Giles, who had voted in Alabama for the previous twenty years, and other Blacks from access to political power.[30] White power was consistent with the social order of peonage within the shadow of the plantation.

Without political power, the freedpeople had little hope of electing their representatives at the state level and thereby fighting Jim Crow legislation on the floor of the state congress. In fact, in both *Williams* and *Giles,* the Court refused to abide by a previous Court precedent. In this previous case, *Yick Wo v. Hopkins,*[31] the Court understood a San Francisco ordinance to be fair on its face (it did not refer to Chinese), but declared it invalid because it was discriminatory in its administration by city officials either closing Chinese laundries or not giving permits to Chinese laundry owners. Justice McKenna was aware of this precedent but still thought a distance of immense proportion separated law from the evil of those whose hands were on the administrative instruments of the law. The formalism of law, as it appeared neutral "on its face" and was legitimized by the Court, would give rise to an evil in the law's application that Giles and other Alabama Blacks experienced because of their race and previous condition of enslavement.

Maintaining legal formalism worked to buttress the growing racial social order. The Court, in the 1915 case of *Quinn v. U.S.,*[32] invalidated Oklahoma's grandfather's law because it violated the letter and the implementation of the law of equality. Sadly, however, by the year of this decision, this type of on-its-face exclusionary law had served its purpose. Oklahoma's reaction to the Court's decision was to bestow permanent registration status on those who had voted in the general election of 1914 when the now-invalidated grandfather law was still active. Oklahoma gave others (Blacks) who were of voting age at the time of the 1914 election just twelve days to get their names on the voter rolls or be disfranchised for life. White supremacy conquered even when losing Constitutionally, for this new law would not be challenged in the Supreme Court for more than twenty years.[33] With the preservation of conservative federalism, there could no oversight, at the state level, when officials deliberately ignored or circumvented the high court's legal formalism.

In the *Quinn* case, Moorfield Storey, a highly competent White, liberal, Boston lawyer, appeared on the behalf of the newly founded NAACP to urge the Court to rule the Oklahoma law unconstitutional.[34] The NAACP, formally organized in 1910 by Black and White liberals, would be in the vanguard of Black protest litigation. The young organization would be the progressive alternative to Booker T. Washington's accommodationism.[35] The alternative goals, as noted in the organization's newspaper, *The Crisis,* with DuBois as editor, would be the abolition of Jim Crow laws, equal educational opportunities for the Black race, enforcement of the Civil War Amendments, and the passage of a federal anti-lynching law. The NAACP hoped that formal law supported by aggressive enforcement would help in the elevation of the "Negro race." With a sizable grant gift from a young White millionaire, the NAACP could begin its legal struggle for power and justice.[36]

The NAACP's litigious struggle reveals much about the limits of legal formalism in bringing about social justice. Desegregation had its obvious limits when faced with the highest stage of White American apartheid. Many Blacks, such as Marcus Garvey[37] and eventually even W.E.B. Du Bois, advocated degrees of autonomy or internal self-sufficiency within the Black community rather than confronting a solid, racist educational structure. By 1933, Du Bois, in controversial editorials, advocated for "voluntary" Black schools that, in part, led to his dismissal from the NAACP.[38] The autonomy of consciousness certainly rose out of the realization that political disfranchisement left the Black community to its own internal resources and that these resources could be mobilized in the interests of these insular communities. These leaders understood how race thinking factored into why the federal Congress withdrew federal protection from their insular communities and left them voteless and thus politically emasculated.[39]

Congressional acquiescence and support of Black political powerlessness can be seen in this body's refusal to enforce section two of the Fourteenth Amendment, which says

> when the right to vote at any election for the choice of elector for the President and Vice President of the United States; Representatives in Congress, the Executive and Judicial officers of a State, or the members of the Legislature thereof, is denied to any of the male inhabitants of such State . . . except for participation in rebellion, or other crime, the basis of representation therein shall be reduced in the proportion which the number of such male citizens shall bear to the whole number of male citizens twenty-one years of age in such State.[40]

Implementing this provision would have surely given any Southern state second thoughts about disfranchising their Black citizens. In 1890, Senator Henry Cabot Lodge of Massachusetts introduced his Force Bill to enforce this provision.[41] Discussions on this bill revived some of the pre-Compromise of 1877 rhetoric and animosities. The devolution of debate along sectional and racial lines prevented the bill from becoming law.

The Court did reconsider the issue of Black political power in cases concerning the exclusionary practices of the White primary system. Primaries are electoral deliberations at the local and state levels. After the Court validated this primary system in *Newbery v. U.S.*,[42] many Southern states followed Texas's lead in developing their own exclusionary primary systems. Texas passed its primary law in 1923. The NAACP, along with Texas resident Dr. L.A. Nixon, filed suit claiming the statute violated his suffrage rights. The statute was explicit: "in no event shall a negro be eligible to participate in a Democratic Party primary election held in the state of Texas." In *Nixon v. Herndon* (1927),[43] the Supreme Court struck down the Texas law because state action was involved in the classification of citizens on the basis of race. Justice Holmes said that the primary law was an "obvious infringement" of the equal protection clause. The Fourteenth Amendment's equal protection clause prohibited a state's administrators from discriminating against its citizens but not individual citizens from discriminating against each other. For Texas Democrats, this was a legal idea strongly suggested by the Court in *Cruiskshank* that the Fourteenth Amendment added, "nothing to the rights of one citizen as against another";[44] thus, the formalism of law cannot be a shield of justice against individuals proactively seeking to solidify the racial caste.

White supremacists in Texas responded to the *Herndon* decision by placing the power to fix political qualifications for participating in the Democratic primaries with the individuals who sat on the Democratic Executive Committee. Those individuals promptly enacted a color qualification that restricted voting in the primary to Whites only. This action led to the second litigated case, *Nixon v. Condon*,[45] in 1932. The Court sided with Dr. Nixon once again, and said that "the party's executive committee had acted under the prompting of state law, and that this, in effect, made the committee an agent of the state."[46] The Court recognized the evil in the Committee's use of its power. Ultimately, the Democratic Party decided to circumvent this second defeat by permitting the individuals within the party to adopt their own White's only rule in 1932. They claimed that this was done without any involvement or direction from the state legislature nor the Executive Committee. In *Grovey v. Townsend* (1935),[47] a unanimous Supreme Court held that the all-White Texas primary was Constitutional because the qualifications were established by individuals with no collusion with the state. Two years later, the Court permitted the use of the poll tax as a voting requirement in *Breedlove v. Suttles*.[48] The NAACP had expended money and time to establish a formalistic body of case law concerning the White primary only to have *de facto* racism continue to achieve what racist *de jure* instrumentalist law was prevented from doing. The one-party solid South was a totalitarian structure that emanated from the social relationship of peonage, sharecropping, and tenant farming. The Supreme Court was not willing to examine the facts on the ground, and instead protected its thinly disguised legitimacy by falling back on a formalistic explanation for supporting the maintenance of racial domination. The limits of legal formalism are clearly seen in this series of cases. The dialectics of law and society and these dialectics' influences on the juridical formation are in constant motion. The strategy constructed by the NAACP to desegregate America was revealed to be deeply flawed because of these dialectics.[49] White power as hegemonic culture essentially involved restricting Black political power, thus the importance of the law cases surrounding the use of the ballot. This culture, in the last instance, permitted the Court to "spontaneously" agree to a conservative federalistic interpretation of the Fifteenth Amendment that gave consent to racial hierarchy. Hegemony, as legitimacy, was clearly seen by Dr. Nixon and the African-American community, peering through the "veil," as a cultural formation of illegitimacy.

The retreat from Reconstruction and the judicial acceptance of exclusionary voting practices had begun in 1876 in the *Reese* case, gained momentum in the *Williams* case in 1898, and reached a high point in *Grovey* in 1935. This progression led to a judicial *coup d'etat* that left the fate of the Southern Black vote in the hands of state officials or private individuals who were eager to return Blacks to a state of political powerlessness and economic dependency. This subjugation developed with the collusion among law, custom, and the hegemonic cornerstone of race. The connection between political rights and economic rights was sourly noted by one Justice Department Commission when he observed, "It is but a step from the evasion of the 15th Amendment to an actual violation of the 13th Amendment."[50]

One of the most devastating economic vestiges of slavery, prohibited by the Thirteenth Amendment was the system of debt peonage.[51] Pete Daniel in his definitive study of peonage noted that by the "dawn of the twentieth century, peonage in the Southern cotton belt was a confusing mass of customs, legalities, and pseudo-legalities. Nearly every Southern state legislature had passed a contract-labor measure."[52] These labor laws made a laborer who signed a contract and who left the job before its completion criminally liable. The law provided that the violator be arrested and either sent to prison (usually on convict-lease terms) or given the opportunity to work out his contract under court-imposed "debt slavery" with the original employer. Southern courts and racial customs permitted peonage to exist within the various sectors of Southern political economy. Black laborers came under the legal control of contract-labor laws whether they worked in the Mississippi Delta cotton belt or "the turpentine areas of Northern Florida, Southern Georgia, Alabama, and Mississippi."[53] Debt-slavery even emerged briefly within Southern railroad construction camps.

Local custom, according to Professor Daniel, usually reigned over court-imposed law. When Black laborers broke contracts, the local police in the cotton belt would arrest the Black laborers, hold them in jail until the planters arrived, and then allow the employers to deal with the prisoners per their interests. The whole system reminded one on the scenario acted out many times before among a runaway slave, the slave catcher, and the slave owner.

This type of labor relations was established in the late 1860s with the infamous "Black Codes,"[54] which were so harsh that the Radical Republicans passed the Anti-Peonage Act of March 2, 1867.[55] One of its provisions contained the following: "Whoever holds, arrests, returns, or causes to be held, arrested, or returned, or in any manner aids in the arrest or return of any person to a condition of peonage, shall be fined not more than $5,000, or imprisoned not more than five years, or both."[56]

The importance of this Act in combating peonage was that the Justice Department had the power to intervene in state criminal cases where a defendant, most times a Black laborer but at times an immigrant,[57] challenged the Constitutionality of the state law (contract-labor) under which he was being tried. The potential "shield and sword"[58] of the Thirteenth Amendment and the Anti-Peonage Act were used periodically by federal authorities to break down this oppressive laboring system. The creatability of this type of law needed a periodic show of activity unless it revealed itself as a complete farce. Periodic would mean a porous shield and a paper sword.

However, the Supreme Court made it very difficult for progressive federal or state authorities to legally protect the civil or economic rights of the freedpeople. Blacks, not being allowed to exercise their political rights, were easily indicted by all-White grand juries and convicted by all-White juries. When sent to prison, the Black victim would be hired out by prison officials to private businesses needing cheap labor. Convict lease and the chain gang became synonymous with White injustice and social class exploitation by the end of the nineteenth century. Governor Talmadge of Georgia explained the goal of this vortex of oppression when he stated "It is to hold the negro down in order to make him work—to keep him poor." This Southern exploitation was the foundation of the New South, and like the Governor stated, its aim was to keep the "Negro" laborer poor, to confine him as far as possible to menial occupations, to make him a surplus labor reservoir and force him into peonage and wage slavery.[59]

The Supreme Court validated Du Bois' "problematic" observation by ruling in the case of *Hodges v. U.S.*[60] The Court said that the Thirteenth Amendment did not give Congress the right to legislate against private individuals and, in this particular case, against individuals who sought to deprive Blacks of their right to make and enforce contracts. The Court said that the Civil Rights Act of 1866 and the Fourteenth Amendment did not give Congress the authority to protect the right to work under a contract agreed on by individuals at the state level. With this decision, the Act of 1866 was literally placed in the dead-letter law file when it came to protecting the working-class rights of Black laborers. The Court, in an *obiter dictum,* noted that the Thirteenth Amendment emancipated the Black man and woman but did "not commit them to the care of the nation; that being citizens, they must look toward their respective states for protection" against armed White men who would threaten, intimidate, and, at times, murder them. Sadly, most understood that every Southern state, by the time of the decision in *Hodge,* had been redeemed by the "Hood and the Cross."[61]

In the *Hodges* case, Justice Harlan, with Justice Day joining his dissent, said that the Thirteenth Amendment not only destroyed slavery, but all the incidents of slavery, and it also gave Congress the power to enforce that right against individuals. Harlan pointed out that the Court had digressed from the *Allegeyer v. Louisiana*[62] (1897) precedent, because in that case the Court said the due process clause of the Fourteenth Amendment included

> not only the right of the citizen to be free from the mere physical restraint of his person, . . . [but also] to pursue any livelihood or avocation, and for that purpose to enter into all contracts which may be proper, necessary and essential to his carrying out to a successful conclusion the purposes above mentioned.[63]

Harlan concluded by saying *Hodges* would place millions of America's Black workers at the hands of state authorities and individuals who would surely deny them their right of contract. The Court, by upholding the bourgeois formal legal contract, would permit Southerners to legalize a social existence for Blacks within the shadow of the plantation.

The Court did provide Constitutional support to the Anti-Peonage Act in *Clyatt v. U.S.* in 1905.[64] However, this decision was limited because of the Court's tortuous reasoning. Justice Brewer, in ordering a new trial for planter Samuel M. Clyatt, construed the peonage statute to indicate that successful prosecution in this area can only take place when the federal indictment can show that a "laborer was held in peonage, arrested with the intention of placing him in peonage, or returned to peonage after having escaped such a condition."[65] Because the federal indictment failed to show this required process, Justice Brewer calmly ruled that "there isn't a scintilla of testimony to show that Gordon and Ridley [Clyatt's Black laborers] were ever therefore in a condition of peonage."[66] Brewer's dictum was legal formalism gone berserk. A mere peek beneath the thin veneer of peonage would illuminate the new emerging exploitative social relations of a Black peasantry with capital's boot on its neck.

To circumvent this judicial shield against peonage, Southern states instituted legislation that made it a crime for a person knowingly to break a contract after being paid an advance by the employer.[67] Usually, the local court would double the fine on the transient laborer and remit him back to his employer or permit a third party, called a *surety,* to pay the fine and lease the laborer into his custody for work until the fine had been paid.[68]

The Court, in two cases involving the same laborer, Alonso Bailey of Alabama, first validated and then invalidated these new laws. In the first Bailey case of 1908, the Court permitted these laws to exist as long as the law was equally applied to both races. However, in the second case, Bailey, with the support of various liberal groups, initiated another test case.[69] In 1911, the Court, with a change in personnel,[70] reversed the first Bailey decision and invalidated Alabama's peonage law. The Court noted that the clause that prosecuted workers for leaving a contracted work place was unconstitutional. The Court also said that these laws were oppressive and contravened the due process clause of the Fourteenth Amendment. It said that "the law of the State did not permit Bailey to testify that he did not intend to injure or defraud . . . he stood, stripped by the statute of the presumption of innocence, and exposed to conviction for fraud upon evidence only of breach of contract and failure to pay."[71] Three years later, the Court took the opportunity to rule third-party sureties to be unconstitutional.[72]

On the whole, these peonage decisions were favorable to Black labor on the formal legal level, but the Court would still be ruling on peonage statutes up to and as late as 1943, when the Court had to invalidate a Florida law.[73] The laxity of federal Justice Department prosecution permitted many of these statutes, supported by local racist *de facto* practices, to languish on the books for thirty years or more.[74]

National attention to peonage was highlighted by such individuals as William Henry Huff, a Black Georgian who fought peonage successfully[75] in test cases, and organizations like the Abolish Peonage Committee of America, the communist-backed International Labor Defense, and the Workers Defense League. The high point of national attention on Black labor under peonage came about because of the 1927 natural disaster of the "Great Flood." In this year, the Mississippi River overflowed its embankments, drowning many inhabitants and starkly revealing the wide "delta" of peonage and, thus, the depths of Black exploitation to a national audience. Authorities arrested Black men or just rounded them up, caged them, and then released them to planters in need of rebuilding their businesses. The Justice Department had its opportunity to aggressively pursue statutory violators of peonage, but it interceded only in an ineffectual way.[76]

The failure of the Justice Department mirrored the failure of other federal agencies. Walter White of the NAACP returned from the Mississippi Delta and wrote a scorching review of the failure of federal relief efforts in the flood area. White cited the use of federal troops holding Black "peons" in "concentration camps"[77] until their planter employers could claim them. This report and other confirming newspaper accounts prompted Secretary of Commerce Herbert Hoover, who was in charge of federal relief, to appoint a "Colored Advisory Committee" to investigate the complaints of the NAACP.[78]

Hoover's committee was chaired by Tuskegee Institute's President Robert Moton, with eleven other Tuskegeeans as committee members. Hoover hoped that a benign report from the "old-Washington" camp would allay or discredit the "paranoiac" outbursts of the NAACP. Attempting to play both sides against the middle, Moton urged Hoover to use this "grave natural disaster" to create a "sense of freedom and hope" for the Blacks in the Delta. Refusing to support White's earlier findings, Moton stressed the need to rehabilitate the area through federal funding. Moton, fearing that White's findings concerning the horrors and failures of the federal effort would alienate federal authorities, believed that soft-pedaling would appeal to the liberal, philanthropic bent of Hoover's federal division. Moton's committee's report lay dormant on Hoover's desk for months.[79]

Exposing the conditions of peonage and the concentration camps of the flood areas to the nation was left up to the NAACP. Between January and March 1928, *The Crisis* ran a series of exposés on the situation of despair and degradation in the Delta. These essays revealed to the public the situation that the Moton report failed to address, but it was too little, too late. By this time, public interest in this great natural disaster had waned. The opportunity to get a federal agency to aggressively pursue and destroy the political economy of peonage, debt slavery, and convict-lease had come and gone.[80]

Taken in total, the disaster, the solidification of Southern custom in state law and in Supreme Court decisions, and the weak response of the federal government led to a spike in the already mass movement of Southern, rural Black workers from plantation to Northern and Southern urban areas. The awareness of being powerless, the fear of being lynched, the feeling that better jobs and more money could be obtained in the urban areas, and the desire to obtain a better education for their children prompted Black men and women to migrate.[81] Such opportunities also reflected the peculiar intra-class relationships between planters who competed for Black laborers and the intersectional competition between Northern industry needing labor and Southern businesses who sought to retain their Black labor. All competitors employed emigrant labor agents.[82] On one level one could say that Black labor, recruited by labor agents, was exchanging one kind of exploitation for another.[83] To stay in the South, to move to another part of the rural or urban South, or to move North was a decision that individual Blacks and entire Black families made as they, of their own volition, moved from a set of social relations that gave them little or no future at all.[84]

The enticement of Black labor from the coercive labor system of the New South clashed with the Northern capital's ideology of free markets and free labor.[85] Political violence, peonage statutes, and licensing statutes were the South's response to the capitalists' worldview. As early as 1875, the Georgia legislature passed a licensing tax of several hundred dollars to punish, stop, or impede "immigrant brokers"[86] from continuing to successfully recruit tens of thousands of Black laborers from the state as they had done in the previous two years. Many Southern states followed Georgia's lead and used their own powers to tax and license occupational categories to address the labor drain caused by labor agents. The U.S. Supreme Court eventually agreed with the idea that a state could place monetary penalties against labor agents in the 1900 Georgia case of *Williams v. Fears*.[87] Both the second *Bailey* case and the *Fears* case reveal the complexity of legal formalism that can appear to be contradictory at times; however, the *Bailey* case sought to legitimize freedom of contract on the ideological level, while the *Williams* case reflected the law's autonomy. A peon's ability to use his or her rights under *Bailey* was eradicated under *Williams*. Freedom of contract without information and money to leave one's present employment and seek opportunities elsewhere revealed the illusory basis of freedom of contract for Southern Blacks within the capitalist social order.

The Black rural to urban migration caused a great deal of economic disruption and race friction, and created the necessity for adjustment on the part of both the White and Black communities. The Whites intended to keep their neighborhoods lily White, and Blacks were determined to acquire a better life in terms of housing and jobs. The clash of these social and economic forces revolved around the law. To prevent race mixing, White legislatures, with the urging of their constituents, passed residential segregation ordinances. These ordinances usually prevented the residence of Whites in all-Negro blocks and Negroes in all-White blocks; divided the city into segregated districts and designated a district for each race; or restricted new residences in mixed blocks to the racial group that had established a majority of the residences in the block.[88] Beginning in 1910, most Southern and border states began to implement this type of legislation.

In 1917, in the case of *Buchanan v. Warley*,[89] the Court ruled unconstitutional laws based on state action that forbade persons to live in specific residential areas on the basis of color. The Court said that "colored persons are citizens of the U.S. and have the right to purchase properties and enjoy the use of the same without laws discriminating against them solely on account of color."[90] The NAACP initiated this test case, but its victory would be undercut by local custom that led to covenant agreements between realtors and citizen groups, acting as private citizens, that restricted whole neighborhoods to Whites only. The Supreme Court validated these racially restrictive covenants in the 1926 case of *Corrigan v. Buckley*.[91] The Court said that the state action prohibition of the Fourteenth Amendment was not involved when private individuals, without the color of law, sought to restrict the holding and selling of property in their neighborhoods to individuals of their race. The Court also noted that such activities could not be compared to vestiges of slavery, as prohibited by the Thirteenth Amendment.

These decisions concerning housing segregation helped lay the basis for the rise of the urban Black ghetto. The law became a major variable in how the configuration of the ghetto and its vanilla suburbs would look for years to come. The Supreme Court, in being formalistic, was able to declare unconstitutional, a blatant violation, based on state action, of racial discrimination by the state of Kentucky. It then used the same legal formalism and said that individuals who discriminate are out of the reach of its power. African Americans who sought to acquire property were left in a powerless state swinging from *de jure* formalism to *de facto* racism.

As stated previously, migration produced race-relation conflict within the changing demography of the urban landscape. However, for those left behind, the demand for Black labor and the processes of production placed further strain on landlord and peasant. As African Americans organized politically to blunt this exploitation by landlords, the legal system responded in kind. In 1919, a confrontation between a Black peasant cooperative and the planter's legal arm-that is, the local sheriff—broke out in Phillips County, Arkansas. In the initial confrontation, a deputy sheriff was killed, and the authorities, with support from the White community, declared a race war and murdered dozens of Blacks. Once the dust had cleared, twelve Black leaders of the cooperative were quickly tried, under mob hysteria, and sentenced to death, and many others received lengthy jail sentences. Two all-White juries took five minutes and another seven minutes to bring back first-degree murder charges and death via the electric chair.[92] On appeal of the death sentences to the Supreme Court, Moorfield Storey argued that Southern custom of racial *lynch law* (speedy trial without proper legal representation and off to the executioner) and the mob that encircled the courthouse prevented a fair and impartial trial. The Supreme Court, in *Moore v. Dempsey*,[93] agreed with Storey, and said that the racial hysteria and Southern custom violated the due process clause of the Fourteenth Amendment. The Court specifically stated that

> If in fact a trial is dominated by a mob, so that there is a departure from due process of law . . . if the state applying no corrective process, carries into execution a judgment of death or imprisonment based upon a verdict thus produced by mob domination, the state deprives the accused of his life or liberty without due process of law.[94]

The question that the Court did not address but would have to deal with was as follows: How can a Black citizen get justice from an all-White grand jury so eager to indict, and an all-White trial jury so ready to convict? Both were the result of the systematic exclusion of Black citizens from the South's jury system, which the Court, in *Virginia v. Rives* (1879),[95] permitted. The Court tried to formalize the procedural rights of Blacks to participate on juries in *Martin v. Texas* (1906),[96] in which they declared that any systematic exclusion of Blacks from juries was in violation of the Fourteenth Amendment. The limitation of this ruling was that the Court said that the mere absence of Blacks from juries, even over a long period of time, was not sufficient proof of jury discrimination, and the burden of proof to prove state action is placed on the Black defendant. Because most Blacks could not afford the cost of investigating and documenting voter rolls, state action could not be substantiated. This decision placed an almost insurmountable barrier between Black citizens and a basic democratic right. The solid South, with the Supreme Court's interpretive permission, continued to use criminal law procedures, *sans* Black jurors, as a weapon to arrest, try, and convict Black individuals in an arbitrary manner.[97]

Separate juries meant separate and unequal justice on a wide variety of social problems. Probably the most critical problem area was that of education. The Supreme Court, during the era of segregation, not only helped in making the Jim Crow legal superstructure, but helped perpetuate this legitimacy in its decision validating the separation of Blacks and Whites in the area of public and private education. The Court, in the case of *Berea College vs. Kentucky* (1909),[98] declared that the State of Kentucky could forbid voluntary interracial associations in private schools. The Court, in support of the appellate state decision, merely noted "the original charter, which does not destroy the power of the college to furnish education to all persons, but which simply separates them by time or place of instruction."[99] This case went even further than *Plessy* in that it racially intruded into the intimate and private associations of individuals outside of public facilities and revised a major point made in the *Civil Rights Cases*. In its decision in these cases, the Court said that discrimination by private individuals is legitimate as long as it is not supported by state action. However, in *Berea*, it was the state of Kentucky that moderated, in a racist manner, the purely private lives of students who made an educational choice to attend an interracial private college.

The thin disguise of Jim Crow judicial reasoning was extended to Americans of Chinese ancestry in the case of *Gong Lum v. Rice* (1927).[100] Chief Justice Taft, speaking for a unanimous Court, declared the word *colored* in a Mississippi statute pertained to Oriental citizens. Taft cited the *Cummings* case and allowed state police powers to classify Chinese as "honorary second-class" citizens and segregate them in all-Black schools. Martha Lum had attended the White school within the Rosedale Consolidated School District for the first time, but was sent home at the noon hour. The Court directed Mr. Gong Lum, daughter Martha, and their lawyer to section 207 of the state constitution that clearly stated that "Separate schools shall be maintained for children of the White and colored races."[101] The Court said that this issue had been addressed too many times in the past and questioned why they had to revisit this issue. Referring to *Roberts v. City of Boston*, *Plessy v. Ferguson*, and *Cummings*, the Court declared, "we cannot think that the question is any different or that any different result can be reached . . . between White pupils and pupils of the yellow races."[102] "The decision is within the discretion of the state in regulating its public schools and does not conflict with the 14th Amendment."[103]

The Court, in the aftermath of *Plessy*, had extended and given judicial protection to a Jim Crow America based on racial, gender, and class inequities. One should always keep in mind that race law was always one step away from or hand-in-hand with class and gender law. One day after a quasi-class decision in *Slaughterhouse* was handed down, the Court rendered *Bradwell v. Illinois*[104] and stooped to proclaim that because Myra Bradwell was a married woman, she could not practice law, the 14th Amendment "privileges and immunities" clause was not applicable in her case, and the "paramount destiny . . . [of a woman is] to fulfill the noble and benign offices of wife and mother."[105] Sexism, class bias, and above all "negro law" became the bailiwick of American jurisprudence in the post-Reconstruction period and first three decades of the twentieth century.

In a way, the Court had reestablished the *Dred Scott* dictum that "the Black man had no rights a White man was bound to respect."[106] Ironically, the Court, in leaning closely toward legal formalism, had forced itself into a juridic corner, one that was clearly marked when the NAACP began its legal campaign to "kill Jim Crow" during the 1930s.[107] With a large monetary fund set up by a young White millionaire, Charles Garland,[108] the Association's legal strategy rested heavily on a belief in legal formalism and its use in elevating the Black community from the depths of Jim Crow. This strategy, developed by the newly appointed lead attorney Charles Hamilton Houston, was to challenge the inequality of the separate but equal doctrine on a case-by-case basis and force local municipalities to upgrade their Black facilities to make them truly equal to those of Whites. The strategy was to make it too expensive for state officials to maintain a separate America. The Supreme Court affirmed this strategy in a formalistic manner in cases that Houston presented before it.[109] The date or period in which the Court began to affirm this civil rights strategy occurred simultaneously with the greatest upheaval within the history of this country's political economy—the Great Depression. NAACP litigation forced the federal judiciary to reassess the legal status of Jim Crow.[110] Southern attitudes concerning education for Blacks were entrenched and firmly expressed in 1908 by Mississippi's Governor Vardaman: "Money spent for the maintenance of public schools for Negroes is robbery of the White man and a waste upon Negroes. It does him no good, but it does him harm."[111] In Southern states, where separate schools had been established, the abysmal disparities of inequality were glaring. Little if any emphasis was placed on educational facilities for Blacks past the high school level. By the 1930s, Black life required more Black professionals to render legal, health, and educational services to this community. The need for these Black professionals became problematic because of the paucity of graduate schools that admitted these students.[112]

Between 1936 and 1938, eight Southern states abided by the separate but equal doctrine by providing out-of-state scholarships for Blacks wanting to seek higher learning at the university level. These out-of-state scholarships for the most part gave Blacks inadequate financial aid and were limited in number. These scholarships received a setback from an unfavorable decision from a lower court restricting the meaning of *substantial equality*. This case, *University of Maryland v. Murray*,[113] established the precedent that substantial equality must be real in terms of the actual cost. The Maryland court went further and stated that these scholarships, with their limited funds and numbers, were not sufficient enough to maintain equality of educational opportunity. The petitioner, Donald Murray, was represented by lawyers from the NAACP.

The NAACP's litigation continued in the case of *Missouri ex rel Gaines v. Canada*.[114] The case developed out of the University of Missouri's refusal of a Black applicant to its law school. Chief Justice Hughes, speaking for the majority opinion, held that Missouri's law school in refusing to admit Lloyd Gaines had violated the equal protection clause of the Fourteenth Amendment. Hughes declared: "by the operation of the laws of Missouri a privilege has been created for White law students which is denied to Negroes by reason of their race."[115] Hughes also said that the out-of-state scholarships were discriminatory because they shifted the burden of maintaining equal opportunity to another state. It was Mr. Gaines' resident state that had the responsibility to do this. The decision, however, did not overrule the separate but equal doctrine; it merely asserted that in states where White students had access to educational facilities and Blacks did not, then Blacks must be allowed into these institutions—that a state's educational institutions must be equal in fact, not just in theory. This victory by the NAACP demonstrated that the Jim Crow social order would have a difficult time passing Constitutional review. Besides the issue of the writ, the Court began to examine how the law was administered instead of relying on how fair it looked on its face.[116] Fair and impartial administration of the law was the test the Court used in the old case of Yick Wo (1883), who claimed that San Francisco's ordinance, although fair on its face, discriminated against Chinese laundry owners like himself in its administration.[117] The Court in the 1930s resurrected this time-honored judicial discretion to ferret out the real workings of the law in action to examine the material contradictions of America's apartheid.

Another progressive trend the Court implemented was to make its own independent examinations of the facts in criminal cases where Blacks had charged that they were denied due process or equal protection of the law. Previously, the Court had relied on the lower court's finding of fact. These types of findings, usually from Southern courts, were biased against the Black defendants.

Law, race, and class litigation erupted out of the Great Depression, which began in 1929, and this litigation confirmed Marx's theory that law is a product of the real clash between opposing social existences within political economy. The total collapse of the political economy of American capitalism ushered in President Franklin Delano Roosevelt (FDR) and the Democrats into the White House and Congress. The collapse also witnessed the Black vote switching from solidly Republican to solidly Democrat, and it would lead President Roosevelt into a confrontation with the U.S. Supreme Court over legal formalism.[118] The collapse also permitted FDR to implement programs of relief, recovery, and reform, and these programs would help establish the capitalist-welfare state.[119] The economic failure led to massive, double-digit unemployment rates, severe contraction in gross national production, and the virtual halt of consumption. For the Black working class and community, the Depression hit harder than it did Whites. As Herbert Aptheker observed, "Whites were starving and Blacks were starving to death."[120] One of FDR's reform measures led to the rise of "industrial jurisprudence"[121] with the passage of the Wagner Act and other pro-labor legislation that helped in the creation of the CIO under Communist Party influence.[122]

The Communist Party USA became very active in Black communities, especially in Harlem, Chicago, and Detroit, and used this presence to advocate for social justice for Blacks caught up in the web of Depression-era poverty and Southern oppression. The *Scottsboro Cases* and the *Herndon Case* are classic examples of this "Red" advocacy.[123] This advocacy by both the Communist Party and the NAACP became a sort of legal insurgency that challenged the Supreme Court to, at least, use legal formalism to prohibit the worst forms of the type of legal instrumentalism that kept Black workers and Black people under the direct heel of Jim Crow and legal custom. The approach that developed between the Communist International Labor Defense (ILD) and the NAACP revealed similar and, at the same time, polar philosophies about bourgeois law. Mark Naison's scholarship on the Communist Party in Harlem reveals this polarity and its effect on both the *Scottsboro* and *Herndon* cases.[124] The 1930s saw the coming of the International's "Popular Front" approach to resisting the rise of fascism.[125] Moscow's Comintern (World Congress) advocated that communist parties in the West reach out and create a broad-based coalition with liberal and progressive organizations to defend "bourgeois democratic rights of the masses." A prime example of how these groups responded to the Popular Front was Adam Clayton Powell, at an ILD meeting, declaring that "he would leave his church [Abyssinian Baptist was the largest Black church in Harlem] if it barred Communists."[126] On another occasion, Powell railed about "his brothers in red."[127] This move to the Red concerned many, as echoed by the Catholic *Interracial Review,* which noted "Communism has come off the street corners of Harlem and is appealing to the educated Negroes, winning among them leaders who shall bring the Black race to Marx."[128] The Popular Front approach was clearly seen when the ILD hired Samuel Leibowitz, a top-notch criminal lawyer, whose fame was established in defending the criminal underside of society, to defend the Scottsboro Boys.[129] When the NAACP became involved in code-fending the boys, there began an ongoing and underlying conflict between the NAACP and the ILD due to their political and philosophical differences and not to how they embraced legal formalism to free either the Scottsboro Boys or Angelo Herndon. The NAACP abhorred the public mass demonstrations organized by the Party in support of the defendants.[130] The Association believed that these mass rallies would be a distraction from the formal legal process and might impair the efforts to win their acquittal. Usually at these rallies, speakers directed verbal snippets at the Association as still being bourgeois and politically backward.[131] This political dissonance was only a sideshow to the actual decisions handed down by the Supreme Court.

The first Scottsboro case, *Powell v. Alabama,*[132] was rendered in 1932 with a seven-to-two holding. This case, like each case, developed out of an accusation of rape against thirteen young Black defendants, several of whom were minors, by two White women of questionable reputation. Thousands of "hooded" Whites encircled the court house demanding the "legal lynching" of the boys for deflowering the purity of White womanhood.[133] A determined state prosecutor said he was going "to ride their Black asses all the way to the governor's mansion." Following the quick trial and conviction in a mob atmosphere, the Communist-led ILD, and subsequently the NAACP, rushed to get appeals to the U.S. Supreme Court. In answering Ozie Powell's charges that he had been denied the right to adequate counsel, the Court examined the trial proceedings and records to clarify the actual facts of the case. The Supreme Court found that the Alabama court had failed to give the defendant reasonable time and opportunity to acquire counsel, thus denying him due process of law as guaranteed by the Fourteenth Amendment.

In the second Scottsboro case, *Norris v. Alabama*,[134] the initial trial judge, Horton, nullified the initial guilty verdict based on medical examination, severe conflicting testimony, and the recantation of one of the women. Judge Horton believed that there was not a scintilla of evidence to warrant a conviction. However, the boys were tried again by all-White juries and sentenced to be executed. On appeal, the U.S. Supreme Court, in examining racial jury exclusion stated "that for a generation or longer no Negro had been called for service for jury in Jackson county . . . that no names of Negroes were placed on the jury rolls . . . established the discrimination which the Constitution forbids."[135] The Court said that Clarence Norris had been denied, in substance and in truth, a fair trial by the all-White jury because the state excluded Blacks from jury service. Essentially, this ruling reversed the *Rives'* decision by shifting the burden of proof concerning discrimination from the defendant to the state. The mere absence of Blacks over a long period of time from jury service would be, for the Court, sufficient evidence of discrimination by the state.

Another case, *Herndon v. U.S.*,[136] became, like the *Scottsboro Cases,* a *cause célèbre* when a nineteen-year-old Communist Party organizer, Angelo Herndon, was arrested in 1932 in Atlanta, Georgia, tried under an amended antebellum slave insurrection statute, and sentenced to die. The statute placed the penalty of death for anyone inciting an insurrection against the state. Angelo Herndon, as a member of the Unemployment Councils organized by the Communist Party USA, was handing out literature that essentially stated that workers, Black and White, will unite against their class exploiters before they would starve to death.[137] In Herndon's first two efforts to *Let Me Live*[138] (the exact name of his prison autobiography), the Supreme Court, using legal formalism, refused to hear this *Rouge et Noir* appeal for justice.[139] With a mass movement of tens of thousands and legal assistance from the ILD, the Herndon case was eventually heard in 1937. The Court used the "clear and present danger" doctrine to rule the slave insurrection statute unconstitutional.[140]

The Court's ability to establish new rules and actively engage them continued in the case of *Brown v. Mississippi*.[141] The Court held that the rack and torture chamber used by the police to extract pre-trial confessions violated the Fourteenth Amendment's due process clause. Justice Hughes' decision made clear that "the rack and torture chamber may not be substituted for the witness stand."[142]

The *Scottsboro Cases* and Ed Brown's case against Mississippi demonstrated that the Supreme Court was abandoning its support of the Compromise of 1877 and thus the *quid quo pro* with Southern White supremacists. By the late 1930s, the Justices began to "look over the shoulder of state trial and supreme courts and inquire into substance; it would no longer be beguiled by the form of law."[143] However, one must keep in mind the ultimate failure of legal formalism as "due procedural rights." A materialist critique of these cases conveyed an understanding that in all of these cases, the Black defendants were accorded their due process of law and still remained in state "lock down" for more than fifteen years. This unjust incarceration destroyed their lives and the lives of their families. They claimed justice and they received all the justice due them within a racialized juridical system that merely changed the form but not the content of a hierarchical structure of capitalist social relations. In fact, all cases witnessed various degrees of *jury nullification* [ignoring the facts within each case] in the initial conviction of the defendants and the state nullification of the intent of the Supreme Court's rulings in favor of the defendants. Racial federalism in form and Constitutional interpretation had changed, but Southern courts still permitted racial custom to impede or prevent any change in content.[144]

With the challenge from the NAACP and the social activism of Black people, be it their changing voting patterns, resistance via migration, union organizing, economic boycotts, and so on, the Supreme Court became an activist court vis-a-vis civil rights issues.[145] The Court, in its progressive decisions, appeared to reject Mencken's suggestion that the Justices are unduly influenced by unenlightened public opinion. Judicial neutrality and objectivism began to be balanced with an activist Court determined to use its power as a shield and sword to protect the civil rights and civil liberties of American citizens.[146] The Court, in these educational and criminal law cases, had, at last, turned the corner and begun to unravel its precedents of White supremacy in accordance with the Compromise of 1877. Turning the corner was a long and slow process, but the country, its executive and legislative branches as well as the judiciary, slowly began to support the civil rights goals of an incipient mass movement for civil rights. This movement dramatically challenged and then smashed the *quid pro quo* of White supremacy laid down in the post-Civil War period.

The Great Depression of 1929 tested the perception that this Constitution was structured to endure for all time because it was made to be adaptable to "various crises in human affairs."[147] The stock market crash of 1929 had stopped the unstoppable—America's great industrial growth. The closing down of industrial plants left millions unemployed, and the job market reflected the raw nature of scarcity. The Black community's economic plight worsened in the North. Not being allowed in lily-White unions and being the last hired and the first fired, the Black worker's economic plight was abominable. In certain parts of the South and mid-West, the dustbowl of agricultural depression occurring since the early 1920s plunged Black sharecroppers and tenant farmers into abysmal misery. In the North, the White middle class, hard hit by managerial layoffs, discharged their Black maids, butlers, and day-help servants. Black women were especially hit hard by these layoffs. This development, in turn, hurt the Black professional class, who found that their blue-collar clients had little money to pay for their services. The Depression affected every aspect of America's society: political, economic, and social. The political economy of monopoly capital was facing its worst crisis.

However, race as an autonomous ideology was largely unaffected by this devastated economy. In fact, the dire times made racism a natural ally for those Whites wanting to blame Blacks for their own economic deprivation. Keeping Blacks powerless was still in vogue for many Southern politicians. This sentiment was echoed by South Carolina Senator E.D. Smith, when he said, "I cannot and will not be a party to the recognition of the 14th and 15th Amendment."[148] The failure of the Republican Party, the party of the Emancipator, to respond to this type of demagoguery and the devolution of Black civil rights was bitterly recognized by a wide variety of Black leadership. One response was that Blacks by the late 1920s and early 1930s had begun to leave the party of Lincoln and to vote Democratic. FDR became the new emancipator, emancipating them from economic despair by giving them rhetorical hope and welcoming them into a "New Deal" of class brotherhood. However, FDR's rhetoric could not change his administration's giving relief aid to Southern state officials who delivered this sorely needed assistance in a race-based, hierarchical manner.[149] One response to this blatant discrimination was the rise of Unemployment Councils organized by the Communist Party USA[150] and the CIO efforts to recruit Black industrial workers across the color bar.[151]

Organizing along new political alignments, this struggle led to renewed efforts to break down the barricades of separation and inequality. In the 1930s, these efforts were personified by the NAACP and the American Communist Party. With the support from progressive labor forces, the NAACP was able to defeat the nomination of Judge John J. Parker of North Carolina to the U.S. Supreme Court.[152] The Association opposed Parker's nomination because he had supported a grandfather clause in North Carolina's constitution and had said that the "participation of the Negro in politics is a source of evil and danger to both races." Labor's opposition was because he upheld, in a circuit court decision, "yellow dog" contracts.[153]

During this period, the NAACP renewed its efforts to get Congress to pass anti-lynching legislation. Its first effort was in 1919, when the NAACP compiled its 105-page pamphlet called *Thirty Years of Lynching in the U.S., 1889–1918.* At that time, the Association persuaded Congressman L.C. Dyer of Missouri to introduce what came to be known as the *Dyer Anti-Lynching Bill,* which after being passed by the House by a vote of two to one, failed in the Senate. Between 1932 and 1935, there were sixty-eight lynchings.[154]

The climate of protest continued in a variety of areas in American life. Social science research began to attack pseudo-scientific theories that claimed Blacks were racial inferiors. Franz Boas and Melville J. Herskovitz provided new and challenging research to refute these false theories. An incipient multiculturalism sentiment developed out of their and other colleagues' research.[155] The American Communist Party helped to build this protest atmosphere by supporting and making a *cause célèbre* of the Scottsboro Cases. The Party insisted on, as stated in their 1936 manifesto, the protection of Black people's rights:

> We demand that the Negro people be guaranteed complete equality, equal rights to jobs, equal pay for equal work, the full right to organize, vote, serve on juries and hold public office. . . . Heavy penalties must be established against mob rule . . . with the *death penalty for lynchers.* We demand the enforcement of the Thirteenth, Fourteenth, and Fifteenth Amendments to the Constitution.[156]

The public pressure from such a wide variety of sources helped cause a shift in public opinion in favor of civil rights and the protection thereof. The Court, not working in a vacuum, recognized this changing mass consciousness. One noted scholar analyzed the relationship between public opinion and the Supreme Court in this manner:

> before there could be much hope that favorable court decisions would be handed down. In the final analysis, the Fourteenth Amendment is worth whatever the courts

and legislature choose to make it from time to time. And what they choose to make it is no more and no less than what the consensus of opinion—not of enlightened opinion mind you, but of general opinion, of mass opinion . . . wants to see it made.[157]

The NAACP and its allies represented both the enlightened and growing mass opinion on race and societal change. American public opinion in the 1930s became very reform minded. Events in Europe, the Depression, and eventually World War II and—most important—the Cold War molded mass opinion in a progressive manner.[158] The Court opinion, after resolving its differences with FDR,[159] began to walk in step with this reform-minded consciousness. It began to slowly chip away at the separate but equal doctrine under the direction of the NAACP via that organization's legal briefs submitted in test cases before the Court itself. Anxious to walk briskly in this new manner, the Supreme Court reviewed these test cases by *writ of certiorari*.[160] Prior to 1931, the Court issued the *writ of certiorari* with great reluctance.[161]

The Supreme Court had to meet the challenge of the growing civil rights movement and had to decide, as with the ruling elites, on what they could live with vis-a-vis the challenge before them. Because the NAACP was arguing that the formal legal equality of separateness should be real rather than ideological, the Court could move away from the blatant racist legalism consistent with the Compromise of 1877 to one that maintained the spirit of the Compromise while at the same time supporting the formalism of equal separateness. The dialectical struggle between law and those who advocated for civil rights revealed the unjustifiable rank ordering and contradictions within a rapidly changing Jim Crow America.[162]

ENDNOTES

1. David Sugarman, ed., *Legality, Ideology, and the State* (London: Academic Press, 1983), 99.
2. See David E. Bernstein, "Roots of the 'UNDERCLASS': The Decline of Laissez-Faire Jurisprudence and the Rise of Racist Labor Legislation," *American University Law Review* 43 (Fall 1993), 85; Michael Les Benedict, "Laissez-Faire and Liberty: A Re-Evaluation of the Meaning and Origins of Laissez-Faire Constitutionalism," *Law and History Review* 3 (Fall 1985); Gail Williams O'Brien, *The Legal Fraternity and the Making of a New South Community* (1960); Jerold S. Auerbach, *Unequal Justice: Lawyers and Social Change in Modern America* (1976).
3. Alfred H. Kelly, Winfred A. Harbison, and Herman Belz, *The American Constitution: Its Origins and Development* (New York: W.W. Norton and Co., 1976), 368–369.
4. Loren Miller, *The Petitioners: The Story of the Supreme Court of the United States and the Negro* (New York: Pantheon Books, 1966), 180. Professor Miller firmly states that "In the Supreme Court's view . . . the Civil War Amendments had changed little, as far as the Negro's constitutional rights were concerned."
5. Brook Thomas, ed., *Plessy v. Ferguson: A Brief History with Documents* (Boston: Bedford/St. Martin's Press of America, 2003), 169.
6. See H. Viscount "Berky" Nelson, *The Rise and Fall of Modern Black Leadership* (Lanham, MD: University Press of America, 2003) 57–58, 62. Professor Nelson does an excellent job in connecting the earlier Niagara Movement to the NAACP.
7. Nelson, 18–19; see also pp. 79, 186.
8. Richard Bardolph, *The Civil Rights Record: Black Americans and the Law, 1899–1970* (New York: Thomas Y. Crowell Company, 1970), 113, citing W.E.B. Du Bois, *The Souls of Black Folk* (Chicago: A. C. McClurg and Co., 1903), 49–54.
9. Bardolph, 180.
10. Nelson, vii–xiv. Nelson asserts that "For most of the twentieth century African American leaders" were proactive in improving the condition of the social and racial class we know as African Americans.

11. See Kelly, Harbison, and Belz, 396, and the section "States Rights and Economic Regulation," 398–410. See also Brook Thomas's analysis of the old *Santa Clara City v. Southern Pacific Railroad* (1886) case, in which the Supreme Court gave corporations Fourteenth Amendment protection as "individuals."

12. See David E. Bernstein, *Only One Place of Redress: African Americans, Labor Regulations, and the Courts from Reconstruction to the New Deal* (Durham: Duke University Press, 2001).

13. Bernstein, 23–45. Professor Bernstein's examination of the rise of licensing laws served as an exclusionary device in the age of enterprise–monopoly capital. See an excellent analysis of monopoly capitalism and Southern tenancy and peonage in Harold Baron, *The Demand for Black Labor: Historical Notes on the Political Economy of Racism* (Somerville, Massachusetts: New England Free Press, 1971), 13–17.

14. Ian F. Haney Lopez, *White by Law: The Legal Construction of Race* (New York: New York University Press, 1996), 1. Professor Lopez clarifies the question, in part, by examining one of the first legislative acts of the "New Republic" Congress, the 1790 Naturalization Act, which limited naturalization to free "White" persons.

15. Miller, 180.

16. Justice Harlan's dissent in *Plessy v. Ferguson,* 163 U.S. 537 (1896).

17. Herbert Aptheker, *Toward Negro Freedom* (New York: New Century Publishers, 1956), 94. See Alfreda Duster, ed., *Crusade for Justice: The Autobiography of Ida B. Wells* (Chicago: University of Chicago Press, 1972); Stephen R. Fox, *The Guardian of Boston: William Monroe Trotter* (New York: Atheneum, 1970); Hannibal Johnson, *Black Wall Street: From Riot to Renaissance in Tulsa's Historic Greenwood District* (Austin: Eakin Press, 1998); August Meier, *Negro Thoughts in America, 1889–1915* (Ann Arbor: University of Michigan Press, 1963). Du Bois quote in Lerone Bennett, Jr., *Pioneers in Protest* (Baltimore: Johnson Publishing Company, Inc., 1968), 244.

18. Nelson, 33. See also Chapter 2, "Rise of the Color Line."

19. Kelly, Harbison, and Belz, 370, "the restoration of federalism occurred at the expense of genuine Black freedom."

20. Morroe Berger, *Equality by Statute* (Garden City: Doubleday, 1967), 81. Robert Harris, *The Quest for Equality* (Baton Rouge: Louisiana State University, 1960), 108. The law permitted registration for any voter (Whites) whose grandfather or ancestor had voted in the election of 1866. Naturally, this law excluded Blacks because the Fifteenth Amendment was not ratified at that time.

21. C. Vann Woodward, *The Strange Career of Jim Crow* (New York: Oxford University Press: 1966), 85.

22. See Darlene Clark Hines, Steven F. Lawson, and Merline Pitre, *Black Victory: The Rise and Fall of the White Primary* (Columbia: University of Missouri Press, 2003).

23. *William v. Mississippi*, 170 U.S. 213 (1898).

24. See the full interpretation of this decision in Loren Miller, *The Petitioners*, 159.

25. Alexander Tsesis, *We Shall Overcome: A History of Civil Rights and the Law* (New Haven: Yale University Press, 2008), 139.

26. *Giles v . Harris,* 189 U.S. 475.

27. *Cummings v. County Board of Education*, 175 U.S. 582. Harlan and his brethrens would not look behind the decision of Georgia school board to close down, for fiscal reasons, a Black public school while permitting the White public school to remain open. The fact was that Georgia's racists would never close down the White school and let the Black school remain open for budgetary reasons. Was this a case of formalism, or instrumentalism gone berserk?

28. *United States v. Reese* 92 U.S. 214 (1876).

29. Enforcement Act 1876.

30. Miller, 160.

31. *Yick Wo v. Hopkins*, 118 U.S. 356 (1885).

32. *Quinn v. U.S*, 238 U.S. 347 (1915).

33. Miller, *The Petitioners*, 221.

34. Miller, *The Petitioners,* 219–220; see also William Hixon, *Moorfield Storey and the Abolitionist Tradition* (New York: Oxford University Press, 1972).

35. Other alternatives that were as viable as these protests were the migration schemes of Pap Singleton and Chief Alfred Charles Sams in the 1890s that helped to found the all-Black settlements in Kansa and Oklahoma. The most important movement was the Marcus Garvey movement of the 1920s. Both Abram Harris and Harry Haywood observed the type of individual recruited by Garvey. Haywood observed that those recruits "had yet shaken the dust of the plantation from their heels . . . [and] embittered and disillusioned by post-war terror and unemployment, saw in the Garvey scheme . . . a realization of their deep-grounded yearning for land and freedom."

See Haywood's *Negro Liberation* (New York: International Publishers, 1948); William and Gilbert Geis, "Alfred Charles Sams and an African Return: A Case Study in Negro Despair," *Phylon* 23 (2nd Quarter, 1962); Walter L. Fleming, "'Pap' Singleton, the Moses of the Colored Exodus," *American Journal of Sociology* 15 (July 1909); Edwin Redkey, *Black Exodus: Black Nationalist and Back-to-Africa Movements, 1890–1910* (New Haven: Yale University Press, 1964); Tony Martin, *Race First: The Ideological and Organizational Struggles of Marcus Garvey and the Universal Negro Improvement Association* (Westport: Greenwood Press, 1976).

36. Genna Rae McNeil, *Groundwork: Charles Hamilton Houston and the Struggle for Civil Rights* (Philadelphia: University of Pennsylvania Press, 1983), 113–114. See also August Meir and Elliot Rudwick, "Attorneys Black and White: A Case Study of the Race Relations Within the NAACP," *Journal of American History* 62, 4 (March 1976), 913–946.

37. Tony Martin, *Race First: The Ideological and Organizational Struggles of Marcus Garvey and the Universal Negro Improvement Association* (Westport: Greenwood Press, 1976).

38. Genna Rae McNeil, 101. See also Pauli Murray, "The Historical Development of Race Laws in the U.S.," *The Journal of Negro Education* 22, 1 (Winter, 1953), 4–15.

39. See Robert H. Brisbane, *The Black Vanguard: Origins of the Negro Social Revolution, 1900–1960* (Valley Forge: Judson Press, 1969).

40. United States Constitution, Fourteenth Amendment, Section 2.

41. Rayford W. Logan, *The Betrayal of the Negro: From Rutherford B. Hayes to Woodrow Wilson* (London: Collier Books 1969), 70–75.

42. *Newberry v. United States*, 256 U.S. (1921).

43. *Nixon v. Herndon*, 273 U.S. 536 (1927). See also Albert P. Blaustein and Robert L. Zangrando, editors, *Civil Rights and the American Negro: A Documentary History* (New York: Trident Press 1968) 396.

44. Donald Lively, *The Constitution and Race* (Westport: Praeger, 1992), 75.

45. *Nixon v. Condon,* 286 U.S. 73 (1932).

46. Richard Bardolph, *The Civil Rights Record: Black Americans and the Law, 1849–1970* (New York: Thomas Y. Cromwell Company, 1970), 212–213.

47. *Grovey v. Townsend*, 295 U.S. 45 (1935).

48. *Breedlove v. Suttles,* 392 U.S. 277 (1937).

49. Genna Rae McNeil, 101–102. Du Bois raised the class question.

50. Pete Daniel, *The Shadow of Slavery: Peonage in the South, 1901–1969* (Chicago: University of Illinois Press, 1972), 10–11. See also Charles S. Johnson, *The Shadow of the Plantation* (Chicago: University of Chicago Press, 1934), 216. See Robert L. Hale, "Some Basic Constitutional Rights of Economic Significance," *Columbia Law Review,* 51 (March 1951), 270–272. See also Thomas E. Edwards, "The Tenant System and Social Changes Since Emancipation: The Negro's Progress in 50 Years," *Annals of the American Academy of Political and Social Sciences,* XLIV (September 1913), 38–46.

51. Daniel, p. 10; *peonage* defined as "a status or condition of compulsory service, based upon the indebtedness of the peon to the master." *Clyatt v. U.S.* 197 U.S. 215 (1905).

52. Daniel, 25.

53. Daniel, 21.

54. John Hope Franklin, *Reconstruction*, 48–49. Slaves Codes modified as Black Codes to regulate to labor of the freedpeople. It permitted "any person to arrest and return to his employer any Negro who quit before the expiration of his contracted term of labor."

55. Robert Carr, *Federal Protection of Civil Rights: Quest for a Sword* (Ithaca: Cornell University Press, 1947), 77.

56. Carr, 77.

57. Pete Daniel; see Chapter V "The Land Where It Never Snows," 82–109. This chapter describes how planters enticed newly arrived Italian immigrants into the Southern peonage system.

58. Metaphor used by Justice Jackson in *Pollock v. Williams* that invalidated Florida's peonage statute. Justice Jackson noted that individual liberties in America are protected by a defensive shield of constitutionalism and a sword of federal enforcement of violators of civil liberties. See Carr, *Federal Protection of Civil Rights*, 3–32.

59. W.E.B. Du Bois, *Black Reconstruction in America, 1860–1880* (New York: Atheneum, 1971), 696. See also Carter G. Woodson, *The Rural Negro* (Washington, D.C.: Association for the Study of Negro Life and History, 1930); Richard Stencer, *The Negro's Share* (New York: Harper and Brothers, 1943).

60. *Hodges v. U.S.,* 203 U.S. (1905).

61. Allen W. Trelease, *White Terror: The Ku Klux Klan Conspiracy and Southern Reconstruction* (New York: HarperCollins, 1971).

62. *Allegeyer v. Lousisina,* 165 U.S. 78 (1897).

63. Kelly, Harbison, and Belz, 414–415.

64. *Clyatt v. United States,* 197 U.S. 207 (1905).

65. Daniel, 16.

66. *Clyatt v. United States,* at 218–219; see also Loren Miller, 191.

67. To control Black labor, Southern states passed "false pretenses" laws that punished laborers who broke contracts after being paid in advance. These laws were struck down by the Alabama Supreme Court. Planters responded with *prima facie* laws that placed the burden of proof on the peon. See Daniel, 67.

68. Miller, *The Petitioners,* 194.

69. These groups helped finance the first case. Included in this group were Booker T. Washington, Oswald Garrison Villard, Ray Stannard Baker, and Attorney General Charles T. Bonaparte. Bonaparte's main interest was crushing peonage pertaining to European immigrants. See Daniel, *The Shadow of Slavery,* 69.

70. There were quite a few five-to-four decisions in this period. A change in personnel sometimes meant the difference between a liberal versus a conservative interpretation of constitutional issues.

71. Miller, 193.

72. *United States v. Reynolds,* 235 U.S. 9 (1914); *United States v. Broughton,* 235 U.S. (1914); see also Miller, 194.

73. Three cases in the early 1940s concerning identical peonage facts as the second Bailey case of 1911. *Taylor v. Georgia* 315 U.S. 25 (1942); *United States v. Gaskins,* 320 U.S. 52 (1944); *Pollack v. Williams,* 322 U.S. 4 (1943).

74. See Daniel, 180.

75. Huff's situation embodied some of the finer features of the runaway clause, slave catcher, and state official scenario. A Georgia planter, William T. Cunningham, pursued four of his runaway indebted Black laborers to Chicago and with the help of Chicago police attained their arrest. With the help of the Peonage Committee, he successfully reopened his case.

76. Daniel, 140–150.

77. Walter White, "The Negro and the Flood," *The Nation,* 124 (1927), 689.

78. Daniel, 149.

79. Daniel, 150–169.

80. Daniel, see Chapter VII, "Two Old Men," 149–169.

81. David E. Bernstein, *Only One Place of Redress: African Americans, Labor Regulations, and the Courts from Reconstruction to the New Deal,* see Chapter One, "Emigrant Agent Laws" (Durham: Duke University Press, 2001). Pete Daniel's book, *The Shadow of Slavery: Peonage in the South, 1901–1969* (Chicago: University of Illinois Press, 1972), is replete with examples of labor agents enticing workers into the "Vortex of Peonage." See also William H. Harris, *The Harder We Run: Black Workers Since the Civil War* (New York: Oxford University Press, 1982), 13.

82. David E. Bernstein, 9, 16–24.

83. Baron, 26. William Forbath, "The Ambiguities of Free Labor: Labor and Law in the Gilded Age," *Wisconsin Law Review* (1985); see *Butchers Union v. Crescent City Co.,* 111 US. 746 (1884).

84. David E. Bernstein, 16. "The Georgia Exodus."

85. See David Montgomery, *Beyond Equality: Labor and the Radical Republicans, 1862–1872* (New York: Vintage, 1967).

86. David E. Bernstein, 12–16.

87. *Williams v. Fears,* 179 U.S. 270 (1900); see facts and analysis in David Bernstein, *Only One Place of Redress: African Americans, Labor Relations, and the Courts from Reconstruction to the New Deal* (Durham: Duke University Press, 2001), 15–19.

88. Bernard H. Nelson, *The Fourteenth Amendment and the Negro Since 1920* (New York: Russell and Russell, 1946), 23. Loren Miller, *The Petitioners,* 246; restrictive covenants developed in San Francisco locking out Chinese citizens. See also Clement E. Vose, *Caucasians Only: The Supreme Court, the NAACP, and the Restrictive Covenant Cases* (Berkeley: University of California Press, 1959).

89. *Buchanan v. Warley,* 245 U.S. 60 (1917).

90. *Buchannan v. Warley* majority dictum; Clement Vose, *Caucasian Only: The Supreme Court, the NAACP, and the Restrictive Covenant Cases* (1959); see also Loren Miller, 250.

91. *Corrigan v. Buckley,* 271 U.S. 323 (1926).

92. Loren Miller, 234. The background of this case gives one a searing glimpse into the inevitable conflict between Black labor and White economic hegemony in the South during this period. In 1919, under the leadership of Robert L. Hill, a Black war veteran, the Philips County, Arkansas, Blacks organized into a fraternal order, the purpose being to pool their monetary resources to attain an anti-peonage lawyer. They hoped to press their claims of peonage violations against area planters. Planter reaction was to accuse Hill of organizing to "massacre" Whites and seize their land. After a shooting that left Whites dead, White mob rampage, over a seven-day period, killed twenty-five Blacks. This farcical trial and sentence was reversed by the U.S. Supreme Court. See excellent account by Walter White, "Massacring Whites in Arkansas," *The Nation* (December 6, 1919); Charles S. Johnson, *The Collapse of Cotton Tenancy* (New York: Books for Libraries Press, 1935).

93. *Moore v. Dempsey,* 261 U.S. 86 (1926).

94. Loren Miller, 235.

95. *Virginia v. Rives*, 100 U.S. 545 (1880).

96. *Martin v. Texas*, 200 U.S. 316 (1906).

97. See Robert Higgs, *Competition, Coercion, and Blacks in the American Economy* (Boston: Cambridge University Press, 1977). See also Randall Kennedy, "The State, Criminal Law, Racial Discrimination: A Comment," *Harvard Law Review*, 107, 3 (April 1994).

98. *Berea College v. Kentucky*, 211 U.S. 26 (1906).

99. *Berea College* case; majority dictum.

100. *Gong Lum v. Rice,* 275 U.S. 78 (1927).

101. Joseph Tussman, *The Supreme Court on Racial Discrimination* (Boston: Oxford University Press, 1963), 19. See also Malik Simba, "*Gong Lum v. Rice*: The Convergence of Law, Race, and Ethnicity," in *American Mosaic: Selected Readings on America's Multicultural Heritage,* eds. Young I. Song and Eugene C. Kim (Englewood Cliffs: Prentice-Hall, 1993), 265–275.

102. Tussman, 22.

103. Tussman, 22.

104. Mary Beth Norton, Carol Sheriff, David M. Katzman, David W. Blight, and Howard Chudacoff, *A People and A Nation: A History of the United* States (Boston: Houghton Mifflin Company, 2008), 461. See also Paula S. Rothenberg, *Race, Class, Gender in the United States: An Integrated Study* (New York: St. Martin's Press, 1995), 336–338.

105. Norton, et al., 461.

106. *Dred Scott v. Sanford,* 19 Howard 393 (1857). Justice Taney's infamous dictum.

107. Professor Genna Rae McNeil refers to Charles Hamilton Houston as the man who killed Jim Crow with his brilliant legal strategy. See her biography *Groundwork: Charles Hamilton Houston and the Struggle for Civil Rights* (Philadelphia: University of Pennsylvania Press, 1983).

108. McNeil, 113.

109. McNeil, 114–115.

110. See Bernard Sternsher, ed., *The Negro in the Depression and War: Prelude to Revolution, 1930–1945* (Chicago: Quadrangle Books, 1969).

111. Loren Miller, 209.

112. Richard Kluger, *Simple Justice: The History of Brown v. Board of Education and Black America's Struggle for Equality* (New York: Vintage Books, 1975), 201. See also Donald G. Nieman, *Promises to Keep: African-Americans and the Constitutional Order, 1776 to the Present* (New York: Oxford University Press, 1991), 136–137.

113. McNeil, 138–139.

114. *Missouri ex rel Gaines v. Canada,* 305 U.S. 337 (1938).

115. Justice Hughes' dictum in the *Gaines* case.

116. The Elaine, Arkansas, case is definitive in how the Court began to take this approach.

117. Ironically, the Court went behind the law in this case concerning Chinese laundries.

118. See Leonard Baker, *Back to Back: The Duel Between FDR and the Supreme Court* (1967); see also William E. Leuchtenburg, "The Origins of President Franklin D. Roosevelt's Court Packing Plan," *Supreme Court Review* (1966), 352–399.

119. Kermit L. Hall, *The Magic Mirror: Law in American History* (New York: Oxford University Press, 1989). See section entitled "Judicial Restraint and the Acceptance of the Administrative and Social Welfare State," 282–283.

120. Personal interview with Dr. Herbert Aptheker at his home, San Jose, California (2001). Dr. Aptheker used this phrase in a scholastic article. This article was based on his experience witnessing hunger and starvation in Southern states as he travelled with his father.

121. Karl Klare, "Critical Theory and Labor Relations Law," in David Kairys, *The Politics of Law: A Progressive Critique* (New York: Pantheon Books, 1982). Klare critique concerns the formalistic relationship between "industrial democracy" and "liberal labor law" that holds out a jurisprudence of well-defined protective rights of labor (see p. 66).

122. Wilson Record, *The Negro and the Communist Party* (New York: Atheneum, 1971), 126.

123. Mark Naison, *Communism in Harlem During the Depression* (Urbana: University of Illinois Press, 1983), 133, 178. See also Robin Kelly, *Hammer and Hoe: Alabama Communists During the Great Depression* (Durham: University of North Carolina Press, 1990). See also Philip Foner, "I.W.W. and the Black Worker," *Journal of Negro History* 55 (1970), 45–64.

124. Naison, 75–76, 82–84, . Professor Naison does an excellent job at explaining and demonstrating with vivid examples of this polarity.

125. See Naison section on *Popular Front*, 169–170.

126. Naison, 87.

127. Naison, 172.

128. Naison, 172.

129. Naison, 80–82; 132–134.

130. The NAACP's approach was to accept law as a "rules" process that could contour via working within the proverbial law box. They believed that social pressure on the law box was disruptive of procedural rules.

131. Naison, see Chapters 6 and 7 for a description of various rallies and minor attacks on the NAACP.

132. *Powell v. Alabama,* 287 U.S. 45 (1932).

133. See Jacqueline Dowd Hall, *Revolt Against Chivalry: Jessie Daniel Ames and the Women's Campaign Against Lynching* (New York: Columbia University Press, 1976). See also Hugh T. Murray, Jr., "The NAACP versus the Communist Party: The Scottsboro Rape Cases, 1931–1932," in *The Negro in Depression and War: Prelude to Revolution, 1930–1945,* ed. Bernard Stenser (Chicago: Quadrangle Books, 1969), 267–281.

134. *Norris v. Alabama,* 294 U.S. 587 (1935).

135. Loren Miller, 272.

136. *Herndon v. Lowrey,* 301 U.S. 242 (1935).

137. Kendall Thomas, "Rouge et Noir: ReRead: A Popular Constitutional History of the Angelo Herndon Case" in Kimberle Crenshaw, Neil Gotanda, Gary Peller, and Kendall Thomas, *Critical Race Theory: Key Writings That Formed the Movement* (New York: The New Press, 1995), 471. See also Carl Swidosh, "The Courts, the Labor Movement and the Struggle for Freedom of Expression of Association, 1919–1940," *Labor History* 45, 1 (February 2004), 61–84.

138. Angelo Herndon, *Let Me Live* (Ann Arbor: University of Michigan Press, 2007; first published by Random House, 1937).

139. Kendall Thomas, 466.

140. See Paul Murphy, *The Constitution in Crisis Times, 1918–1969* (New York: Harper Row, 1972). See also Zechariah Chaffee, *Free Speech in the U.S.* (Cambridge: Harvard University Press, 1941).

141. *Brown v. Mississippi,* 297 U.S. 278 (1936). See also Richard Cortner, *A Scottsboro Case in Mississippi: The Supreme Court and Brown v. Mississippi* (Jackson: University Press of Mississippi, 1986).

142. Loren Miller, 279. In another case of torture, *Chambers v. Florida,* 309 U.S. 227 (1940), the Court said that a confession based on a coercive interrogation over several days and nights could not stand the test of due process of law.

143. Loren Miller, 280.

144. Even though one talks about the progressive *Scottsboro* decisions, the boys still spent very lengthy prison terms because of local autonomous Southern injustice.

145. The Supreme Court consistently supported the NAACP position that separate but equal must be substantially equal. See law school cases out of Oklahoma and Texas.

146. Except for the incarceration of Japanese Americans, this trend tended to be true.

147. *Bank of United States v. Deveaux*, 5 Cranch 1.

148. Earl Black and Merle Black, *The Rise of Southern Republicans* (Cambridge: Harvard University Press, 2002), 43.

149. *The Raw Deal* was another name that Blacks gave FDR's New Deal. This term was based on the discriminatory practices on many New Deal programs. See Leslie H. Fishel, Jr. "The Negro in the New Deal Era," in *The Negro in Depression and War: Prelude to Revolution, 1930–1945*, ed. Bernard Sternsher (Chicago, Quadrangle Books, 1969), 7–28.

150. Record, 108.

151. The CIO's major objective was "to bring about the effective organization of the working men and women of America regardless of race, color, creed, or nationality." Quoted in Bernard Sternsher. Essay by Herbert R. Northrup, "Organized Labor and Negro Workers," 127–149.

152. Bernard Nelson, 100–101.

153. Loren Miller, 257–258. See Bernard Nelson on the issue of "yellow dog" contract.

154. Barton J. Bernstein and Allen J. Matusow, eds., *Twentieth Century America: Recent Interpretations* (New York: Harcourt, Brace, and World, 1969), 289.

155. Melville J. Herskovitz and Franz Boaz wrote extensively on cultural pluralism and provided an anti-racist intellectual forum for debate that influenced America's social consciousness. See John Gershenhorn, *Melville J. Herskovitz and the Politics of Knowldege* (Omaha: University of Nebraska Press, 2004); Vernon Williams, Jr., *Rethinking Race: Franz Boas and His Contemporaries* (Lexington: University Press of Kentucky, 1996).

156. Bardolph, 188.

157. Nelson, 57–58.

158. See Mary L. Dudziak, *Cold War Civil Rights: Race and the Image of American Democracy* (Princeton: Princeton University Press, 2002). This is a strong thesis. The question that her research poses is, "Why desegregate?" America had just defeated the two major threats to American democracy—Germany and Japan. Winning the hearts and minds of Third World–people and thereby winning the Cold War could not be achieved without securing the rights of America's minorities via the dismantling of Jim Crow.

159. See Baker, *Back to Back: The Duel Between FDR and the Supreme Court* (1967); see also Leuchtenburg, "The Origins of President Franklin D. Roosevelt's Court Packing Plan," *Supreme Court Review* (1966), 352–399.

160. The *writ of certiorari* permits the Court to cast a broad net and select hot cases from the lower courts of appeals. The term *certiorari* means "to be informed of" and permits the Court to "inspect the proceeding conducted in a lower court to determine whether there have been irregularities." Quote on p. 230 of Kermit L. Hall, *The Magic Mirror: Law in American History* (New York: Oxford University Press, 1989).

161. See Kermit L. Hall, 277. "The Supreme Court review was made overwhelmingly discretionary through the writ of certiorari."

162. See Alexa B. Henderson, "FEPC and the Southern Railway Case: An Investigation into the Discriminatory Practices of Railroads During World War II," *The Journal of Negro History* LXI, 2 (April, 1976), 173–187. Charles H. Martin, "Race, Gender, and Southern Justice: The Rosa Lee Ingram Case," *The American Journal of Legal History*, volume 29 (1985), 250–268; Mary L. Dudziak, "Desegregation as a Cold War Imperative," *Stanford Law Review*, volume 41, No. 1 (1988), 61–120.

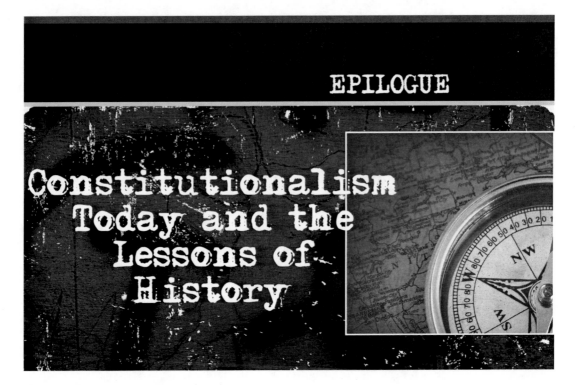

Constitutionalism Today and the Lessons of History

During the 1940s, the NAACP's social engineers won cases before the U.S. Supreme Court that struck down White primaries (*Smith v. Allwright,* 1944), ruled illegal segregation on interstate transportation (*Morgan v. Virginia,* 1944), and said that court-enforced racial restrictive housing covenants were unconstitutional (*Shelly v. Kramer,* 1948). *Amicus curiae* briefs from the State Department and the Justice Department supported the Court's position. This support by the federal state had to do with the emerging Cold War and the propaganda of Communist Russia, which argued that it was hypocritical of the United States to claim that they were the leaders of the free world when lynching, rape, and Jim Crow were as American as apple pie. Secretary of State John Foster Dulles said and understood that the United States could not win the hearts and minds of Third World–people when their phenotypical counterparts in the United States were treated as second-class citizens in the United States. An earlier recognition of this fact was clearly understood by President Truman when, in 1948, the Democratic party issued the document "To Secure These Rights." This document was a clarion for a federal attack on Jim Crow. The United States Supreme Court's Constitutional "salvo" was the 1954 case of *Linda Brown v. Board of Education—Topeka, Kansas.* In ruling, the Court stated that separate but equal as doctrine was unconstitutional because it has a "detrimental effect upon the colored children." A more critical understanding of this case points out that the hegemony of racism also had a similar detrimental effect upon White children.

CIVIL RIGHTS AND BEYOND

The Civil Rights Movement in the late 1950s and 1960s had constitutional law on its side and, to many others, God almighty. Law, faith, and race and class struggle were revealed in sit-ins, pray-ins, and wade-ins that desegregated public eating places, churches, and pools. In 1964, President Johnson issued Executive Order 11246, which forbade job discrimination and required "affirmative action" by corporations receiving federal contracts. Congress passed the Civil Rights Act of 1964, the Voting Rights Act of 1965, and the Fair Housing Act of 1968. The U.S. Supreme Court validated this legislation in *Heart of Atlanta Motel v. U.S.* (1964), *Katzenbach v. McClung* (1964), *South Carolina v. Katzenbach* (1966), and *Jones v. Alfred H. Mayer Co.* (1968). The NAACP continued to push the Court to extend Linda Brown's struggle, and in 1970, the Court did just that. In *Alexander v. Holmes County Board of Education* (1969) and in *Carter West Feliciana Parish School v. Board* (1970), the Court mandated no more "deliberate speed" for school boards who attempted to obstruct the principles of *Brown,* but "full speed" ahead, even if it meant busing to achieve racial balance in America's schools. The Court's aggressive approach would continue in *Swann v. Charlotte–Mecklenburg Board of Education* (1971), when it ordered 13,000 students bused. These victories in the South were tempered by the Court's inability to do likewise in the Northern and Western areas of the country. In the 1973 Denver case *Keys v. School District No. 1*, the Court refused to order a citywide desegregation plan that limited, on a school-by-school basis, any plan for racial balance. The Court said that each school must be guilty of "intentional" efforts at school segregation. This conservative legal trend continued in 1974 in the case of *Milliken v. Bradley*, when a court-ordered citywide suburban plan in Detroit was overruled by the U.S. Supreme Court. The High Court reasoned that local suburban schools should not be included arbitrarily, even if the goal was noble.

The end of the Civil Rights Movement, coupled with the election of conservative president Richard M. Nixon, signaled a major shift in public policy support and the federal state's support for desegregation. With the help of Nixon's Supreme Court appointees, the Court became known as the *Nixon Court* or the *Burger Court* (after Warren Burger, the chef justice appointed by President Nixon). The contradictions between legal formalism and instrumentalism can be seen during this period. The Court began to chip away at the recently achieved legal progress. However, the Court did initially uphold the anti-job discrimination clause, Title VII of the 1964 Civil Rights Act, in *Griggs v. Duke Power* (1971). However, the Court then reversed and modified the *Griggs* ruling in the 1976 case of *Washington v. Davis*. Both cases involved the interpretation of the new 1972 legislation, the Equal Employment Opportunity Act, which strengthened Title VII. The anti-job discrimination and affirmative action requirements of Executive Order 11246 divided the nation over such ideological terms as *reverse discrimination* and *preferential treatment*.

The Court addressed these ideological terms first in *Regents of University of California v. Bakke* (1977). In examining Alan Bakke's claim of being "bumped" because of the law school's preferential admission quota policies, the Court ruled in Bakke's favor but suggested that race can continue to be a valuable tool in admission policy *sans* quotas. Within this collusion between formalism and instrumentalism, the Court, in 1979 and 1980, respectively, upheld a private corporation's preferential treatment program that helped minority workers gain new skills (*United States Steelworkers of America v. Weber*) and a congressional program that "set aside" ten percent of federal funds for minority-owned businesses (*Fullilove v. Klutznik*).

The conservative leaning of the Burger Court eventually appeared in the case of *Mobil v. Bolden* (1980), when the Court established the "intentional" or "motivational" legal principle to ferret out individuals who discriminate. To prove discrimination, the intention of the discriminator must be proved. This was a decisive change from the "results-oriented" Warren Court, which had assumed that if it walks like a duck, quacks like a duck, and looks like a duck, then it must be a duck. The difficulty of proving intentprotected many racists who went underground. However, the victory of Ronald Reagan in the 1980 presidential election further solidified the country's slide into the abyss of conservatism, as revealed in 1982, when the Reagan administration filed an *amicus curiae* brief in support of the closeted White racist Bob Jones University. Bob Jones claimed its tax-exempt status, withdrawn by the Internal Revenue Service, was unconstitutional. The IRS claimed that Bob Jones practiced discrimination and therefore could not receive federal funds. The Supreme Court ruled in favor of the IRS. Reagan's revenge was to use the ideological term *reverse discrimination* to have his Justice Department file various *amicus curiae* to support White men or White businesses threatened by Black progress initiated by affirmative action programs. This approach was successful in the case of *Firefighters v. Stotts*, 1983, and *Wygnat v. Jackson*, 1986. In both cases, the Court used "White seniority" to protect those at the top from newly hired minorities.

A change in Court personnel (Reagan appointed Anthony Kennedy to replace retiring Justice Powell) gave Court conservatives a majority. This led to the direct subversion or elimination of affirmative action programs in such cases as *Martin v. Wilks,* 1980; *Patteson v. McLean Credit Union,* 1989; *Ward's Cove Packing Company v. Antonio,* 1989; and *Richmond v. Croson,* 1989. In a rare turn of events, Justice White broke with the conservative majority. He sided with a slim liberal majority and supported a tax-increase to poverty-stricken neighborhood schools in *Missouri v. Jenkins*, 1990. In addition, this new liberal majority also upheld affirmative action goals that increased the number of minority broadcast-owned stations in *Metro Broadcasting v. Federal Communication Commission*, 1990.

President Reagan's imprint on conservative judicial activism cannot be overlooked. His judicial appointments to the High Court (e.g., Black conservative Clarence Thomas replacing Black liberal social activist Thurgood Marshall) as well as David Souter and William Rehnquist led to decisive decisions reflecting a conservative mood in White America. The Court ruled that schools be released from judicial oversight when they began to dismantle Jim Crow in *Board of Education of Oklahoma City Public Schools v. Dowell* (1990) and *Freeman v. Pitts* (1992). Betraying the freedom summers of voter registration and the victims of Klan Terror, the Court, with Souter writing the opinion, diluted minority political power in *Johnson v. DeGrandy* (1994). In this decision, the Court said that the Voting Rights Act does not require Florida's reapportionment plan to increase Black and Hispanic voting power. The social impact of this conservative legal chill under the recent Bush administration was ultimately revealed in one of two cases concerning the University of Michigan. In *Gratz v. Bollinger* (2003), the Supreme Court struck down the use of race as an evaluative variable in the university's affirmative action undergraduate admissions plan. And consistent with *Bakke*, the Court said the University of Michigan's law school could use race as one of many variables in the law school's efforts at attaining diversity—*Grutter v. Bollinger* (2003). Obviously, even with the social stratification of minorities, race and class converged in these two cases. The election of President Obama will ultimately signal another shift in the trajectory of constitutionalism, race, class, and the law. His tenure as president will enable him to appoint new justices to the Supreme Court who will reflect his liberal, social activist, realist, progressive, and instrumentalist approach to law, society, and social change.

SUGGESTED READINGS

Mary L. Dudziak, *Cold War Civil Rights: Race and the Image of American Democracy* (Princeton: Princeton University Press, 2000).

Alan David Freeman, "Legitimizing Racial Discrimination Through Antidiscrimination Law: A Critical Review of Supreme Court Doctrine," *Minnesota Law Review*, 62 (1978), 1049–1119.

Susan Goldberg, "Equality Without Tiers," *Rutgers Law School (Newark)* 2 (2004), 482–582.

Nathan Hakman, "Political Trials and the Legal Order: A Political Scientist's Perspective," *Journal of Public Law*, 21 (1972), 73–126.

Thomas Kleven, "The Supreme Court, Race, and the Class Struggle," *Hofstra Law Review,* 9 (1981), 795–858.

Donald E. Lively, *The Constitution and Race* (Westport: Praeger, 1992).

John B. McConahay, Courtney J. Mullin, and Jeffrey Frederick, "The Uses of Social Science in Trials With Political and Racial Overtones: The Trial of Joan Little," *Law and Contemporary Problems*, 41, No. 1 (1977), 205–229.

Donald G. Nieman, *Promises to Keep: African-Americans and the Constitutional Order, 1776 to the Present* (New York: Oxford University Press, 1991).

Lewis Steel, "Nine Men in Black—Who Think White," *New York Times Magazine (Sunday),* October 13, 1988, 56–122.

Alexander Tsesis, *We Shall Overcome: A History of Civil Rights and the Law* (New Haven: Yale University Press, 2008).

INDEX

A

Abolitionist movement, 17
Act of 1875
    rhetoric used, 95
Adams, J.
    slavery and, 35
Adams, J. Q., 49
African Americans community, 7–8
African labor
    legal control, 19
    legal statutes and, 24
    and political economy, 17
    poor Whites and, 20–21
    status of slavery, 23
America
    civil war, 44
    constitutional law, 1
    democratic slave economy, 8
    law transformation, 45
    racial domination in, 8
    Revolution and Constitutional Convention, 29
    Whiteness and social relationships, 102
American Constitutionalism, 11
Amistad, 5
Anglo-saxon race, 110
Anti-Peonage Act
    Clyatt v. U.S. in 1905, 124
    of March 2, 1867, 96, 123
Atlanta Exposition speech, 101
Australian ballot, 97–98
Authoritarian social structure, 30

B

Balbus, I., 3–4
Baron, H., 18
Bestor, A., 47
Bill of Rights, 57
Bingham, J. A., 70
Blackburn, R., 19
Black community
    A. M. E. church review, 113
    Black labor, 89
        force, 6

legal definition of equality, 90
    rights, 90
    White terror, 92
Black Marxism, 11
    in New Orleans, 107
    railroad corporations, 107–108
"Black Gold" transportation, 19
Black Reconstruction, 82
Boston Female Antislavery Society, 50
Bradwell, M., 129
Breen, T. H., 19
Brown, H. B.
    Plessy case decision, 110
Burgess, J. W., 84

C

Capitalism, 9
Capitalist–slave relationships, 25
Cases
    Abelman v Booth, 55
    Abelman v. Booth, 95
    Alice Jones vs. Leonard "Kip" Rhinelander, 9
    Allegeyer v. Louisiana, 124
    Berea College vs. Kentucky, 128
    Bradwell v. Illinois, 129
    Breedlove v. Suttles, 122
    Buchanan v. Warley, 127
    Civil Rights Cases, 118
    Clyatt v. U.S. in 1905, 124
    Collins v. America, 63
    Commonwealth v. Aves, 62
    Commonwealth v. Carver, 60
    Commonwealth v. Jennison, 35
    Corrigan v. Buckley, 127
    Cruikshank Case, 118
    Cummings v. Board of Education, 107
    Dred Scott v. Sanford, 53, 55
    Elkinson v. Deliesseline, 51
    Ex parte Virginia, 95
    Farwell v. Boston, 59
    Giles vs. Harris, 120
    Gong Lum v. Rice, 128
    Gregson v. Gilbert, 19

Cases (*continued*)
    Groves v. Slaughter, 51
    Grovey v. Townsend, 122
    Herndon v. U.S., 132
    Hodges v.U.S., 124
    Hudgins v. Wright, 9
    James vs. Bowman, 93
    Jennison v. Caldwell, 35
    Logan v. U.S., 111
    Major v. State, 61
    Mima Queen v. Hepburn, 37–38, 48
    Missouri ex rel Gaines v. Canada, 130
    Moore v. Dempsey, 128
    Newbery v. U.S., 122
    Nixon v. Condon, 122
    Nixon v. Herndon, 122
    Norris v. Alabama, 132
    Pace v. Alabama, 106
    Plessy v. Ferguson, 102, 105–106, 109
    Plessy v. Ferguson, and Cummings, 129
    Powell v. Alabama, 131
    Prigg v. Pennsylvania, 95
    Quinn v. U.S., 120–121
    Quock Walker v. Jennison, 35–36
    Roberts v. City of Boston, 46, 129
    Rodney v. Illinois Central Railroad, 63
    Scottsboro Cases and Ed Brown's case, 132–133
    Scudder v. Woodbridge, 56, 59
    Somerset v. Steward, 52
    State ex rel. Abbott v. Hicks, 108
    State v. Hale, 60
    State v. Jim, 62
    State v. Mann, 56, 58
    State v. Will, 61
    Strader v. Graham, 55
    Strauder v. West Virginia, 95
    Texas v. White, 71
    United States v. La Jeune Eugenie, 50
    University of Maryland v. Murray, 130
    U.S. v. Harris, 93, 106
    U.S. vs. Cruikshank
        compromise in, 91–92
    U.S. vs. Reese, 92
    Virginia v. Rives, 95, 128
    Virginia v. Rives and jury rights cases, 118
    Willard v. State, 63
    Williams v. Fears, 126
    Williams vs. Mississippi, 119
Cincinnati meeting of 1891, 97
Citizens' Committee to Test Constitutionality of
       Separate Car Law, 108
Civil Rights Acts, 6, 93–94, 124

Civil Rights Cases, 95, 105
Civil war
    constitutional standards of, 106
Colored Farmers' National Alliance, 97
Communist International Labor Defense (ILD), 131
Congressional Act of 1970, 35
Conklin, R., 7
Constitutionalism and freedpeople, 69
Constitution, color race in
    all-White general elections, 119
    Alonso Bailey of Alabama, 125
    Anti-Peonage Act in
        Clyatt v. U.S. in 1905, 124
    Anti-Peonage Act of March 2, 1867, 123
    Berea College vs. Kentucky, 128
    Black Codes, 123
    Black community, 121
    Black labor, 126
    Black professionals, 129–130
    Bradwell v. Illinois, 129
    Buchanan v. Warley, 127
    Civil Rights Act of 1866, 124
    civil rights movement, 118
    Civil War Amendments, 118
    colored advisory committee, 125
    communist party USA, 131
    Corrigan v. Buckley, 127
    court's interpretations in, 118
    Crow, J. system, 119
    debt-slavery, 123
    de facto practices, 125
    Dred Scott dictum, 129
    enforcement act of 1870, 120
    FDR, 130–131, 134
    Force Bill, 121
    Fourteenth Amendment, 122
    Georgia legislature
        licensing tax of, 126
        White and Black communities, 127
        Williams v. Fears, 126
    Giles vs. Harris, 120
    Gong Lum v. Rice, 128
    Harlan's
        dissent in *Plessy*, 119
        legal lynching, a la Colfax Massacre, 119
    Hodges case, 124
    Jeffersonian Democracy and the Calhoun principles, 120
    Justice department
        failure of, 125
    Maryland court, 130
    monopoly capitalism, 118
    Monroe Doctrine, 120

Moore v. Dempsey, 128
NAACP, 118, 121–122
Negro race, 121
Newbery v. U.S., 122
Norris v. Alabama, 132
Plessy decision, 117
Plessy v. Ferguson, and Cummings, 129
poll tax, 119–120
popular front approach, 131
Powell v. Alabama, 131
Quinn v. U.S. in 1915, 120–121
Reese case, 120
Roberts v. City of Boston, 129
Scottsboro Cases and Herndon Case, 131
south's effort, 119
Supreme Court 1896-1936
    redeeming decisions, 119
surety, 124
thirteenth amendment, 123
University of Maryland v. Murray, 130
Virginia v. Rives, 128
Walter White of
    NAACP, 125
white juries, 123–124
Cover, R.
    Justice Accused, 63
Crandall, P., 46
The Crisis, 126
Crow, J., 8, 79, 102, 120, 129, 131, 135
    law, 105–109, 112
    legal superstructure, 128
    political economy, 118
    system, 89, 119
Cruikshank, W., 92
    case, 118
Curtin, P. D., 18

D

Daniel, P., 123
Darwinian racialism, 110
David Walker's Appeal, 51
Davis, A., 5
Day, T., 31
Day, W., 93
DeBow, J. D. B., 57
Declaration of Independence, 30
De Felice's Encyclopedie, 30
Democracy in America, 33
Democrats and liberal republicans, 92
Desdunes, D. F., 108
de Tocqueville, A., 10
    Democracy in America, 33

Dicey, A. V.
    equalization of unequal social beings, 4
The Dispatch, 113
Douglas, S. A., 54
Douglass, F., 2, 8
DuBois, W. E. B., 84
Duke's Laws, 24

E

Economy and Society, 3
Emerson, J., 54–55
Enforcement Act, 71, 92
England
    African labor in, 18
    Africans commerced into colony, 19
    "Black Gold" transportation, 19
Equality defined, 30–31
European Industrial Revolution, 17

F

Federalism, 7
    defined, 32
Ferguson, J. H., 109
Fetishism of commodities, 5
Field, J. S.
    philosophical approach, 111
Foner, L., 17
Formalistic law, 5
Formal Style of law, 47
Franklin Delano Roosevelt (FDR), 130–131, 134
Franklin, J. H., 101
Freedman Bureau Act in 1865, 70
Freedom lawsuits, 36–37
Free-labor system, 71–79
Freeman, E., 5
Free soil/federal power of antislavery, 44
Fries's Rebellion, 32
Fugitive Slave Act
    of 1793, 52, 95
    of 1850, 53
Fuller, M.
    emancipation proclamation, 110
    illinois constitutional convention, 110

G

Garfield, J. A., 83–84
Garland, C., 129
Genovese, E., 17–18
    hegemonic function of law, 4
Georgia legislature
    licensing tax of, 126

Georgia legislature (*continued*)
  White and Black communities, 127
  Williams v. Fears, 126
Grady, H., 79
Gramsci, A., 3–4
Gramscian theory, 60
Gray, H., 111
Great Depression, 11, 133

H
Hall, K., 17
Hamilton, C., 129
Handlin, M., 18
Harlan, J. M., 95, 111
Harlan, M.
  dissent in *Plessy,* 119
  legal lynching, a la Colfax Massacre, 119
  rights of freedpeople in, 106–107
Harris, J. C., 100
Hayes, R. B., 106
Hegemony
  concept of, 4
  understanding, 5
Helper, H. R., 59
Herndon, A., 131
Herskovitz, M. J., 134
Higginbotham, A. L., 19
Hoffman, F. L.
  *Race Traits and Tendencies of the American
    Negro,* 101
Holmes, O. W.
  political and economic stimuli, 10
Horwitz, M., 44
Howard, J. M., 70
Howard, O. O., 79
Howell, R. F.
  myth of judicial neutrality, 105–106
Human development
  in sixteenth and nineteenth centuries, 18

I
Iberia
  slave trade, 18
The Impending Crisis and How to Meet It, 59
Indian Removal Act of 1832, 49
Indian slavery, 21–22

J
Jackson, A., 46
Jefferson, T.
  rationalization and justification, 29–30
  right of revolution theory, 30

Johnson, A.
  biography of, 21
Johnson, S., 31
Justice Accused, 63

K
Kansas–Nebraska Act of 1854, 54
Klan violence with Constitutional leeway, 6–7
Ku Klux Klan Act, 93
  of 1871, 71

L
laissez-faire Constitutionalism, 78
Laws
  civil rights, 6
  defined, 1
  law of womb, 37
  liberty and inequality, 23
  master-and-slave relationships, 9
  race and, 10
  rule of, 4
  of slavery
    use as instrument of class domination, 55–64
  treating unequals as equals, 6
Legal formalism, 3
Legitimacy, 5
Liberator, 50
Liberty and inequality, 22–23
Little, J. A., 5
Llewellyn, K., 47
Locke, J.
  Second Treatise, 30
Loring, E. G., 50
Lum, M., 129
Lynch law, 7
Lynd, S., 33

M
Madison, J., 31
  census, veiws on, 33
  Federalist, 32
  slavery and consequences, 36
Market revolution, 44
Marshall, J., 45
Martinet, L. A., 107
Marx, K., 17
  theory of law, 1–2
Maryland's law, 23
McClendon, J. Dr., 9
Mediterranean, slave trade, 18
Miller, A. S.
  myth of judicial neutrality, 105–106

Miller, L., 54
Miller, S. F., 91, 110
Mississippi, 119
Missouri Compromise of 1820, 55
Monopoly capitalism, 7
Morrison, A., 9
Moton, R., 126

N

NAACP. See National Association for the Advancement
    of Colored People (NAACP)
Nash, K., 61
National Association for the Advancement of Colored
    People (NAACP), 95, 121–122
  and allies, 135
  and American Communist Party, 134
  Black civil rights, 133–134
  civil rights of African Americans, 118
  Dred Scott dictum, 129
  Dyer Anti-Lynching Bill, 134
  great depression of 1929, 133
  Hoover's committee, 126
  Missouri ex rel Gaines v. Canada, 130
  and the social activism of Black people, 133
  Thirty Years of Lynching in the U.S.,
    1889–1918, 134
Native-American populations
  mortality rate, African labor, 18
Negro, racial formalism and betrayal
  compromise of 1877, 94
  economic and racial vision, convergence, 89
  hotel accommodation cases, 94
  national citizenship rights, 91
  national entrepreneurial context and Supreme Court
    decisions, 95
  northern society, 95
  Supreme Court, role of, 89
Negro Seamen's Act, 50
Neo-revisionists, 2
New Orleans Crusader, 107
Newton, H. P., 5
The New Tribune, 113
New World
  colonial societies, 20–21
  slavery, 9, 17
  social relationships of race and class, 20
  world market and, 18
The New York Times, 79
Nicholls, F. T., 109
North of Slavery, 46
Northwest Ordinance, 33
Notes on Virginia, 31

O

Obitum dictum, 57
O'Neal, J. B., 61–62
"One drop rule," 9
Order of Divine Providence, 109
Organic law, 70

P

Parker, J. J., 134
Peckham, R., 111
Penn, W., 24
Phillips, S. F., 109
Plessy, H. A.
  case, 111–112
  Donohoe's Magazine, 113
  state's racialist law, 108–109
Political economy and conflict of laws, 44
Popular front approach, 131
Populism
  race and class
    African-American response, 101–102
    agrarian populists and Black and White,
      coalition, 96
    Anti-Peonage Act of 1867, 96
    Australian ballot, 97–98
    Black agrarians, 97–98
    Black blood and toil for, 97
    Boss Rule and Monied Elites, tools, 97
    Bourbon Democrats, 97
    Cincinnati meeting of 1891, 97
    Colored Alliance, 99
    Colored Farmers' National Alliance, 97
    convict lease system, 98
    coup de grace of, 99
    debt, 96
    Democratic White supremacist elites, 96
    ex-Populist and landed gentry, 99–100
    farmers and freedpeople, 97
    Louisiana writer, 101
    North American Review, 100–101
    peonage, 96
    Southern Alliance, 98
    Southern Alliance and Democrats, 99
    Southern economy downturn in, 96
    Southern Populism, failure of, 99
    Tennessee (White) Populists, 98
    White agrarians, 98
    White supremacy and Negro-phobia, 100
Portuguese, "Black Gold" transportation, 19
Powderly, T. W., 97
Prado, C. Jr., 17
Prigg case, 52

Procedural rules of law, 5
Punch, J., 21

Q

Quasi-free laboring system, 19

R

Race
  based hierarchical social structure, 22
  critics, 8
  defined by law, 9
  federalism and freedpeople, 71–79
  materialist conception of, 8
  ruling planter class, 22
Reconstruction Acts, 70
Reese and other voting rights cases, 118
Republican of Springfield, 113
Revisionists, 2
Rights of inheritance, 9
Rule-of-law procedures, 5

S

Second Treatise, 30
Shiras, G. Jr., 111
Simpson, O. J., 5
Slaughterhouse cases, 118
  of 1873, 90–91
Slavery
  Africans and, 23
  defined, 17
  early development, 4
  fugitive slave clause in Ordinance, 33
  law favoring freedom and, 21
  for life, 19–20
  production of agricultural commodities in New
    World, 18
Smith, H., 100
Smith, V., 25
Social consciousness, 4
Somerset case, 54
South Atlantic system, 20
Southern agrarian–plantation economy, 45
Southern Alliance and Democrats, 99
Southern formal legal rules system, 7
Southern law of slavery, 60
Southern Populism, failure of, 99
State sovereignty/extraterritoriality for slavery, 44
Stevens, T., 70
Storey, M., 128
Stowe, H. B., 57
Supreme Court, 89
  Black civil rights, 101–102

civil rights legislation, 90
compromise of 1877, 90
formulation of, 34
laissez-faire capitalism and hierarchical racialism, 90
language and theory use, 90
law of slavery, 55
Szentes, T., 18

T

Taney, R. B., 48
Tannenbaum, F., 17
Tourgee, A. W., 109
  argument on, 109–110
  column in Chicago *Inter Ocean,* 108
Traditionalist, 2
Trans-Atlantic slave trade, 18–19

U

Unitarian religious consciousness, 30

V

Virginia's law, 23

W

Walker, J. C., 108–109
Walker, Q., 5, 46
Walvin, J., 19
Warren, C., 95
Washington, B. T., 101, 118
Watson, A., 18
Watson, T., 99
  People Party's first Congressman-elect, 97
Weber, M., 3
Western criminal law, 57
Westin, A., 107
Whiskey Rebellion, 32
White community
  agrarians, 98
  domination, 6–7
  racism, 17
  ruling class, 8
  White women
    intermarrying with Negroes or slaves, 22
White Terror, 78
Williams, E., 17
Wilmot, D., 53
Woodward, C. V., 99, 112
Worcester Railroad decision, 59
Wo, Y., 130

Z

Zong case, 19